Great Stone Circles

Great Stone Circles

FABLES FICTIONS FACTS

Aubrey Burl

Yale University Press • New Haven and London

Dedicated with much affection to

PROFESSOR DEREK SIMPSON, FSA

my supervisor of years ago, now colleague and friend,
with whom many sites in Britain, Ireland and Brittany have been visited,
including the Golf in Edinburgh.
'I'll bring them over, sir'.

© 1999 Yale University

Designed by Kate Gallimore
Typeset in Sabon by Best-set Typesetter Ltd., Hong Kong
Printed in Italy

Library of Congress Cataloging-in-Publication Data
Burl, Aubrey.
      Great stone circles: fables, fictions, facts/Aubrey Burl.
           p. cm.
      Includes bibliographical references and index.
      ISBN 0-300-07689-4
      1. Stone circles–England. 2. Megalithic monuments–England. 3. Stonehenge
(England) 4. England–Antiquities. I. Title.
GN805.BB665 1999
936.2–dc21   98-34056
                                      CIP

Title-page: Boscawen-Un, Cornwall.

CONTENTS

ACKNOWLEDGEMENTS

I am grateful to the Cumberland and Westmorland Antiquarian and Archaeological Society for allowing me to include Chapter Two about Long Meg and Her Daughters, a paper from the Society's *Transactions 94*, 1994. Equal appreciation is expressed to the Wiltshire Archaeological and Natural History Society for its permission to use Chapters Eight, Nine and Ten about Stonehenge, first published in the Society's *Magazine*, volumes *84, 87, 90*, of 1991, 1994 and 1997. Each of the four chapters has been updated and lengthened.

Sincere thanks are offered to Stan Beckensall for allowing me reproduce his excellent drawing of the elaborate carvings on Long Meg. Andrew Lawson located Richard Atkinson's photograph of the Stonehenge anthropomorphic carving for me. It is in the archives of the Trust for Wessex Archaeology, Salisbury, Catalogue no. P51598, Print No. 2036. I am also indebted to Pamela Colman, Sandell Librarian, Wiltshire Archaeological Society; Max Milligan; Peter Saunders, Curator, Salisbury and South Wiltshire Museum; Cheryl Straffon, editor of *Meyn Mamvro*; and Dr Olwen Williams-Thorpe, Department of Earth Sciences, The Open University.

As always I am appreciative of the guidance of my long-standing and patient editor, John Nicoll. Many improvements and corrections were made to the text and references through the meticulous concern of Kate Gallimore.

Finally, I wish to state my deep gratitude to the two editors, Alex Gibson and Derek Simpson, and the many colleagues who so willingly contributed essays to the unexpected delight of a Festschrift dedicated to me, *Prehistoric Ritual and Religion*, 1998. Such unsolicited gifts are rare and there is no greater honour in the academic world than to receive one. I value it greatly.

LIST OF FIGURES

INTRODUCTION

Stone circles fascinate. They perplex. They seldom satisfy.

In 1773, shortly before the Boston Tea Party, Samuel Johnson made archaeology's most outrageous statement about a stone circle. It was a waste of time, he grumbled. 'To go and see one druidical temple is only to see that it is nothing, for there is neither art nor power in it; and seeing one is quite enough'.[1]

Even for his own unromantic time, the dreary Age of Reason, he was wrong. Druidical temples had been luring the curious for years. Places of mystery they were then and they remain so today when the mythical hobgoblins, giants and druids of previous centuries have been supplanted by rather less improbable guardians of the dead, hill-top worshippers and astronomer-priests. The rings mutate, as they have always done, into whatever shape popular imagination demands.

Imagine a stone circle on a fine holiday weekend. It is crowded. Wild flowers are trampled. Birds keep their distance. Children scramble over stones. There are four distinct groups of visitors, three of them earnest in their enquiries, the fourth a cheerful though perhaps perplexed company of tourists.

There are objective researchers, the Scientific-Investigative: demographers and mathematicians precisely assessing the weight of stones to determine the size of theoretical work-forces, computing the tumbled, half-buried, broken stones for evidence of numeracy and counting-systems, measuring and planning the ring for proof of its Pythagorean geometrical design. Astronomers peer from stone to stone searching for alignments to the sun, moon or any bright star that fits.

Nearby are archaeologists. They excavate, tabulate, conserve but, sadly, often refuse to speculate. Pusillanimously reluctant to think about prehistoric people they dehumanise the circle, metaphorically finding megaliths rather than men, wood rather than women. Mark Antony knew better: 'You are not wood, you are not stones, you are men'. 'The proper study of mankind is man', agreed Alexander Pope.

The third type of explorer is the Subjective-Emotional. They touch stones for electro-magnetic tingles. A sub-group dowse with rods for quivers of subterranean undercurrents and aquastats. Companions dangle pendulums over stones with the weight swinging clockwise for good, anti-clockwise for evil – or the other way round depending on one's sex. The gyrations are counted in tens to reveal the age of the ring. Deep in their concentration many of the investigators, scientific or subconscious, pass unknowingly through a spectral ley-line that radiates like an Exocet out to spires, turrets, dew-ponds and death-roads. Courteously, rods are lowered to make way for mystics in search of the elusive Mother-Goddess.

Quite apart, cameras click at an innocent coach-party in their brightest and best as they queue to pose, one by lagging one, in front of the only stone that an impatient book-illustrator wants to photograph for its carvings before the evening shadows darken it into obscurity.

The result of much of this may be little more than the creation of a wished-for world that never was. We must accept that it was real but different human beings who erected and used these rings. The difficulty is to know what kind of people they were. Images of mathematically-minded Neolithic scholars or of sensitive diviners locating

Plate 1 Visitors to the Rollright Stones.

centres of spiritual emanations may be no more than phantoms of the modern mind, as unrealistic as the brute described in an article of 1861 entitled, 'Traces of our remote ancestors'.

That user of a stone circle was depicted 'as one among a band of trembling votaries, drawing near to the rudely pillared enclosure-temple, canopied only by the blue vault of heaven, and swayed by terror, or blind hope, or ruthless savagery, at the will of the stern interpreters of a dark and merciless superstition'. And if this over-dramatises the male the female was worse. 'Why should we task fancy to repicture the women? They were probably more degraded in mind than the men, unclothed, long-haired, prematurely withered – meet helps and mates to such lords. In one word, they must have been the "squaws" of White hunter and warrior savages, instead of Red ones'.[2]

Despite the delightful political incorrectness the picture is no more unrealistic than kinder but idealistically utopian visions of the past. Any recreation of distant societies must take note of the skeletons, artefacts, structures, art, social stratification, ways of life, every physical piece of evidence that has survived to be interpreted. Science analyses the facts. Art gives them life. Prose states. Poetry explains. Shakespeare, as always, understood this.

> Imagination bodies forth
> The forms of things unknown, the poet's pen
> Turns them to shapes, and gives to airy nothing
> A local habitation and a name.
>
> *A Midsummer Night's Dream*, V, 1, 14–17.

Pottery and postholes are little more than pathways to people. Whenever archaeology departs from that fundamental premise it impoverishes the past.

To the uninformed it might seem that little has been learned since 1843. 'No one can doubt, I apprehend, but that this stone circle was originally constructed by the aboriginal Britons, under the superintendence of the Druids either as a temple, or a court of justice, or both, as Druidical circles were used for worship and for seats of judgement'.[3] Few would contradict this excellent example of a circular argument.

Plate 2 An ancient Briton by John White, Virginia Expedition 1592.

The reality is that stone circles can be explained and this book is an attempt to do so. It is neither a guide nor a general study. It is a debate that uses twelve attractive and informative rings in much more detail than is normally possible in order to remove some of the uncertainties that befuddle research into the problems of prehistory. The sites have been chosen because each encapsulates a particular problem and provides an explanation. Four of the chapters have been published in archaeological journals but have since been updated and expanded for a wider readership. The remainder have been written especially for this book. Each chapter is concerned with a significant aspect of stone circles: their legends, their construction, age, design, distribution, art, astronomy and purpose (Fig. 1).

Legends surround stone circles and Chapter One on the Rollright Stones explains how they developed. Stories of girls turned to stone, of witchcraft, of stones going down to drink at midnight rivers, these are common currency amongst megalithic rings. It has been believed that there are vague prehistoric memories of real events in these tales. The truth is that most are fables of the early eighteenth century or later. The history of the Rollright Stones epitomises this modern making of myths.

Like the Rollright Stones Long Meg and Her Daughters in Chapter Two had legends attached to the ring. But far more relevant to the prehistoric truth is an understanding of the circle's megalithic art and the astronomical alignment built into the site.

The three circles of Stanton Drew form a complex that is unique in the differing sizes of the rings and their layout. Chapter Three provides a vivid example of prehistoric landscaping.

Chapter Four describes the four Land's End circles of Boscawen-Un, Boskednan, Tregeseal and the Merry Maidens which attract hundreds of visitors each year to enjoy the mystery and the challenge of these silent monuments. But what can be seen today is very different from the rings that prehistoric people knew.

Stone circles have been dismissed as rude stone monuments. In a characteristic prehistoric paradox, the un-megalithic, megaxylic Woodhenge disproves this. Examination of this complicated site in Chapter Five reveals not only careful planning but also numeracy and the use of a unit of measurement.

Stonehenge contains a cornucopia of questions to be considered in Chapters Six to Ten. After (6), an Introduction, (7) asks how the bluestones from south-west Wales reached Salisbury Plain 140 direct miles away; then (8), why the outlying 'solar' Heel Stone does not stand in line with the midsummer sunrise and why it is not the Heel Stone; (9) why the Slaughter Stone was not used for sacrifice but does confirm the existence of a Megalithic Yard; and (10) why Stonehenge, this most British of stone circles, is not a stone circle and is not British.

The book ends with a reconstruction. In 1862 William Linton wrote of the singular erections known as Druidical circles. He remarked on the conflict between 'evidence of great mechanical power' and 'a degree of skill and intelligence incompatible with a barbarous state of things'.[4] As Chapter Eleven explains the building and use of Swinside demonstrates a definite compatibility between the power and the 'barbarity'.

Little of this might be known to the day-trippers wandering around a typical circle but the facts have been gleaned from the four hundred years of wonderings by earlier visitors to the silent ring.

At night ghosts are there, 'a fayre felde of folkes' who have gone before: John Aubrey on horseback making a scribble of notes; William Stukeley dreaming of a divinity of druids; William Borlase seeing sacrificial victims roped to perforated pillars; Daniel Defoe wondering at the heaviness of the blocks; John Keats groaning at the dreary ring of stones on a drearier moor; the Rev. Charles Henry Hartshorne riding to stone circles in Shropshire, the Rev. Henry Rowlands imaginatively sketching them in Druidical groves on Anglesey; and with the dawn of the present century and the motor car more substantial figures.

Sir Norman Lockyer, Alfred Watkins, and the half-forgotten pioneers, Fred Coles, John Conlon, Captain, later Rear-Admiral, Boyle Somerville, G. F. Tregelles, R. G. Collingwood, John Ward, faded sepia snapshots but memorable for their investigations that scraped away the encrusted misconceptions of what the rings had been. The fantasies persist.

It was not always so. Five thousand or more years ago men and women had their own beliefs fashioned by their own, long-lost needs. They were skilled. They knew

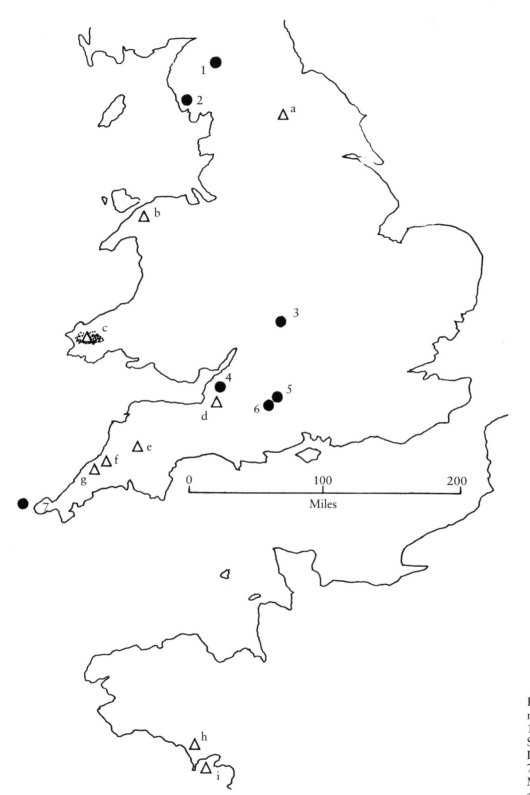

Fig. 1 Map showing the major, 1–7 and minor, a–g, sites.
1. Long Meg and Her Daughters; 2. Swinside; 3. Rollright Stones; 4. Stanton Drew; 5. Woodhenge; 6. Stonehenge; 7. Boscawen-Un, Boskednan, Merry Maidens, Tregeseal.
a. Thornborough; b. Llandegai; c. Preseli Mountains; d. Priddy; e. Grey Wethers; f. Hurlers; g. King Arthur's Hall; h. Crucuno; i. Kergonan.

which stones would last, they knew how to lay them out, erect them, knew that there was a sun and a moon, carved symbols, met inside the rings for ceremonies that might appal the modern mind.

The circles in this book clear away a little of the mist that persists in drifting slowly, unevenly, across these marvels of the megalithic past.

PART ONE
Fables, Fictions and Facts

Plate 3 *(previous pages)* Limestone blocks at the Rollright Stones, 'Corroded like worm eaten wood by the harsh jaws of time' (William Stukeley).

Plate 4 *(above)* The western arc of the Rollright Stones.

Chapter One

The Rollright Stones, Oxfordshire

THE GROWTH OF A LEGEND

I know that some will nauseate these old Fables: but I doe profess to regard them as the most considerable pieces of Antiquity, I collect: and that they are to be registred for Posterity, to let them understand the Encroachment of Ignorance on Mankind: and to learne what strange Absurdities Man can by Custome and education be brought to believe.

John Aubrey, *Monumenta Britannica*, I, 1665–93, 66.

FACTS AND FABLES

In 1967 Jacquetta Hawkes wrote that 'Every age has the Stonehenge it desires – or deserves'.[1] It is an aphorism illustrated perfectly by the ways in which stone circles have been interpreted over the centuries. For generations these chronological chameleons have provided a challenge for the serious enquirer and simultaneously a paradise for the escapist. Whether in Tudor times or today they have impartially accommodated scholarship, superstition and self-delusion. Learning has not eliminated legend. Nor has research hindered romance. People have persisted in believing what they wish to believe and ever since the Middle Ages fact and folklore have been enforced bedfellows.

John Aubrey's 'old Fable', quoted above, concerned the Somerset circles of Stanton Drew. By folklore they were a wedding-party turned to stone for dancing on the sabbath. Similar legends of petrifaction were attached to other megalithic rings such as the Hurlers and the Merry Maidens in Cornwall and the Rollright Stones in Oxfordshire. In times of little science but much superstition when giants, fairies and witches were realities of the mind such a punishment for sinners was as good an explanation as any for stone circles whose existence was otherwise beyond understanding.

The rings have been differently explained from century to century. The history of the Rollright Stones epitomises the changes. Some forty strides across the ring consists of a few tall standing stones and many stumps and lumps of leprous limestone. Just outside is an isolated pillar, the King Stone. To the east, at the far edge of a field, are the ruins of a chambered tomb, a portal-dolmen known as the Whispering Knights.

The circle is on a long and winding ridge some twenty miles north-west of Oxford, in between Little Rollright to the west and Great Rollright to the east. The straggling

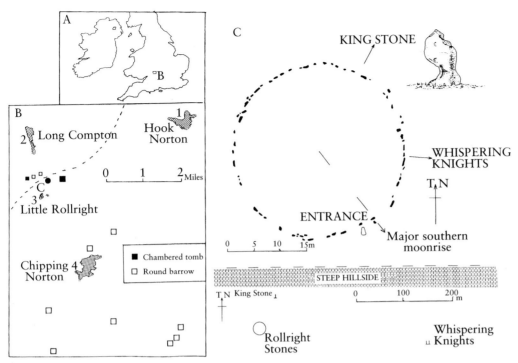

Fig. 2 Map and plan of the Rollright Stones, Oxfordshire.

village of Long Compton is hardly a mile to the north. Somewhere, four miles to the east, is the lost tenth-century battleground of Hook Norton (Fig. 2).

The recorded history of the ring is not a collection of truths worn thin by time but a series of changing credulities that reveal more about the obstinacy of parochial belief than the objectivity of clear thinking. Two contradicting modes of thought endured. The facts ploddingly accumulated by antiquarians did little to erode the persuasiveness of folklore.

It was popularly accepted that the Rollright Stones were the bodies of a Danish king, Rollo, and his men metamorphosed by a witch who turned herself into an elder tree which bled if cut. Chippings from the stones were powerful amulets against the Devil and from illness. Fairies lived in caves under the outlying stone. With them slept Rollo's warriors who would awaken one day 'and rule over the land'.

There may be frailties of truth in such whimsies, folk-memories fragile as cobwebs, so faint that they are almost undetectable, faded distortions of associations with water, of seasonal assemblies, celebrations. Stories of pixies who were powerless against iron have been thought to be warped recollections of Bronze Age natives unable to resist the iron swords of Celtic invaders.[2] Others believed fairies to be sanitised versions of witches who had held sabbats in the midnight circle. How this folklore came about and how comparable unreason still persists despite the increasing awareness of what the stone circle was in prehistory is a pattern repeated at megalithic ring after ring in western Europe.

The Rollright Stones were probably erected in the Late Neolithic period around 3000 BC and the ring was still in use in the Bronze Age. It is likely to have been abandoned around 1000 BC. Then, for a millennium, nothing is known of it until the early centuries of Roman Britain.

The limestone pillars stand in a broad but inconspicuous bank. Excavations in 1986 revealed that it had been heightened in Roman times and the ring's interior made level perhaps to convert the circle into a cock-fighting arena.[3] This mute evidence is all that exists in the silence of a further nine hundred years.

CHRISTIANITY AND HEATHENISM

The Dark Ages, Saxon kingdoms, Viking invasions left no word about the ring which may, like many others, have been a centre in which the corrupted memories of old rituals lingered. In spite of Christian teaching repugnant rites of sexuality and the worship of pagan deities continued at megalithic rings, chambered tombs and standing stones. The Church fulminated censoriously but impotently against the blasphemy.

> The Councils of Arles in 452, and Tours in 567, the Archbishop of Bourges in 584, Childebert in 554, Carloman in 742, and Charlemagne all condemned the superstitious regarding of stones, fountains, trees etc, and enjoined the destruction of the venerated objects. Patrick, Bishop of the Hebrides, desired Orgylus to found a church wherever he should find standing stones.[4] In 959 the Saxon king, Eadgar, issued an edict 'against enchantments, necromancies and divination' and ordered priests 'totally [to] extinguish heathenism and forbid well-worshipping'.

It was pious but impracticable. Paganism persisted and would persist even into modern times.

THE MIDDLE AGES: STONES AND SUPERSTITIONS

By the late eleventh century through a combination of politics and geography the Rollright Stones almost entered history. In 1086 Domesday Book recorded a Warwickshire hamlet, *Contone* or *Cumtune*, 'the settlement in the short, broad valley'. It would be another two hundred years, in 1299, before it became Long Compton as its huts, cottages and farmsteads straggled farther and farther along the Stratford–Oxford road.

Also in Domesday Book but in Oxfordshire was *Rollendricht*, 'the estate with special, local, legal rights belonging to Hrolla', a land-holding which included the stone circle as well as the villages of Great and Little Rollright. Military confusion followed. At the battle of Hastings twenty years earlier the minstrel knight, Taillefer, had chanted the stirring 'Song of Roland', inspiring the Norman cavalry to charge the Saxon ranks. A hopeful descendant of Hrolla may have misinterpreted the estate's name of *Rollendricht* or *Rollandri* thinking that it referred to Roland, an ancestor who had fought a battle near the circle. The *Anglo-Saxon Chronicle* did refer to a fight in 916 at Hook Norton four miles away. It was fought. But not by Roland who had been killed in 778.[5]

To the mediaeval peasant with his hopes of Heaven and dread of Hell stone circles were supernatural, the work not of humans but of unworldly creatures, ogres, wizards, hobgoblins, the Devil. Merlin the magician had carried Stonehenge, 'the Giants' Dance', from Ireland. Elva Plain, a ring in the Lake District, was called *elfhaugr* by Vikings, 'the place of imps and elves'. Satan, ever busy, ever destructive and ever incompetent perpetually interrupted the building of a church at the fine stone circle of Swinside. So wondrous were these alien rings that their stones could not be counted.

They were the petrified bodies of sinners, they were known to move, to dance, to uproot themselves and at hallowed days of the year trudge to brooks to drink at midnight.

Then, suddenly, the Rollright Stones became archaeological. An account, refreshingly uncontaminated by rural gullibility, was tacked on to a list of the miracles of Britain by an early fourteenth-century cleric in Cambridge.

'In Oxenefordensi pago sunt magni lapides . . .' In the Oxford country there are great stones, arranged as it were in some connection by the hand of man. But at what time this was done, or by what people, or for what memorial or significance, is unknown. Though by the inhabitants that place is called Rollendrith.[6]

At what time . . . by what people . . . is unknown. It was honest, it was objective and it was the first serious comment about the circle. But the legend of the petrified king was unmentioned. It had not yet been invented.

TUDOR TIMES: HISTORY AND WITCHCRAFT

Early in the sixteenth century John Leland, the itinerant antiquarian, used the ring as no more than a reference to the 'bigge Stone a 3. Miles West from *Rolleriche* Stones . . . And Palmer's Sun told me, that this Stone of certente is the Marke, and not *Rolleriche* Stones'.[7] It was the Four Shire stone near Moreton-in-Marsh at the junction of Gloucestershire, Oxfordshire, Warwickshire and Worcestershire.

In popular imagination giants and Satan were still favoured as the makers of stone circles but during the sixteenth century there was growing scepticism about magic, myth and Merlin whose marvels had been chronicled in Geoffrey of Monmouth's twelfth century fabulous but unhistorical *History of the Kings of Britain*. With the gradual realisation that the distant past had been inhabited by real people scholars turned to the mundane but more reliable texts of the Venerable Bede and the *Anglo-Saxon Chronicle* in which verifiable events such as the Viking invasions were recorded.

It was still believed that giants had existed in ancient times because the fossilised bones of mammoths had been mistaken for men. It was the renaissance of empirical thinking and in this revision megalithic rings became the works of man and were thought to be Roman or Danish cenotaphs, memorials to slain warriors.

The 1586 Latin edition of Camden's *Britannia* claimed only that the Rollright Stones were men turned to stone but the 1610 English version was more specific. The ring was an 'ancient Monument . . . to wit, certaine huge stones placed in a round circle' which the common people said were 'sometimes men, by a wonderfull *Metamorphosis* turned into hard stones', a king, five knights and an army. 'These would I verily thinke to have been the monument of some victorie and haply, erected by *Rollo* the Dane, who afterwards conquered *Normandie*'. But the stones were blemished. 'Without all forme and shape they be, unaequal; and by long continuance of time much impaired'.[8]

A contemporary, the poet Michael Drayton, in his prolix *Poly-Olbion*, 1613, celebrating the glories of Britain, patriotically reversed the result of the battle, deeming the stone circle

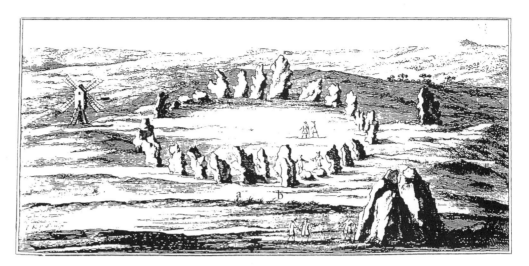

Fig. 3 A sketch of the Rollright Stones from Camden's *Britain*, 1610, showing the undamaged entrance with the two external portal stones (a, b) in the foreground. Three tourists stand by the Whispering Knights.

> ... *Rollright* (which remaines
> A Witnesse of that day we wonne upon the Danes)

but in his critical notes to the poem the lawyer and scholar, John Selden, derided petrifaction 'as a tale not having his superior in the ranks of untruth'. As for the Rollright Stones, 'to suppose this a monument of that battell, fought at *Hochnortin*, seems to me in matter of certainty, not very probable; I meane being drawn from *Rollo*'s name'. Realism was replacing romance.[9]

Camden's most interesting information about the stones was not simply that for the first time the ring was stated to be circular and had been built by human beings. More important was the accompanying illustration which showed a windmill to the south, the outlying King Stone with no hedge between it and the circle, and the Whispering Knights chambered tomb. It also contained a feature which is so badly damaged today as to be almost unrecognisable, a portalled entrance at the south-east composed of two circle-stones with two more pillars, side by side, just outside them (Fig. 3). No comment was made about it and this culturally informative piece of prehistoric architecture was overlooked for another two hundred years.

Every age has what it desires – or deserves. It is an irony of megalithic studies that at the very time that living beings were taking the place of phantoms and fiends in stone circles another fantasy emerged. Witchcraft. James I of England, when James VI of Scotland in 1597, had written *Daemonologie* after being terrifyingly convinced that he had been in danger of death by sorcery. Years later he decided that there was a defect in English law whereby only witches found guilty of causing death could be executed. In 1604 the law was changed, all proven witches were to be put to death.

There had been few witch trials in the Middle Ages. Between 1560 and 1680 there were hundreds. In Elizabeth I's reign Bishop John Jewel returned from Switzerland, the hotbed of sternly moral Calvinism. 'What a company and number of witches be within England' he raged. Persecution was inevitable. Calvin himself was unyielding. 'There are witches and ... they must be slain ... God expressly commands that all witches and enchantresses shall be put to death, and this law of God is a universal law'.[10] The hitherto unexplained reason for the petrified Rollright Stones was that they were the handiwork of a malicious witch.

By repute covens had gathered at the circle ever since Tudor times although there is no conclusive proof of this. Nor is there any record of a formal prosecution for witchcraft in the Cotswolds. On the other hand, a sixteenth-century commission in Oxford reported rumours of sabbaths being held at the stones and Cotton Mather, American clergyman and witch-fanatic, declared that witches assembled in the city 'in Hellish Rendezvouses'. It has also been claimed that during the reign of Charles I (1625–49) a woman 'was hanged for attempting to kill her sister's child by means of witchcraft. She was said to have attended countless sabbaths at the Rollright Stones and on Boar's Hill outside Oxford'.[11]

Down the mile or more of steeply winding and busy road northwards from the circle there is a sandstone effigy of a woman in the porch of Long Compton church. Contorted, cracked, eroded, with an 'eerie and malevolent smile' it was locally muttered that she was a witch turned into stone, her feet resting on what may be a cat, her 'familiar'. With her fastidiously networked hair, flat cap, fitted bodice and flowing skirt the figure is more probably that of a mediaeval woman moved from the church when the clerestory and chancel were added in the first half of the fifteenth century.[12]

There is no question that fears of witchcraft were strong in the Midlands. In March 1619, Joan Palmer and her daughters of Bottesford in Leicestershire were put to death in Lincoln for casting mortal spells on the two sons of Francis Manners, sixth Earl of Rutland. The elaborately carved and painted tomb in the church is said to be the only one in England to mention witchcraft, 'Two sonnes both wch dyed in their infancy by wicked practise and sorcery'.[13]

Closer to the Rollright Stones, only nine miles from Long Compton, Joan Perry, suspected of being a witch, and her two sons, John and Richard, were hanged in 1661 for the murder of William Harrison of Chipping Camden who had disappeared while collecting estate rents. John Perry, Harrison's servant, freely confessed to the crime. Yet next year Harrison returned, alive, well and telling the fatuous story that he, a seventy year old man had been kidnapped and sold into slavery in Turkey. Witchcraft, a false but unextorted confession, a non-murder, a preposterous explanation. Unastonishingly, the mystery is known as the Camden Wonder.[14]

In the opening decades of the seventeenth century there was little archaeological progress at the Rollright Stones but the legend was developing well. That sinners had been turned to stone had been believed since the Middle Ages. The later gloss that the wrongdoers were a king and his army arose from the misidentification of Rollo as an invading Dane when he had really been the innocent landholder of *Rollendricht*. The illusory king had come to Rollright after his victory at Hook Norton. By the 1600s the malice of a witch accounted for the petrifaction. Rollo had been turned to stone by the spite of a hag who discovered intruders on her land.

The awkward facts that Rollo had gone to Normandy in 876 'and he reigned fifty years' and that the Hook Norton affray did not occur until 916 were ignored.[15] And the legend would grow. Problems remained. It was still unclear what trickery the witch had used to dupe the unwary king. Nor was it known why she had transformed herself into a tree. Over the following hundred years, a heyday for the flourishing of legends, explanations were forthcoming.

THE SEVENTEENTH CENTURY: THE BEGINNINGS OF RESEARCH

Archaeology made advances. In his manuscript notes of 1665–93 John Aubrey, that dedicated, ever-curious antiquarian and assiduous fieldworker, quoted measurements

Plate 5 The northern arc of the Rollright Stones.

for the circle, recorded an excavation and suggested, with typical diffidence, that the ring was pre-Roman. Danes went. Druids came.

In 1675 at Oxford he met Robert Plot, author of *The Naturall Historie of Oxfordshire*, 1677, who told him about the stones. The circle is less than twenty miles from Oxford and it is possible that Aubrey rode out to see it. If so, the visit is unrecorded. In his *Monumenta Britannica* he used information partly from Plot, partly from Camden's *Britannia* but largely from his own knowledge of comparable monuments.

He knew something of the legend. 'The common people call them by the name abovesaid [Roll-rich], and dreame that they were sometimes Men, by a wonderful metamorphosis turned into hard stones. The vulgar verse is:

> When Long-Compton I shall see,
> Then King of England I shall be.

which a man, if he goes a few paces forward, may see'. This was not personal observation. It came word for word from Camden.

He added valuable notes. There were no carvings on the stones which 'except one or two, the rest are not above four foot and a half high' [1.4m]. The ring was a true circle of 36 paces, about 32.9m, very close to the modern survey of 33 ± 1m.[16] Having seen lines of stones at Avebury and Stanton Drew he thought that the outlying King Stone might be the sole survivor of a similar avenue 'though now decayed by Time'.

A common acquaintance of Plot and Aubrey, Ralph Sheldon had 'industriously dug in the middle' of the ring without success and Aubrey was gently critical of the excavation. He already knew that in 1678 a Dr Toope had found human bones not in but outside the Sanctuary stone circle near Avebury.

Ralph Sheldon of Beoley Esq (my honoured friend) told me, he was at some charge to digge AD 167–[?] within this Circle to try if he could find any Bones but he was sure that no body was buried there; but had he digged without the circle and neer to it, it is not unlikely he mought have found Bones there; as at the Temple [the Sanctuary] above Kynet aforesaid.[17]

Aubrey's most profound insight was the deduction that stone circles like the Rollright Stones must have been erected much earlier than was commonly believed. From correspondents in Ireland, Scotland and Wales he learned that megalithic rings existed where neither Danes nor Romans had been. And from a folk-tale that St Patrick had destroyed a heathen ring in Ireland 'we may from hence infer that the Circle of Stones . . . was before the planting of Christianity in this Country'.

Collating the amassed material he concluded that there was clear evidence that 'these monuments were pagan temples: which was not made-out before, and that also (with humble submission to better judgements) offered a *probability* that they were *Temples* of the *Druids*'. His concept of Druids – 'They were two or three degrees I suppose less salvage than the Americans' – was very different from the image of philosopher-priests advocated by his successor in the study of stone circles, William Stukeley. As by 'Americans' he was alluding to atrocities committed by Indians on European settlers in New England the comparison was not flattering.[18]

Classical authors had stated that Druids had been barbaric, sacrificing victims by disembowelling so that from the agonised contortions auguries of the future could be divined. At a time when witches were burnt alive and when the hanging, drawing and quartering of the Gunpowder Plot conspirators was still remembered such practices would have seemed entirely credible.

There is an interesting connection between Aubrey and Stukeley whose own megalithic researches began around 1710, thirteen years after Aubrey's death. One of Aubrey's most voluminous informants was Dr Thomas Gale, Dean of York, and it was his son, Roger, landowner and scholar, who became the close friend of Stukeley. Gale visited the Rollright Stones in 1719.

By the end of the seventeenth century the eastern side of the portalled entrance had collapsed and a hedge had been planted between the ring and the King Stone. The untidiness did not impress that indefatigable horsewoman, Celia Fiennes who, having passed the Four Shire stone, 'Came to Rowle Stone, where are many such greate stones as is at Stonidge, one stands upright, a broad Stone Called the King's Stone, being the place a Saxon King was secured against his enemies: thence to Broughton'.

Twenty years later Daniel Defoe was more enthusiastic about the 'second Stonehenge; being a ring of great stones standing upright, some of them from 5 to 7 foot high' [1.5, 2.1 m]. Educated opinion was now thinking of stone circles as monuments of the dead. Uneducated opinion was firmly attached to older ideas. Defoe had passed many standing stones in Wales of which it seemed 'next to impossible, that all the power of art, and strength of man and beast could carry them, and the people make no difficulty of saying the Devil set them up there'.[19]

Plate 6 The fallen stones and portals of the south-east entrance.

THE EIGHTEENTH CENTURY: DRUIDS, DREADS AND JUDAS

On Wednesday, 19 August 1719, Roger Gale wrote to Stukeley about the Rollright Stones. With stories of local witchcraft abundant it is significant that his version of the popular rhyme was subtly different from Aubrey's couplet in which the King had spoken to himself. Gale quoted:

> If Long Compton thou canst see . . .
> Then King of England thou shalt be

as though an unknown person, probably a witch, was luring the ambitious man to his doom.

Gale was dismissive. 'Last Satturday morning I had the satisfaction of seeing the stones called Rollrick, which are but a molehill to a mountain in comparison to those we saw at Stonehenge and at Abury'. But he did provide the first set of detailed field-observations. The ring was not circular, being about 32 m north-south by 30.2 m, with stones set together as though 'intended to form a close wall'.[20] They stood by the hedge between a field and heathland. The twenty-two stones were thinnish and of unequal sizes, a few over 1.4 m high some only 0.6 m. At the north was one larger, 2.1 m high and 1.7 m wide. There was no sign of a bank or an avenue.

The outlying King Stone 'is a great stone which the countrey fancies represents a man on horseback'. It was about 76 m to the north-east and was 2.4 m high, 2.1 m wide but only 30 cm thick. Being so slender Gale thought it must have been extracted from a nearby quarry, a notion 'which . . . much displeased my landlord that came from Chipping Norton with me to show me this petryfied court, which is the creed of the countery, and he that contradicts it is lookt upon as most audacious free-thinker'.

Stonehenge was surrounded by prehistoric burial-mounds but Gale noticed no barrows near the Rollright Stones, 'only a bank about 10 yards [9 m] north of

Plate 7 The bent pillar of the King Stone.

the King, in length about 20 yards, breadth 7 [18 × 6.4 m], flatt and uneven on the top, as if made out of the rubbish of the neighbouring quarry'. He added that although Long Compton could not be seen from the King Stone, 'if you step a yard to the north of him it discovers itself over the top of this bank which intercepts it from his view'. The bank, lying ENE–WSW, was in fact much bigger, some 90 m long, 40 m wide and 1 m high. Over the following centuries quarries by the lane severely truncated it.

Stukeley decided that it was a long barrow. He had already seen the circle in 1710, 'a very noble monument; the first antiquity of this sort that I had seen; and from which I concluded these works to be temples of the ancient Britons . . . Nought pleased me better'.[21] Yet despite returning in 1724 he had little original to say. Obsessively interested in Avebury and Stonehenge he was content to rely on Gale's account just as he had used the work of John Aubrey and Edward Lhuyd, the Welsh antiquarian, often without acknowledgement.

After his ordination in 1729 the clarity of his archaeological thinking was blurred by religious prejudice. As a mission he chose to use stone circles 'besides preserving the memory of these extraordinary monuments . . . to promote as much as I am able, the knowledge and practice of ancient and true Religion'. His intention was to combat the heresy of free-thinkers who were attacking the orthodoxy of the Church. It was virtuous but it was not archaeology.[22]

As Stuart Piggott explained, 'the learned would read about stone circles and thence would gently be drawn to the Druids, and before they knew where they were the beauties of the ancient patriarchal religion, foreshadowing the whole doctrine of the Church of England, would be presented so persuasively that any free-thinking ideas would be put to rout'.[23] To this end stone circles became proto-Christian churches in which amiable Druids performed decorous rites of worship. It was an argument that may have appealed to the erudite but to the more populous unlearned there always lurked behind Stukeley's flaccid ministers the more appealingly gruesome image of gore-spattered priests and blood-dripping altars.

Stukeley's spurious transformation of Druids was a nuisance. At Rollright his most worthwhile contribution came from his experienced eyes that detected the numerous round barrows on the heath like the cemeteries around Stonehenge. There were several shallowly scooped-out round basins known as pond barrows and there was also a disc barrow, a spacious earth-banked circle with a delicate central mound. On Salisbury Plain such 'fancy' barrows often contained the cremations and luxurious possessions of wealthy Early Bronze Age women.

In a sketch Stukeley showed two round barrows just west of the King Stone with a third, stones tumbled on it, a little farther away. Later known as Gough's Barrow it was probably a Neolithic tomb covering a megalithic chamber.[24] Agriculture has ploughed these mounds into extinction and it is only Stukeley's records that prove that years after its construction the Rollright Stones, like Avebury, Stonehenge and other great Neolithic rings, became the heart of a Bronze necropolis. 'Another argument of its being a Druid temple, is taken from the barrows all around it'.

Stukeley wrote briefly but poetically about the circle which consisted of flattish slabs of various shapes and sizes, maybe once, he thought, of about sixty blocks, 'many stones have been carried away within memory to make bridges, houses &c'. The condition of the survivors was vividly evoked. Of oolitic limestone which had weathered badly they were 'corroded like worm-eaten wood, by the harsh jaws of time'. It cannot be bettered.

The ring was not Danish. It was Druidical. Its position, its many stones and its dimensions were the proof. Gale's estimated diameter of 105 ft [32 m] was a multiple of Stukeley's theoretical Druids' Cubit. 'We suppose this is not measured with a mathematical exactness; but when we look into the comparative scale of *English* feet and cubits, we discern 60 cubits'. His arithmetic was biassed. The cubit being 52.8 cm in length sixty would measure not 32 m but 31.7 m.

He casually mentioned the 'merely Monumental' portal-dolmen on its low mound to the east of the Rollright Stones, twice terming it a 'kistvaen' but never calling it the Whispering Knights which had not yet become another bogus enhancement to the legend. Stukeley scoffed at petrifaction, dismissing the prejudices of natives who 'take it very ill if any one doubts of it; nay, they are in danger of being stoned for their unbelief'.

He recorded a local custom. In 1722 he had seen the enormous if debatable long barrow of Shiplea Hill near Cossington in Leicestershire. He wrote that on its top 'are several oblong double trenches cut in the turf, where the lads and lasses of the adjacent villages meet upon Easter-Monday yearly, to be merry'. There were others along the Fosse Way, 'and such a one I formerly found at Rowldrich stones . . .'. Near the

Plate 8 A peacock butterfly on a northern stone.

King Stone was 'a square plat, oblong, form'd in the turf' and 'hither, on a certain day of the year, the young men and maidens customarily meet, and make merry with cakes and ale, the remains of the very ancient festival here celebrated in memory of the interr'd, for whom the long barrow and temple were made'. He did not specify the date of the merrymaking. A later informant, William Parry, learned nothing more of any annual feasting.[25]

During the eighteenth century a gaggle of fatuities embellished the folk-stories. A fragment chipped from the stones would be a talisman against misfortune. If a stone were removed it would bring ill-luck to the culprit. The stone might also return to the ring of its own accord. A witch, by now given a name and believed to have been from a nearby village was accepted as the cause of the petrifaction. She survived as an elder tree that grew stunted and straggly alongside the circle. It was a collection of misunderstandings, mistranslations and escapism that excited unsophisticated visitors.

'P.S.', wrote Parry in 1742, 'I have, as hundreds have done before me, carried off a bit from the king, his knights and soldiers, which I intend to send or keep for you'.[26] A sketch by Stukeley in 1724 had already shown a shallow concavity low down on the outlier's eastern side. Over the decades this was hammered and hacked into a deep gouge until, in 1883, the battered pillar was engirdled protectively by ugly iron railings.

The fragments were mementoes to some, amulets to others. Welsh drovers on their way to the great Banbury cattle market were repeated offenders, taking pieces 'to keep the Devil off' despite the persistent superstition that the wheels of the drover's cart would lock insolubly as a result. So prized were the chippings that a man told Sir Arthur Evans that he been offered as much as a pound for one at Faringdon Fair twenty miles away.[27]

Although it was believed that possessing a bit brought good fortune it was also known that removing a whole stone ensured calamity. Humphrey Boffin, a farmer at the time of the Civil War, 'fetched the King Stone' to bridge a culvert. Ominously, eight strong horses strained to shift the load to Long Compton even though descending the hill. Put firmly in place across the water the slab was found on the bank next morning. Eerie noises had been heard during the night. The stone was reset. It shifted again. A single horse easily returned the ominous stone to the circle. If this had not been warning enough Roundheads later drowned Boffin in his own well.[28]

Another story stated that the heavy capstone of the Whispering Knights had been dragged away. The misguided and eventually horror-stricken thief 'could have no rest till he removed it back again'. A third tale had a miller take a stone to dam the brook that drove his waterwheel. It failed. Every night the water drained away. He blamed witchcraft. 'There are enough witches in Long Compton to drag a waggon load of hay up Long Compton hill'. In 1936 Leslie Grinsell was informed that the tallest stone of the ring had been carted to Little Rollright only for two men to be killed on the way.

Paradoxically, years before these mishaps John Aubrey wrote that at the circle-henge of the Devil's Quoits a few miles away 'one of these stones was taken down by a farmer about y[e] year 1680 to make a brigde of'. No apparition appeared. The 'brigde' survived.[29]

That such country dreads of disturbing ancient places are exceptionally old is not supposition. There is historical evidence. Compiling a 'history' in the early ninth century, a heap, he said, of all he found of rumours and marvels the Welsh monk, Nennius, wrote, 'There is another wonder in the country called Builth. There is a mound of stones there [Cefn Carn Cafall], and one of the stones placed on the top has the footprints of a dog [Arthur's] on it . . . Men come and take the stone in their hands for the space of a day and night, and on the morrow it is found upon the stone pile'.[30]

Stories of the uncountable Rollright Stones, of stones that dance at midnight, that go down to drink as the ring does at a nearby spring either on New Year's Day or when the stones hear the church bells of Long Compton, such tales may have origins just as deep in time. The fable of the elder tree is certainly as old.

In AD 959 King Eadgar demanded that 'every priest zealously promote Christianity and totally extinguish every heathenism; and forbid . . . the vain practices which are carried on with various spells, and with *frid-splotten* [sanctuaries], and with elders and with various other trees . . .'.[31] Eight centuries later the heathen Rollright Stones had its own elder tree.

Having turned the king and his men into stones the witch inexplicably transformed herself into an elder. A gloss added that were the tree to be cut it would bleed. It is a fable with an arboreal background and it can be dated. Parry informed Stukeley that 'there was, in the memory of man, an elder tree growing in the ditch betwixt the king and his soldiers, which the shepherd boys would often be cutting to please their curiosity of seeing a juice springing up from the wound as red as blood'.[32]

The elder is a hedgerow tree and its link with witchcraft at the Rollright Stones cannot be much older than 1677 when a drawing in Plot's *Naturall Historie*, Tab. XVI, 364, showed a hedge between the ring and the outlier. It had not been there in 1610. Nor did Aubrey mention it.

With its white flowers and red Autumn berries the elder exudes a bloodlike liquid if cut while blossoming in late Spring. The tree has evil associations. A branch taken into the home would bring the Devil with it. The Holy Cross was said to have been made of it. Judas hanged himself on an elder whose rubbery fungus was called Judas's ear.

> Judas he japed . with Jewish silver
> And after, on an elder tree . hanged himself.
> William Langland, *Vision of Piers Plowman*, Passus I, 67–8.

Which is why its wood stinks.

Widely considered to be capable of curing ailments the tree's health-giving virtues provided an obvious connection with witches who were notorious for their skill in concocting herbal potions. With its bleeding and with its sacrilegious ancestry it is not surprising that the elder, so close to the stone circle, should be imagined as an erstwhile witch.[33]

Then, through the misconstruing of a place-name and ignorance of history the witch was given a local habitation and a name, a fictitious Mother Shipton of Shipton-under-Wychwood, a village eight miles south of the ring. Having been insulted by the king she turned the army to stone.

It was the wrong witch, the wrong date and the wrong village. The 'witch' was a confusion with the better known Yorkshire prophetess, Mother Shipton (1488–1561), née Ursula Sontheil, of Knaresborough, who died over six centuries after Rollo. The village which was the root of the mistake, and by coincidence where Eustace, father of the Piers Plowman poet lived, was wrong. Only the credulous could interpret Shipton-under-Wychwood as 'the home of Mother Shipton in the wood of the witch'. The prosaic and proper translation is 'the sheep-farm in the forest of the Hwicce', a minor Saxon tribe who settled in the lands around the Severn Basin.[34]

By now the legend was full-grown. The witch had met the king on his way to conquer England. She promised him easy success.

> Seven long strides shalt thou take, and
> If Long Compton thou canst see
> King of England thou shalt be.

The warrior eagerly stepped forward towards the edge of the slope only for Gale's long mound to block his view. The witch cackled.

> As Long Compton thou canst not see
> King of England thou shalt not be.
> Rise up! Stick! And stand still, stone,
> For King of England thou shalt be none.
> Thou and thy men bleak stones shalt be
> And I myself an eldern tree.

Plate 9 The imprisoned King Stone.

Stories expanded. The ruin of the portal-dolmen, its five gaunt stones leaning together like secretive men became known as the Whispering Knights, murmuring traitors plotting against their king. Girls who eavesdropped would hear the name of their future husband. By the nineteenth century less innocent fertility customs became the vogue. If at midnight on Midsummer's Eve village girls ran unclothed around the circle they would see the man they were to marry. The King Stone acquired sexual powers. Childless wives rubbed their bare breasts on it hoping to become pregnant. One midnight an infertile woman from Snowshill was glimpsed naked by the stone.

> In his early career he [Jahweh] was a stone god, phallic in shape . . . elsewhere throughout the world we find in like manner a certain class of phallic gods who are specially conceived as givers of fertility and to whom prayers and offerings are made by barren women who desire children. And the point to observe is that these gods are usually (perhaps one might even say always) embodied in stone pillars or upright monoliths.[35]

The erect outlier had become a fertilising organ.

THE NINETEENTH CENTURY: VICTORIAN VIRTUES

Entertaining though this was it did not inhibit serious research. Just as the so-called Age of Reason had been followed by the Romantic period when Lake poets, Gothic novels and legends were *à la mode* so in turn that whimsical time was followed by a mechanical century of engineers and scientists who made detailed measurements, maps and plans. Druids were refashioned from wild-eyed seers into sober astronomer-

Plate 10 The imprisoned Whispering Knights.

priests. It was also the age of emergent county archaeological societies, Ordnance surveyors, systematic fieldwork and imperfect excavations.

The first good plan of the Rollright Stones, complete with elevations of the stumps and pillars, was made by Dryden and Lukis in 1840. In 1855 Beesley noticed that the ring stood on a long trackway from north-eastern to southern England, an ancient ridgeway whose existence was endorsed by Sir Cyril Fox in 1932.

'It was possible to travel along the Jurassic outcrop . . . from the Humber to the upper Thames, Gloucestershire and Salisbury Plain', a spine of limestone high above the swamps and forests of the Midlands. Situated at the narrowest part of this conspicuously steep, high ground the Rollright Stones had been erected on a prehistoric way leading to the rich Wessex territories of Avebury and Stonehenge. It was strategically placed at the junction of other routes from the west 'high on the edge of the Welsh uplands' along which, in historic times, cattle were driven along the hills 'to avoid the toll-gates in the Clun valley'.[36]

No longer an isolated monument but one whose site had been specifically chosen as a link in a widespread network it was also found to contain something that connected it with a region 200 miles away. In 1866 Bonney reported that 'at "Long Meg & Her Daughters" (Cumberland) and at Rowldrich (Oxfordshire) we find two stones placed in advance of an opening in the ring as if to form a kind of portal'. With this perceptive rediscovery of the entrance came the awareness that the design of the ring was comparable to the great stone circles of the Lake District. The significance of this, however, would not be understood for more than a century.[37]

That champion of the ubiquitous King Arthur, James Fergusson, was insensitive to such architectural grace-notes. 'It is an ordinary 100-foot [30 m] circle', he wrote in 1872, 'and the traveller . . . is sure to be dreadfully disappointed'. On the highest, rawest part of the countryside the ring was 'a sort of monument that boys of any of our larger schools could set up in a week . . . Certainly nothing that a victorious army, of say even 1,000 men, could not complete between sunrise and sunset in a summer's day'. Fergusson invoked an 'army' because of his obsessive belief that the circle commemorated the site of one of Arthur's battles, a wish as unrealistic as the legends of Rollo and Roland. He was in error by more than three thousand years.[38]

By the late nineteenth century so many stones had been despoiled for souvenirs that in 1882 the owner, Mr Bliss, 'replaced all the stones possible in their original positions for before that they seem to have been neglected in every way and were gradually growing less'. The complex of ring, outlier and tomb was scheduled in 1883 as a protected monument and an HM Office of Works sign was set up warning of prosecution for 'any person wilfully injuring or defacing the same'.[39]

MODERN TIMES: EXCAVATIONS, AXES AND ALIGNMENTS

The book by T. H. Ravenhill, *The Rollright Stones and the Men who Erected Them*, 1926, revised and enlarged in 1932, is an indispensable addition to the literature of the ring and has contributed greatly to the understanding of the circle. Living at Little Rollright Ravenhill could comfortably visit the circle a mile away, undertaking minor but vital excavations. And engaging the expertise of eminent scholars he made several profound observations.

Ravenhill noticed that care had been taken to set the unweathered and flattish sides of the slabs inwards to create a smooth-faced interior, a wish for elegance that is a characteristic of many circles including Stonehenge and Avebury in Wessex and Castlerigg in the Lake District.

He remarked on the curious honeycombing caused by weather on the limestones and how closely they were packed together. Originally 'the Circle must have presented the appearance of a circular stone wall'. Gale had seen this, 'some of them pitcht so close together, edge by edge, that it is evident that they were intended to form a close wall'. Lukis also agreed. The stones were 'as close together as their irregular outlines will allow'. In a region occupied by henges with continuous banks broken only by an entrance early stone circles with contiguous blocks may have been megalithic imitations of these earthworks.

In 1925 Ravenhill discovered a fragment of a human cheekbone in the chamber of the Whispering Knights. The following year, with two colleagues, he sank three trial pits around Stukeley's 'long barrow' proving that the mound was a natural outcrop. Just to its south the King Stone had been set up in a stretch of deeper earth 'as far up the slope as possible without having to dig into the rock, the base of the stone probably resting against the edge of the strata, which here have a considerable inclination'.[40] Its chosen position may have been a compromise between setting it at the head of the

Plate 11 The collapsed portal-dolmen of the Whispering Knights.

rise to be conspicuous to passers-by on the lower slopes, and the difficulty of quarry-
ing a stonehole in the rock-hard limestone.

Ravenhill criticised the belief, strong in the years around 1900, that the outlier
had been an astronomical marker. In 1907 Taunt claimed that it stood in line with
the midsummer sunrise and that another stone in the north-eastern arc of the ring
had a perforation through which 'the sun shines at its rising on December 21st'. As
the midwinter sunrise always occurs at the south-east there was an obvious hole in
the argument. But as late as 1930 J. Harvey Bloom confidently asserted that the
circle was 'in Stone-Age days a mighty temple to the Sun'. Ravenhill disagreed.
'Quite obviously', he wrote, 'the King Stone is too far to the north for such a purpose'.

Twenty years earlier, in 1906, Sir Norman Lockyer, Director of the Solar Physics
Laboratory, had anticipated Ravenhill. From the centre of the ring the King Stone,
about 76 m outside the Rollright Stones, did not stand at 49° in line with the midsummer sunrise. Lockyer thought that it probably recorded the ascent of an
unspecified star. Ravenhill was unconvinced. 'Modern archaeology is even more sceptical about star orientations than it is about solar orientations'.[41]

After Ravenhill research remained almost motionless for thirty years. The *Victoria County History, Oxfordshire*, 1939, simply repeated what had been said by Beesley, Evans and Ravenhill. Even the county archaeological society, founded in 1853, added nothing. The circle was left to harmless devices in which fables were supplanted by foibles.

In 1925 Alfred Watkins wrote that the stones were part of a straight landscaped ley-line from Long Compton church to Chipping Norton church and castle four miles away. In 1978 this distance was quadrupled by a newly-discovered ley from Arbury Iron Age camp, through Cropredy Bridge, scene of the Royalist victory in AD 1644, to Wroxton's fine fourteenth-century church, to another camp, then to the Madmarston third-century BC multivallate hillfort, finally reaching the Rollright Stones which had been put up three thousand years earlier.

Leys were not the only attraction. Dowsers with rods and pendulums strolled purposely about the ring, still do, enquiring which stones were male, which female, which beneficial, which evil. Spirals of energy were detected. In 1977 the Dragon Project was instituted 'to examine the possibility that energy anomalies might be associated with stone circles'. Using sensitive instruments 'to measure the intensity of the energy fields around the stones and the variations produced in them at sunrise in various seasons' ultrasonic discrepancies were noticed but the results were inconclusive. Regrettably, in recent years there have been less scientific episodes at the circle, reports of sexual indulgences, sabbats, even animal sacrifice. They are not described here.[42]

Alexander Thom's work is. In the early 1960s, measuring to the estimated centres of the Rollright Stones' holes, he concluded that this was a true circle with a diameter of 103 ft 6 in [31.6 m], its circumference of 325 ft [99 m] being almost precisely 120 Megalithic Yards of 0.829 m [99.5 m]. There were signs of an entrance, a 'gateway', at the south-east.

From the ring's centre the King Stone had a compass-bearing or azimuth of 29° and would have stood in line with the bright star, Capella, α Aurigae, in 1750 BC.[43] The date is astronomically impeccable but it is unlikely that Capella had been chosen as a target. Even had the circle been set up no earlier than 2500 BC the star, which was drifting steadily northwards by $1^{1}/_{2}$° each century, would have risen nearly 10° or 15 m to the east of the outlier. It is proper to note, however, that Thom's date was obtained independently of four C-14 determinations from the excavations of two round cairns near the King Stone in the 1980s. Corrected they averaged 1792 BC, almost fifty years earlier than the proposed stellar date.

In *The Stone Circles of the British Isles*, 1976, 295, the present writer suggested that the King Stone had been erected where it was so that from down the hillside it would have guided travellers to the stone circle which was out of sight from the northern side of the ridgeway. This is still feasible.

In the same book this author grossly underestimated the original number of stones, proposing twenty-two, but noted that the site was an isolated megalithic ring in an area of henges: Barford, Condicote, the Devil's Quoits, Hampton Lucy, Westwell, and the two mini-henges of Deadman's Burial. In a landscape of shallow clay loams the atypical stone circle was probably the assembly-place of pastoralists inhabiting a territory of some twenty square miles.[44]

In 1982 and 1984 the excavations of cairns near the King Stone was part of a wider field survey between 1981 and 1986 by the Oxford Archaeological Unit under the direction of George Lambrick. There were limited excavations in the circle and at the Whispering Knights where flint implements were discovered within 9 m of the tomb: a plano-convex knife and scraper. The Rollright Stones themselves were examined for lichens that could identify those slabs that were undisturbed, and there was extensive plotting of flint scatters with the intention of updating 'Rollright's regional archaeological context'. The results were published in Lambrick's two attractive booklets of 1983 and 1988.

The excavations near the King Stone raised the possibility that the pillar had been set up as a grave-marker for Site 4, a 17 m wide round cairn that lay just NNW of the long, natural mound. Radiocarbon assays from secondary cremations of 1420 ± 40 bc (BM-2427) and 1540 ± 70 bc (BM-2430) with calibrated midpoints of c. 1734 BC and 1887 BC are of Early Bronze Age date. A tiny round cairn, Site 3, to the west of the King Stone covering an infant's cremation and a collared urn, yielded comparable dates of 1370 ± 90 bc (BM-2429) and 1530 ± 50 bc (BM-2428), the central equivalents of c. 1674 BC and 1874 BC.[45]

The King Stone is a problem. For proponents of archaeo-astronomy the conjunction of the Capella 'date', 1790 BC, and the four unrelated C-14 assays averaging 1792 BC prove that the stone had been put up to commemorate the burials. To sceptics the stellar alignment is an illusion. There is little evidence of star-lines in any prehistoric monument of western Europe. It is arguable, indeed probable, that the burials were laid against a pillar venerated for its antiquity and already a thousand years old, maybe even older than the adjacent ring.

Despite this uncertainty much had been learned about the complex. Originally the Rollright Stones had been a true circle. Subsequently the uprooting and replacing of many stones caused so much irregularity that the diameter of 33 m could not be quoted with a deviation of less than ± 1 m. With caution this can be refined. Using a combination of John Barnatt's precise plan and Thom's method of planning from the middle of the stoneholes, not difficult with blocks averaging only 41 cm thick, a diameter of about 32.9 m is feasible.

Except for the entrance at the south-east the ring was formed of over a hundred slabs standing shoulder to shoulder. They were crudely graded in height and weight. Those at the north-west were taller and a third heavier than those opposite by the entrance. They stood in a low broad bank with a 20 m wide gap at its south-east whose terminals were at the east and south. Central to the opening was the portalled entrance, 5 m wide, formed of four stones which had apparently been selected for their opposing shapes. From inside the ring the circle-stone on the left, number 35, was a flattish block but its partner, 37, was a thin pillar. Outside it the fallen stone, 38, was a thick slab that may have stood radially to the circle. Its partner, 36, opposite the flat-topped circle-stone, 35, was a slender pillar. Such alternation of shapes is a pattern known in many pairs of standing stones as well as the famous contrasting sarsen cylinders and lozenges of the Kennet Avenue at Avebury. Whether these combinations of 'female' flat-topped blocks and 'male' pointed pillars were chosen as forms of fertility symbolism remains debatable.[46]

The Rollright Stones, the King Stone, the Whispering Knights presented few difficulties for their builders. Constructed of surface slabs lying conveniently close, none weighing more than six tons, the entire complex could have been dragged and

Plate 12 The Rollright Stones looking towards the east.

erected by a work-gang of twenty in three weeks. Fergusson's estimate had not been far from the truth.

The Rollright Stones was a 'Cumbrian' stone circle. It was the correct size, shape, was of numerous, almost contiguous stones, was embanked, had cardinal point orientations and a portalled entrance, all distinctive architectural traits of the great rings of the Lake District.[47] One of its functions may have been to act as an entrepôt on a trackway along which stone axes from the Langdale mountains were taken southwards to the rich settlements of Wessex. It may even have been designed using a Cumbrian unit of measurement.

It may be no more than numerical coincidence but whereas the circle's hypothetical diameter of 32.9 m is not a exact multiple of Thom's Megalithic Yard but an uneasy 39.7 it is one that is integral to a length of 0.794 m being almost exactly 42 of those units. This hypothetical 'Cumbrian Yard' fits other Lake District rings: 36 at Swinside, 40 at Brats Hill, 42 at Elva Plain, 42 at Castlerigg. Local units, differing from region to region, are suspected elsewhere. The Lake District question will be analysed statistically in Chapter Eleven.

Seductively, the King Stone stands about 96 units outside the circle. If there is significance in this it does not follow that the distance was measured from the ring. Instead, planners may have counted from the outlier when setting up the stone circle.

Like the Heel Stone which probably stood long before the sarsens of Stonehenge and like the thin but bellied outlying pillar of Long Meg, a needle of lean sandstone quite unlike the chubby porphyritic boulders of the Cumbrian ring, in the beginning the King Stone may have been a single standing stone for a settlement near the trackway. Later the Rollright Stones were built alongside it and, finally the cairns in a protracted prehistoric sequence of: Early Neolithic ridgeway; King Stone; Whispering Knights; Late Neolithic Rollright Stones; Early Bronze Age disc- and saucer-barrows; and Middle Bronze small cairn burials.

The ring had an astronomical refinement. Like other Cumbrian circles with external portals such as Swinside and Long Meg and Her Daughters, the builders neatly arranged the pair of stones on one side of the entrance, here the two on the north, to form an alignment. Standing in a 1.2 m long line the two were easy to sight along. The combination of latitude 52°, azimuth 142°.5, and horizon height, $-0°.03$, produced a declination of $-29°.3$, that of the most southerly rising of the moon.

At the Rollright Stones the juxtaposition of a portal dolmen, a type of chambered tomb well-known in Wales, and a Cumbrian entrance circle, suggests that both the tomb and the ring were distant outliers of a tradition of western megaliths.[48] Portal dolmens like the Whispering Knights are known in western Wales and in Somerset. There are Oxfordshire counterparts at Enstone, Langley and Spelsbury. The distribution implies an influx from the west onto the congenial Cotswold soils.

Entrance circles, though presumably later, have a similar pattern. There may have been two at Ffridd Newydd, Dyfed, between a pair of portal dolmens at Carnedd Hengwm South and Cors y Gedol a mile away.[49] There are others south of the Lake District at Gamelands, Westmorland, and at the Druids' Circle, Penmaenmawr near Conway. The discovery in Oxfordshire of axes both from the Langdale and from the Welsh Group VII axe-factory of Graig Lwyd near the Druids' Circle indicates the exporting of those implements in the centuries around 3000 BC.[50]

There is indirect support for the belief that the Rollright Stones had an early date. About nineteen miles to the ssw assays were obtained from the ditch of the once-great circle-henge of the Devil's Quoits near Stanton Harcourt. Their dates of 2060 $\pm$ 120 bc (HAR-1887) and 1640 $\pm$ 70 bc (HAR-1888) hint at occupation there from late in the Neolithic to well into Early Bronze Age times, perhaps from 2800 to 1900 BC. Discovery of Late Neolithic grooved ware in a posthole fits well with this time-span.[51]

'In the Oxford country there are great stones arranged as it were in some connection by the hand of man. But at what time this was done, or by what people, or for what memorial of significance is unknown'.

It is over six hundred years since those words were written. Through the following centuries, slowly, unsurely, like waving away mist with one's hands, truths have been glimpsed. At what time? Probably around 3000 BC. By what people? By men and women of the Late Neolithic, pastoralists, members of loosely-linked societies trading or bartering or presenting gifts of ritual objects such as stone axes, people of an open-air grooved-ware cult. Of what significance? So much has been recovered since those despairing words of the early fourteenth century.

Camden stated that the ring was circular. Aubrey gave its size. The sharp eyes of Stukeley noticed that its had become the focus of a Bronze Age necropolis. Amongst the diversions of popular whimsies the ring's importance grew when Beesley noted that it stood at the junction of trackways from the north-east to southern England and from Wales to the Midlands. Bonney recognised the portalled entrance whose position at the south-east of the circle faced the Whispering Knights and also the line of gentlest approach. The comparative density of flints there suggests that there may have been settlements on the lower ground to the south and that this was the direction from which neighbouring people approached the ring.[52]

Enthusiastic claims that the King Stone was an astronomical marker were unfounded but coarse alignments that included the moon and two cardinal points are akin to others in Lake District circles. A connection with the exploitation of Cumbrian stone for axes strengthens the comparison.

Within this latticed panorama of emigration and traffic in which the Rollright Stones has to be envisaged as a staging-post between Yorkshire, Cumbria, Wales and Wessex there are intimacies for the ring itself. With an internal area of some $835\,m^2$ it could have accommodated an assembly of one hundred and fifty participants without crowding. Its heaviest stone, no more than three tons, could have been set up by a dozen or so workers. Centuries earlier even the six-ton capstone of the Whispering Knights could have been manoeuvred into place by thirty labourers. There is no need to imagine a vast concourse. The congregation may have included men, women and children, even others from distant parts gathering at seasonal times of the year. 'Of what significance . . .' may ultimately be answered. At present it remains speculation.

The circle of the Rollright Stones was used by people who looked to the skies in their ceremonies. It was a meeting-place, a market, a sanctuary, even a temple. But not everything can so easily be explained.

In June 1991, Mark Rylance, now artistic director of the Globe Theatre, and the Phoebus Cart company performed *The Tempest* inside the ring. Midnight matinees were arranged. The play was, after all, 'about the elements'.

There was instant disruption. Mobile phones failed. A stopwatch lost ten minutes an hour. Quartz watches went wrong. Actors forgot their lines. A dancer saw 'strange lights, with peoples' eyes looking like diamonds'. During the production a gale of driving rain lashed across the muddy and exposed field. 'Here's neither bush nor shrub to bear off any weather at all, and another storm brewing', groaned Trinculo.

At the end the players applauded the audience. All two hundred drenched spectators cheered the cast. Before the play began a spokesman remarked that 'the Rollright Stones is a very atmospheric site'.[53]

Plate 13 Long Meg with her 'daughters' in the background.

Chapter Two

Long Meg and Her Daughters, Cumbria

PAST BELIEFS, PRESENT THOUGHTS AND PREHISTORIC
TIMES

*The name by which this monument is known appears to have no connection
with the original constructors, or with the purposes for which it was erected.*
C. P. Kains-Jackson, *Our Ancient Monuments*, 1880, 12.

For burdened travellers the stone circle of Long Meg and Her Daughters situated just
east of the River Eden, two and a quarter miles north of Langwathby and five and a
half miles north-east of Penrith, was a comfortable distance across two fords from the
three henges at Eamont Bridge six miles to the south-west (Fig. 4).

It is the fifth biggest of all the stone circles in Britain and Ireland. No cromlech in
Brittany exceeds it. Even the greatest, Ménec East near Carnac, 7,634 m², is smaller.
With diameters of 109.4 m east-west by 93 m Long Meg's area is 7,991 m² (0.8 ha),
fully twenty-five times larger than the average ring, and the circle is greatly exceeded
only by the enormous outer ring at Avebury whose interior is almost eleven times larger. Other circles such as Stanton Drew Centre, 10,315 m², the Ring of Brodgar, 8,435
m², and Avebury South, 8,326 m², are more spacious than Long Meg but
only marginally so.[1] It must be assumed that these enclosures were vast because
they were for huge assemblies, probably both men and women, from the surrounding
countryside.

First systematically surveyed by C. W. Dymond and then by Alexander Thom, Site
L1/7, many questions remain about this famous ring, not the least being the origin of
its name.

FROM MEDIAEVAL TIMES TO AD 1900

As long ago as 1600 Reginald Bainbridge, 'scolemaster' of Appleby, informed William
Camden of 'certaine monuments or pyramides of stone . . . commonlie called meg
with hir daughters . . . They are huge great stones'. In 1904 there was an unsubstantiated report that the Castlerigg circle was also known as 'Meg and her Daughters' but
of this there is no confirmation.[2]

Meg, a hoyden or coarse woman according to the Oxford English Dictionary,
has sometimes been equated with the Elizabethan Margaret Selby, second wife of
Sir William Fenwick of Wallington Hall close to Morpeth in Northumberland.[3]

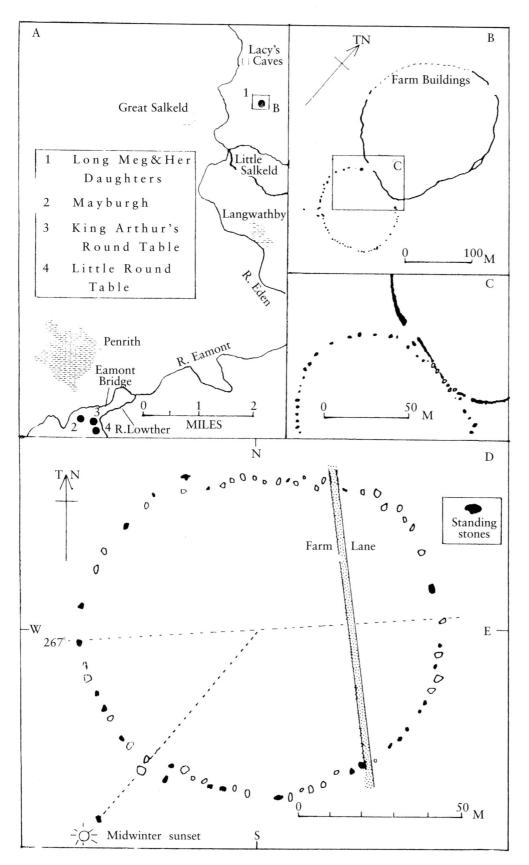

Fig. 4 Map and plan of Long Meg and Her Daughters, Cumbria.

Nicknamed Meg of Meldon she was said to be a witch whose idiosyncracy it was when not seeking frantically for a misplaced treasure to sit in a stone coffin amidst the ruins of Newminster Abbey near her home.

The identification is unlikely. Apart from the discouraging fifty hilly miles of Pennines between Morpeth and Little Salkeld Lady Selby was born too late. Newminster Abbey was not dissolved until 1537 so 'Meg' and her coffin must have been after that date. She was certainly alive in 1606 when her daughter was betrothed. References to a 'Long Meg' existed long before either of these dates.[4]

The stature and skinniness of this mythical woman gave rise to the saying, 'as long as Meg of Westminster'. In his *History of the Worthies of Britain*, 1662, Thomas Fuller wrote, 'This is applyed to persons very tall, especially if they have Hop-pole-heighth wanting breadth proportionable thereunto. That such a gyant woman ever was in Westminster, cannot be proved by any good witness'.[5]

Because her supposed gravestone was exceptionally long a pamphlet of 1582, *The Life and Pranks of Long Meg of Westminster*, concluded that she must have been a giantess but Fuller believed that 'her' stone was no more than the marker of a mass grave of monks who had died of plague. 'If there be any truth in the Proverb, it rather relateth to a great Gun, lying in the Tower, commonly call'd long Megg, and in troublesome times . . . brought to Westminster . . .'.

The gun was Mons Meg, a powerful cannon taken back to Edinburgh Castle in 1829. Forged in Flanders it was acquired by James II of Scotland on his marriage to Mary of Gueldres in 1449. It was enormous. Some 4 m long it was capable of firing a stone ball over one and a half miles and was used to bombard and wreck the keep of Norham Castle in 1513. Fifteenth-century gunners gave such gigantic pieces pet names such as 'Foul mouthed Meg' and 'Dulle Griet' (Mad Meg), and it seems that 'Long Meg' was a popular mediaeval catch-phrase applied to any long and slender object, very apt for the tall and scrawny 3.8 m high pillar of red sandstone standing south-west of the ring of her seventy or so daughters.

Witches and stone circles are seldom associated. Where they are, as at the Rollright Stones in Oxfordshire, it is the witch that casts the spell. Sometimes the rings were trysts where witches gathered. Scottish megaliths such as the Clava cairn at Auldearn or the Lang Stane o'Craigearn are examples. But only Long Meg is composed of petrified witches. Her name probably dates from the late fifteenth century, the time when fear of witchcraft was becoming a hysteria and an age when uninformed superstition imagined that the stones of circles were the ossified bodies of sinners.

The vague 'seventy or so' daughters results from the tradition that the stones were uncountable. Given the half-buried fragments of boulders amongst the stones of the irregular ring it is understandable that estimates have varied. In 1610 Camden said there were 77 pillars. John Aubrey, using Sir William Dugdale's imperfect record, stated 'about two hundred in number'. Stukeley 'counted' on hundred in 1725, later amending this to 70. Hutchinson made 67. Wordsworth, who visited the ring, 'that family forlorn', in 1833 imploring Long Meg to reveal her secrets, 'Speak, Giant-mother', but receiving no reply, said there were 72 daughters as well as Long Meg. Dymond's accurate 1875 survey recorded that there were 69, including Long Meg, of which 27 were erect. Nine years later Lukis could find only 67, 24 of them upright. By mischance in 1933 Collingwood said there were 57. Thom plotted 66.[6]

The discrepancies may be fortunate. It is rumoured that the first exact count will break the spell put on a sabbat of witches by the magician, Michael Scott, who turned the gaggle of unholy hags to stone. Anyone establishing their true number will re-animate the coven, probably to the teller's discomfiture.[7]

There are other stories. The pillars are girls turned to stone for dancing on the Sabbath. If a piece were broken off Long Meg she would bleed just as the witch at the Rollright Stones would do. More confusingly, the unwearying traveller Celia Fiennes who visited the circle in 1698 wrote of 'Great Mag and her Sisters [sic], the story is that these soliciting her to an unlawfull love by an enchantment are turned with her into stone'. This enigmatic reference to pre-nuptial sex may have prompted the diarist to add that 'the stone in the middle which is called Mag is much bigger and have some forme like a statue or figure of a body'.

In July 1752, George Smith denied this. 'The vulgar notion that the largest of these stones has breasts, and resembles the remainder of a female statue is caused by the whimsical irregularity of the figure, in which a fervid imagination may discover a resemblance of almost any thing'.[8]

Smith was right. Except for the spirals and arcs on her eastern face Long Meg is undecorated. Anthropomorphic representations of a protectress of the dead, symbolised by pairs of breasts in high relief like those in Breton *allées-couvertes* such as Tressé, Kerguntüil and Mougau-Bihan, are unknown in Britain. Here, except for Stonehenge, where motifs do exist in stone circles they are abstract and of undeciphered significance.[9]

Celia Fiennes had been told about the counting. 'The rest are but soe many craggy stones, but they affirme they cannot be counted twice'. The reason for this, common amongst stone circles, may have been the damage they had suffered.

In August, 1725 Stukeley saw how badly the ring was being treated. A ditch ran across it from east to west, the northern half ploughed and planted, the southern in a common. Nor were the stones safe. 'Many are standing, but more fallen, and several carried away; but lately they have destroyed some by blasting, as they call it, i.e. blowing them in pieces with gunpowder; others they have sawed for mill-stones'.[10]

Worse was to come. Towards the end of the eighteenth century the owner of Salkeld Hall and of Long Meg, Lt-Colonel Samuel Lacy, created an 'antiquity' by enhancing some caves on the bank of the Eden, transforming them into an elegant grotto complete with paid 'hermit'. He then began the demolition of something genuinely ancient.

> The late Colonel Lacy, it is said, conceived the idea of removing Long Meg and her Daughters by blasting. Whilst the work was being proceeded with under his orders, the slumbering powers of Druidism rose in arms against this violation of their sanctuary; and such a storm of thunder and lightning, and such heavy rain and hail ensued, as the Fell-sides never before witnessed. The labourers fled for their lives, vowing never more to meddle with Long Meg . . . All lovers of antiquity must be thankful for the providential throwing of cold water on so wicked a design.

Perhaps alarmed by this manifestation of the supernatural Lacy had a change of heart. 'Part of the ground within the area of the monument is ploughed', wrote Hutchinson, 'and heretofore the fences of the fields intersected it, so that from no quarter a proper view of the whole circle could be had, to take a drawing of it; but Mr Lacy, to gratify the curious, is removing those obstacles'.

Dangers remained. In the mid-nineteenth century some stones were shifted but the farmer 'couldn't get a crop whatever, danged if they didn't put them all back again'.[11]

What could not be replaced were two cairns that had stood at the centre of the ring. Bainbridge, writing to Camden around 1600, mentioned that 'Ther are within the compass of these stones two great heapes of small stones under the wiche, they say, that the dead bodies were buryed ther'. The cairns were there almost a century later. From Dugdale's unpublished notes John Aubrey transcribed, 'In the middle are two Tumuli, or Barrowes of cobble-stones, nine or ten foot high'. From curiosity he enquired about 'the Giant's bone, and Body found there. The body is in the middle of the orbicular stones'.

Whether this meant that before 1693 the cairns had been dismantled and a burial discovered is unrecorded. Certainly by 1725 the ring was empty. 'In the middle of the circle', commented the observant Stukeley, ' are two roundish plots of ground, of a different colour from the rest apparently, and more stony and barren'.

In the revised 1695 edition of Camden's *Britannia* there was scepticism about the cairns. 'The heaps of stones in the middle of this monument, are no part of it; but have been gather'd off the plough'd-lands adjoyning, and . . . have been thrown up here together in a waste corner of the field'.

This is improbable. As Clare Fell has observed, 'it seems extremely unlikely that two heaps of stones would be thrown up in the centre, as this would impede ploughing within the circle. In all probability two burial cairns formerly existed here'. The fact that they were removed to make room for crops strengthens the belief in their prehistoric origin, erected inside a long-hallowed sanctuary, a phenomenon known elsewhere. Five cairns lie inside the ring of Brat's Hill on Burn Moor. The circular outlines of others are still detectable inside Castlerigg, a circle sometimes wrongly called the Carles as though the stones were 'ceorls' or husbandmen ossified for some misdeed. The error comes from a misreading of Stukeley who actually wrote, 'They call it the Carſles, and, corruptly I suppose, Castle-rig'.[12]

The addition of cairns and barrows to stone circles was commonplace in the Early Bronze Age. A round barrow was raised on the bank of the Arbor Low circle-henge in the Peak District. A miniscule chambered tomb was squashed inside Callanish. Long Meg's prehistoric cairns were probably secondary intrusions.

Fergusson, with his obsession that every circle and standing stone was a Dark Age Arthurian cenotaph, decided that Long Meg was the gravestone of a chieftain who had fallen in one of Arthur's six battles in Cumberland, conflicts commemorated by names such as King Arthur's Round Table and Arthur's Pike hill near Moor Divock. Cumbrian locals, scoffed Fergusson, could never have invented them because 'The boors of that land had no literature – no learning'.

Stukeley, rather more sensibly, believed the stony, barren patches where the cairns had stood 'probably were the immediate places of burning the sacrifices . . .'. Such druidical horrors appealed to the eighteenth century and Hutchinson visualised a dramatic function for Long Meg which 'from its vicinity to the altar, was used for binding the victim'.[13]

FROM AD 900 TO THE PRESENT DAY

Plate 14 The fallen south-western entrance with the outlier beyond.

Despite the flat land to west and east the ring of Long Meg and Her Daughters was built on a wide sandstone terrace sloping so pronouncedly down to the north that the circle's north-east arc is 6 m lower than Long Meg at the south-west.

The stones were local except for the triassic sandstone of Long Meg which came either from the banks of the River Eden one and a half miles away, or from the hard beds of the Lazonby Fells across the river to the west. The other boulders were glacial erratics lying nearby: a few mica schists and granites from Scotland; many Borrowdale volcanics from the Lake District; and some quartz porphyries from the same region.[14] They are massive. Although there are a few relatively small stones of no more than four tons the average block weighs nine tons or more and demanded the strength of forty labourers to manoeuvre into position. Two huge boulders on the major axis, almost east-west of each other, are up to thirty tons in bulk. Such monsters could have been moved only by well-organised gangs of at least 135 workers.

On the western side of the circle are traces of a low bank, 3.5 m wide but only a few centimetres high. Whether this is prehistoric or simply the results of ploughing could be resolved only by excavation.[15]

In contradiction to Wordsworth who called the site 'a perfect circle eighty yards in diameter' the ring has a noticeably flattened northern arc so that the north-south diameter is 16 m shorter than that from east to west. Fergusson was the first to recognise this, remarking on its imperfect layout. Dymond was content to call it 'an irregular oval' as though it was no more than a badly-laid out ring and it was not until 1900 that a geometrical explanation was offered for its assymmetrical shape.

George Watson speculated that it was a well-planned east-west oval based on two 91 m wide semi-circles with centres 18.3 m apart. Long Meg, he theorised, was the survivor of four outliers at the corners of a rectangle around the oval, each of them in line with a solstitial rising or setting. The enormous east and west blocks had been altars and from the centres of the semi-circles thirty calendrical risings and settings of the sun were indicated by stones in the oval. Long Meg was in line with the midwinter sunset.[16]

His theory was ingenious but almost completely wrong in its measurements, construction and alignments. Decades later Alexander Thom deduced that the site was one of his Type B flattened circles based on two right-angled triangles whose sides were 22, 66 and 70 Megalithic Yards, 0.829 m, long. The erratic positions of some stones, he thought, had been caused by the downward flow of earth over the centuries.

Solifluction is doubtful. A more plausible explanation for the straightened north arc is that it was erected against the south side of a vast ditched enclosure, about 220 m SSE–NNW by 190 m, possibly a settlement site. It was pear-shaped, flattening out where the ground rose. There, against the southernmost of several entrances, 'the north portal of the [stone] circle appears to turn slightly east to turn directly into the enclosure entrance', presumably to allow access from one to the other.[17]

If so, they were contemporaries, the circle arguably being the later if only by a few years. Its northern stones are closer together, smaller, narrower, lighter than elsewhere as though it had been too dangerous to erect heavier ones against an existing ditch. The precaution was justified. Several blocks subsequently fell onto the upper silts of the trench.[18]

So far from being one of Fergusson's 'rude stone monuments' the architecture of the 'circle' is complex. There appear to be two entrances, one now incomplete at the north-west and a second at the south-west where two great boulders frame a wide gap outside which a pair of great blocks act as portals. That the two entrances are not diametrically opposite each other is not unusual. The same is true at Stonehenge, Arbor Low and several henges.

At the south-west, some 18 m beyond the portals, stands Long Meg, the tapering sandstone pillar, 3.8 m high and weighing about nine tons. From the middle of the ring it is not central to the entrance but is in line with the western circle-stone and portal. Almost rectangular in section its surfaces are roughly weathered except the east side which is smoother and angled 64° from True North. This is a full 20° from the bearing between the middle of the circle and Long Meg and is a good reason for believing that the pillar was there long before the ring. If not, from the evidence of other sites, the flattest and best edge should have faced the circle. The additional fact that it bears megalithic art adds strength to this observation.

In 1835 Sir Gardner Wilkinson noticed a concentric circle of four rings around a central cup carved on the outlier. Some years later Professor Simpson examined the stone and claimed to have found seven sets of motifs. A more reliable survey by Harvey in June 1940, when the light was excellent, traced three unarguable groups.

The light quickly deteriorated. 'It was only the fortunate chance of arriving at exactly the right moment, and having a piece of chalk, that enabled a complete record to be made'. Although faint the carvings were real and more have recently been noted and recorded by Beckensall.[19]

The topmost carving, about 1.5 m from the base of Long Meg, has a central cup, three surrounding concentric circles 22 cm in diameter and the upper quadrant of a fourth. A slanting groove or gutter, tangential to the middle circle, extends outwards to the WNW. Fifteen centimetres SSE of this set is a continuous anti-clockwise spiral, 25 cm across, of four turns around a central cup. The third group, also 25 cm across and about 60 cm above the ground consists of two small concentric circles with the upper two-thirds of two more above them.

Such art does not conform to classical cup-and-ring styles but is more akin to the early passage-tomb repertoire with spirals, guttered rings and grouped arcs. Chevrons carved on the nearby Glassonby ring belong to the same school.[20] Bradley has observed that at Long Meg 'the uprights of the circle itself are entirely undecorated but the one outlier is of a different raw material and is profusely carved with motifs found in passage tomb art. This stone is also located on the axis of the midwinter sunset as viewed from the centre of the circle'.[21] Excitingly, one of the symbols, the spiral, may be astronomically informative.

Watson was the first to suggest that Long Meg was aligned on the midwinter sunset. Morrow reversed this, preferring to think of a prehistoric observer around 1150 BC using the outlier as a backsight, looking towards the circle-centre and the midsummer sunrise but with no foresight to direct the eye the 'sightline' would have been undefined and unusable. The 'date', calculated on the rising of the bright star Arcturus, α Boötis, in a northerly mountainous notch, was a stellar misconception. Other than the sun, stars had no connection with Long Meg.

Alexander Thom concurred with Watson. After a characteristically meticulous survey in 1954 he calculated that with Long Meg's latitude, 54°.72, an azimuth from the circle-centre to the outlier of 223°.4, and a horizon height of 1°.1 the declination would be −24°.17, that of the midwinter sunset long before 4000 BC. That this was when Long Meg was erected should not be taken literally. The sun's extreme risings and settings drift along the skyline so slowly over the centuries that an error by the builders of only $^1/_2$° when setting up the pillar, hardly 60 cm over a distance of some 74 m, would change this solar 'date' by over 3,000 years.[22]

What is most intriguing about the sightline is not that it existed. An interest in the sun and moon is well-attested amongst the Neolithic and Bronze Age societies of western Europe and to detect a solar line at Long Meg is no surprise. But that it was physically carved, like a celestial advertisement, in a symbol that was widely-understood is unexpected.

In an error-filled but stimulating book Brennan described how day by day on its six-month journey northwards towards midsummer the sun's shadow casts tight, clockwise spirals, but much looser anti-clockwise ones as it moves back towards midwinter. The well-known spiral on the midwinter pillar of Long Meg is an anti-clockwise one. So are two others recorded by Beckensall, one 90 cm above it, the other, almost eradicated, 35 cm from the ground at the south edge of the stone (Fig. 5).

This could be no more than coincidence but Brennan did cite many other examples of the same occurrence: at Newgrange, at Barclodiad-y-Gawres, at Cape Clear in

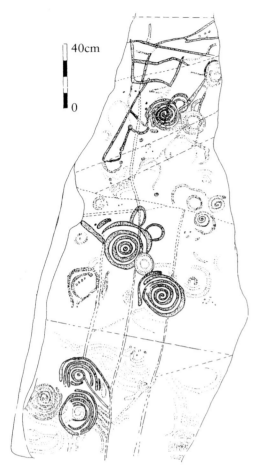

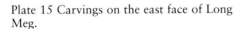

Fig. 5 Carvings on Long Meg from a rubbing by Stan Beckensall.

Plate 15 Carvings on the east face of Long Meg.

County Cork, at Knowth and elsewhere. Long Meg, therefore, may possess one of the first megalithic symbols to be understood in modern times.

Interestingly, in September 1995 a spiral was noticed at the circle of Castlerigg nineteen miles to the south-west. It was carved on an eastern stone of the circle, at the end of an unexplained internal rectangle. Against it a second stone bore a lattice-pattern. Like Long Meg they marked a solar position but not that of the equinox. Because the south-eastern horizon was slightly higher than the north-eastern the midpoint between the midsummer and midwinter sunrises was slightly south of true east. The stones stood there, halfway between the sunrises. Predictably the spiral was clockwise.[23]

It might be asked why it is that Long Meg is not framed in the middle of the wide entrance but this would have offered a 'window' 7° wide. Instead, the alignment was very neatly determined from the interior of the ring by the two bulbous stones on the western side of the entrance and the sharp foresight of Long Meg rising beyond them. This 24 m long line ensured accuracy. There was no need to find the centre of the circle. An observer just sighted along the three stones. Similar constructions exist at Swinside, at Ballynoe in County Down and at the Rollright Stones.[24]

Like several other great Cumbrian rings Long Meg contained not only a calendrical line but one to a cardinal point.[25] At Castlerigg and Swinside it was the north, at Mayburgh the east, at Long Meg the west. Unlike the calendrical settings these cardinal lines are rarely accurate to more than a degree or two. The writer believes that circle-builders were concerned not with the abstract concept of a cardinal position but with the point midway between two solar extremes, at Long Meg presumably that between the midwinter and midsummer settings. Had the western skyline been level this would have been at True West, 270°. The horizon at Long Meg, however, was nearly a degree higher to the south-west causing the sun to disappear below the horizon sooner. This 'pulled' the midpoint a little to the south so that the gigantic western boulder stood not at 270° but at 267°, equidistant between the observed winter and summer settings. What looks like cardinal inaccuracy to today's investigator was solar precision to the people who set up the stone.

Such astronomical revelations are only part of many advances made in the study of stone circles over recent decades. Much has been discovered since the centuries when Long Meg and others were blood-spattered druidical temples. Territories are becoming apparent[26] with a variety of monuments in them. On the eastern rim of the Lake District at Long Meg there was not only the enclosure and the great circle but the kerb-circle of Little Meg and a second, much smaller stone circle, seen by Stukeley but now destroyed, some hundred metres wsw of the outlier. About 6 1/4 miles to the ssw there was the cluster of three architecturally disparate henges of Mayburgh, King Arthur's Round Table, and the Little Round Table.[27] The same distance nnw of Long Meg were circles and cairn-circles at Broomrigg.[28]

The similar spacing intimates that there were settled tracts with boundaries delimited by the natural features of rivers, fells and marshes. In Cumbria the great stone circles are spaced about ten miles apart but their territories must have differed greatly in size just as today's cities, towns and villages do.

It is possible to make estimates of the differences. As an example, using the combined criteria for three circles of their areas, their average weight of stone, their heaviest stone and the number of workers needed to set it up, quite constant relationships emerge. The smaller the ring the lighter the stones, the fewer the labourers. The converse also applies (Table 1).

On the arbitrary assumption that an assembled congregation would occupy about half the ring and that rather than being packed in like the audience of a pop concert they each had a comfortable body-space of a metre around them then, in ascending order, the theoretical size of community for each of the circles would be: 104 for Grey Croft, 149 for Castlerigg, and 1,540 for Long Meg and Her Daughters. That these ratios are not entirely fanciful is supported by today's numbers of inhabitants of the nearest town: Gosforth, Keswick and Penrith: about 1,000, 5,500 and 12,250 respectively.[29]

Plate 16 The outlier and stone circle looking towards the north-east.

TABLE 1. Relationship between modern populations and the size of stone circles.

	Internal Area m^2	Average Stone Ton Weight	Heaviest Stone	Minimum Work-force
Grey Croft	539	2.5	3.7	20
Castlerigg	722	4	15	70
Long Meg	8,011	9	30	135

The projected figures for prehistory are almost certainly wrong but the proportions are probably near the truth. The hypothetical population of Long Meg, even if wrong by a factor of two or three, still implies that there were sufficient people for several groups of workers to have been erecting stones at the same time. Comparable suggestions have been made for co-ordinated gangs digging the ditches of henges such as Stonehenge.

What remains unknown is whether all members of a territory participated in the ceremonies or whether some were excluded by sex or age. With a postulated thousand or more people at Long Meg one might guess that every one took part. Otherwise the population would have been extremely large.

The rings must have been for natives but their presence in the challengingly mountainous region of the Lake District is best explained by a connection with the stone-axe industry. As long ago as 1933 R. G. Collingwood perceived this. Although, as was

Plate 17 Showing the great size of the stone circle, Long Meg rises in the background.

usual then, he was doubtful about astronomical alignments, he declared that 'the stone circles and the axes thus hang together and seem to demand explanation as the relics of a single people'.[30]

When this was is better known today. Exploitation of the tuffs from the Langdale screes had a long duration between about 3800 and 2200 BC. Great rings such as Long Meg, Castlerigg and Swinside are likely to be early in this period, some confirmation coming from a C-14 assay of 2,525 ± 85 bc (GU-1591), calibrated to *c.* 3275 BC, from the Lochmaben Stane, the survivor of an oval ring on the far side of the Solway firth.[31] Its remote situation implies that it was later than rings at the heart of the industrial area.

The spaced locations and size of these early stone circles suggest that they were places where natives and strangers met at agreed times of the year established by a solar calendar. In Australia aborigines also bartered or exchanged stone axes. 'The tools were traded along known routes by stages and . . . these journeys were arranged to coincide with seasonal festivals of magical and social significance'.[32]

Long Meg and Her Daughters may be seen partly as a staging-post to which visitors from Yorkshire and elsewhere came regularly to acquire the precious axes and partly as a centre where local people gathered, coming from nearby settlements and from isolated farmsteads miles away, assembling at the death of the year in the shortest and darkest days to supplicate for the return of summer, light and warmth. The ring may be one of Britain's oldest stone circles, erected in the years around 3000 BC.

'The thing is not so wonderfull as that of Stonidge', shrugged the matter-of-fact Celia Fiennes but it astonished the more sensitive William Wordsworth. 'Though it will not bear a comparison with Stonehenge, I must say, I have not seen any other relique of those dark ages which can pretend to rival it in singularity and dignity of appearance'.

Plate 18 The rough blocks of Stanton Drew.

Chapter Three

Stanton Drew, Somerset

AVENUES AND ALIGNMENTS

Stanton-Drew, where is to be seen a monument of stones like those of Stone-henge *in Wiltshire; but these being not altogether so big as the* Stone-henge *ones, nor standing in so clear a plain, the hedges and trees mix'd among them have made them less taken notice of.*

William Camden, *Britannia*, 1695, 79.

Even larger than Long Meg and Her Daughters the central stone circle and its two smaller rings and avenues at Stanton Drew are members of a group of multiple rings in south-western England including the four Priddy henges, the three Hurlers on Bodmin Moor and the three erstwhile Tregeseal circles at Land's End.[1]

Because so many stones are fallen or missing at Stanton Drew the site seems unpromising, offering few insights into the nature of the societies that raised and used the complex. Implausible legends rather than plausible archaeology have appealed to many otherwise disappointed visitors. But the belief that the circles have nothing to tell us is wrong.

Recent research removes the need for pessimism. It can be shown that the site was carefully landscaped around 2800 BC by people possessing elementary numeracy and considerable surveying skills. They also respected earlier Neolithic monuments and integrated them within the layout of the circles. Tradition was combined with innovation. Containing architectural traits from the large stone circles of the Lake District subtle astronomy was also built into the pattern of the splendid but short-lived megaliths of Stanton Drew.

There was an earlier astonishment. A magnetometer survey by English Heritage in 1997 revealed two unsuspected features. Inside the great central circle there were nine concentric rings, 23 m to 94 m in diameter, of large postholes, over four hundred of them forming an immense timber structure that may have preceded the megalithic rings, probably unroofed, perhaps lintelled, carved and painted. Outside the stone circle was a 7 m wide ditch, 135 m in diameter around the circle with a 40 m wide entrance at the north-east. Nothing can be seen of it today.[2]

THE MEGALITHIC MONUMENTS AT STANTON DREW

Below Wales, by the side of the Bristol Channel, is the largest stone circle in western Europe after the outer ring at Avebury. Two much smaller rings flank it to the

Plate 19 An aerial view of the three rings, from the south-west.

north-east and ssw. The three circles stand in a 366 m long but angled line, the central an enormous 114.6 m in diameter. They lie just south of the River Chew in a valley, Broadfield Down rising steeply to the west, the Mendips to the south. Following extensive Neolithic forest clearance the countryside was open with scattered hazels and miles of grassland, an ideal environment for open-air stone circles. With the remains of two avenues, a Cove (a three-sided, unroofed setting of tall slabs) and an outlying stone, Hauteville's Quoit, the group is remarkably similar to Avebury but separated from that monstrous earthwork and its megalithic rings by 30 miles of prehistoric forest and marshes (Fig. 6).

That early eighteenth-century enthusiast for Avebury, the antiquarian, William Stukeley, noticed the likeness. 'Now what could be plainer than the conformity between this work and Abury? the same situation, near the spring of a river, upon a knoll in a large valley, guarded from severity of weather by environing hills: here is the cove of three stones; the circle of twelve; that of thirty stones;

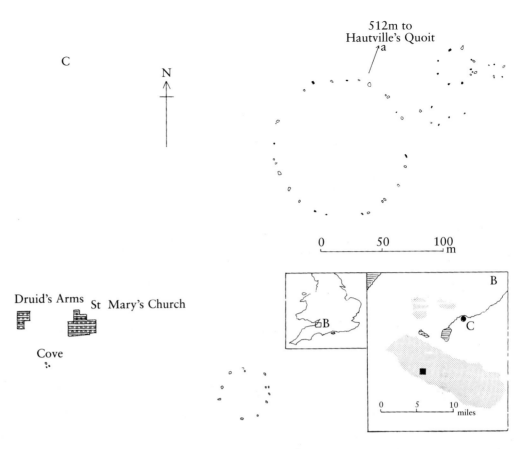

512m to
Hautville's Quoit

C

N

0   50   100
              m

Druid's Arms St Mary's Church

Cove

B

C

B

0   5   10
              miles

Fig. 6 Map and plan of Stanton Drew.

all set at the same intervals of thirty foot [9.1 m]; here are the concentric circles'.[3]

The Stanton Drew rings are a brecciated mixture of local limestones and sandstones probably from the Harptree ridge three or four miles to the south. On a low river-terrace this once-great site now seems disappointingly unobtrusive, its very spaciousness and toppled stones reducing the impression it makes. The rings seem almost without meaning, lying remotely from each other and their coarse, fallen blocks do not assist the imagination. Two centuries ago a visitor wrote that 'In 1784, I went . . . on May the nighteenth to see the remains of a supposed Druid Temple at Stanton Drew. The first appearance did not offer anything which seemed to deserve a second attention'. He was unimaginative.[4]

The remoteness of the circles hindered research. Just as Avebury was not noticed until 1649, and even then only by accident, the even more isolated Stanton Drew had to wait until 1664 when John Aubrey, visiting his grandmother at Burnett Manor in the nearby parish of Compton Dando, was told about the rings. 'Twas a strange chance, you may say that I should come to know this old Monument, which lies so very obscure in a place far from any great Roads'.[5]

THE NAME

Stanton Drew had nothing to do with Druids. Despite Aubrey's conjecture that 'It is very probable that the village hath its name of Drew from the Druids' he was cautious enough to add, 'Drew is the name of an ancient Family in the Western parts', and that was the explanation.[6]

Stanton Drew is a composite name. In the Anglo-Saxon Charters and in Domesday Book the hamlet was known only as *Stantune*, 'the homestead by the stones'. The 'Drew' was added in the thirteenth century when the Drogo or Dreux family became the landowners.[7]

HISTORY OF RESEARCH

The first recognition that the stones were of importance came with the building of the Norman, perhaps Saxon, church of St Mary's, deliberately erected between the Great Circle and the Cove presumably to discourage pagan practices at the stones.[8]

Then, for centuries, the circles, so far from large towns, were disregarded by outsiders and maltreated by their rural owners. 'Mr Aubrey, that indefatigable searcher-out of antiquities [was] the first that has observed it', wrote Stukeley in an unusually generous tribute.[9] When John Aubrey visited the rings he was unable to understand their layout because of agricultural cultivation and rural destruction. 'When I saw it, the corn [barley] being ripe I could not survey the stones so exactly as I would . . . As hard as these stones are they make a Shift to brake them with sledges, because they so incumber their good land, and they told me they are much diminished these fewe yeares'.[10] There were other difficulties.

On 23 July 1723, William Stukeley went to Stanton Drew with the Rev. John Strachey. His ever-curious eye noted that 'Near Stanton Drue, in a *trivium* [a crossroads] is an old elm-tree made infamous for the bloody trophies of judge Jeffry's barbarity, in the duke of Monmouth's rebellion; for all its broad-spreading arms were covered over with heads and limbs of the unfortunate countrymen'.[11] The tree was at Pensford where twelve men were condemned to death in September 1685. One, William Mangell, pleaded not guilty, was tried in the morning and hanged in the afternoon.

Stukeley's companion, Strachey, more single-minded about the circles, regretted that the rings are 'so Intermixt with Hedges & Inclosures & distant from a great road that they have not so much taken notice of by Antiquarys'.[12] The great central circle was split in three by the hedges of fields for cattle. To its north-east the confusion of a ring and two avenues with standing, fallen and broken stones, some dragged out of position, caused Stukeley to interpret the overgrown litter as five concentric circles with a ditch and quickset hedge cutting through them. Several stones were on the far side, two or three lying in the trench. The third ring, well to the SSW, was half in pasture, half in an apple-tree orchard. Between it and the Cove in another orchard was a dovecote.[13]

Convinced that philosophical druids had landscaped their rings as images of the heavens Stukeley decided that the SSW circle with its twelve stones represented the solar month and the lunar year (Fig. 7). The central was a Temple of the Sun and the north-east stood for the five lesser planets.[14]

In 1740 the younger John Wood, architect of Bath's elegant Royal Crescent, followed the same reasoning but with different results. At Stanton Drew, the 'Oak Man's Town', the SSW circle was the Sun because it was bigger than the north-eastern 'Moon' Circle. The central was the Earth's year as its circumference was 'just 365 Jewish Yards' of 0.96 m, an error of twelve cubits or 11.5 m. Like Stukeley Wood believed the north-east to be a quintuple circle. Outlying stones including Hauteville's Quoit were

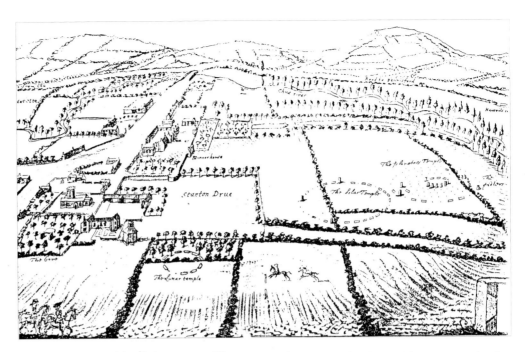

Fig. 7 Stukeley's sketch of the lunar, solar and planetary temples at Stanton Drew.

the lesser planets of Mercury, Mars, Jupiter and Saturn. The Cove, 'three stones in the Garden by the Church', was the altar of Venus.[15] Neither Stukeley nor Wood could have known of Uranus, undiscovered until 1781, nor Neptune, 1846, and Pluto, 1930. Wood concluded that 'The Works of *Stantondrue* form a perfect Model of the *Pythagorean* System of the Planetary World'.[16]

He fantasised about the druids. Stanton Drew was their university, Wookey Hole, the famous cavern, being an initiation centre. The university had four outlying colleges: Harptree with its many round barrows was an institution for bards and poets; the geometrical megaliths of Exmoor formed a centre whose priests made human sacrifices to obtain prophecies; Stonehenge was the place where druids raised spirits from the infernal depths; and the fourth college at Avebury was for philosophers.[17]

Because of the crops, the hedges and other obstructions Aubrey, Stukeley and Wood all misinterpreted the tumbled stones of the north-east ring and the two avenues of that circle and the central as four or five concentric rings. The first to recognise the chaos as the wreckage of two simple circles and their avenues was Benjamin Donne, an eminent eighteenth-century cartographer.

THE MEGALITHIC COMPLEX

Following his earlier planning of 1872 and 1874 C. W. Dymond, FSA, CE, 'sometime Chief Engineer for the London to Bristol portion of the Great Western Railway',[18] resurveyed the rings in June 1894 with the Rev. H. T. Perfect of Stanton Drew. Their 'new and accurate instrumental plan at a scale of 50 feet to the inch' [600:1] is framed inside St Mary's church. The replanning established all three rings as circles rather than ellipses as is still occasionally suggested.[19]

The smallest of the rings, the north-east circle, stands on uneven land in a cramped area that declines noticeably towards the north, and abruptly to the east where the River Chew may originally have flooded. The circle is 29.6 m in diameter, its eight stones all of dolomitic breccia and apparently 'positioned on the principle of opposing pairs equidistant from the centre, as distinct from arrangement on the circumference of a circle precisely marked out from the centre with the aid of a cord.[20] It may originally have been provided with two outlying portal stones standing just beyond an entrance-gap at the east.

It is sometimes said that the ring's stones are substantially taller and heavier than those of the other circles but this is only minimally true. With an average length of 3.2 m the blocks are little longer than the median 2.8 m of the central ring.[21] The heaviest, at the south-west, 3 m high, raddled, blotchily red and wrinkled like elephant's skin, weighed about thirty tons and would have demanded the strength of a hundred workers to haul upright.

The central ring is more problematical, particularly as a large old elm tree near the middle fell in 1962, its tumbled roots disturbing and effectively destroying any evidence of a prehistoric feature. The circle is on the only expanse of fairly level ground. Different surveyors have computed different diameters for the circle varying from as little as 91.4 m by Stukeley to as much as 380 × 347 ft (115.8 × 105.8 m) by Wilkinson. Thom, unsure of the size of the central ring, tentatively proposed 372 ft 3 in (113.5 m), about 137 of his Megalithic Yards of 0.823 m. Wood recorded 378 ft (115.2 m). So did Philip Crocker, 378 × 345 ft (115.2 × 105.2 m) in 1826. Dymond measured the circle as 368 ft (112.2 m). A mean between the parameters of 112.2 m and 115.2 m, 114.6 m would seem acceptable, making the ring rather bigger than Avebury's southern circle but not approaching the enormity of its Outer ring.[22]

With an internal area of more than 10,000 m^2 the enclosure must have been planned to accommodate a vast concourse of people. Even setting aside half the arena for officiants and allowing each onlooker a comfortable body-space of 2 m^2 the circle could have held two thousand men and women, the dispersed population of families in a territory of many square miles around Stanton Drew.

Because of the haphazard disposition of prostrate stones, some fallen outwards, some inwards, some sideways, the original number is debatable. Even probing failed to decide how many there had been. Realising that breaks in the ring were not part of its original plan and that modernday farmers had toppled obstructive stones into pits Stukeley anticipated the technique of bosing, 'percussing the surface of the ground with a weighted rammer, and listening to the sound thus produced'. On the undisturbed ground the sound is a dull 'thud' but over filled pits or stones, more resonant like a 'thoomp'. Stukeley was aware of the principle. Buried stones, he observed, 'may be found by knocking with one's heel upon the spot, whence there is a sound'.[23]

His companion, John Strachey, was more draconic. 'Several of these Stones have of Late Years been Undermined, thrown down and buryed by one John Cowly tenant on ye farm where they stand. But ye Parched grass over them in dry Weather plainly discover where they lye as I proved by thrusting down my Sword to several of them'.[24] Further long droughts in the summers of 1887 and 1893 permitted recognition of other buried stones by their covering of parched grass.[25] They were not evenly spaced, from 8.2 m to 8.5 m apart. Today some twenty-seven are visible and allowing for some removed or buried in the wide gaps at north-west, ESE and south, presumably to facilitate ploughing, an original number of thirty-two stones is reasonable.

The SSW circle, 44.2 m in diameter, contains twelve stones, all now prostrate, of dolomitic breccia and sandstone. They lie on a ridge on the very flat brow of a knoll 14 m above their partners. The site provided a wide overview of the other rings.

THE AVENUES

From the north-east ring John Aubrey noticed a short but disrupted avenue, 32.9 m long and 8.5 m wide. He speculated that, 'The Stones a a a a &c seeme to be the remainder of the Avenue as at Kynet and reach in length about halfe a quarter of a mile'.[26] The ten stones suggest that four pairs had been added beyond the two outlying stones at the entrance. Such portalled entrances were developed in Cumbria at large Late Neolithic rings like Swinside and Long Meg and Her Daughters. At Avebury, probably at Stanton Drew and on Dartmoor such settings were enhanced by the addition of further pairs of stones to form short avenues that provided dignified approaches to the circles.[27] At Stanton Drew the avenue was disrupted by a hedge beyond which the avenue ended where the land sloped down steeply to the flood plain of the River Chew.[28]

From the central circle a second avenue, once of eight stones of which four stand, joins the first. Both are splayed, narrowing to 9.1 m against their circles. Originally the linked avenue ended at the former bank of the river.

There are indications, as there are in the Kennet avenue at Avebury, that the two avenues were secondary to the circles. The great circle's avenue has pillars of silicious breccia different from those of the ring. Its stones are graded, the tallest portal 2.4 m high, much bigger than those of the ring. Its companions decline to a mere 1 m down the slope. The mineralogy of the other avenue also is different from its ring. Although the stones nearest the circle are large, 3.1 m and 3.7 m long, the remainder are so displaced, one smashed into three fragments against the entrance, that it would be overconfident to claim grading for them.

Plate 20 The two side slabs and fallen back-stone of the Cove.

'The church of Stanton Drew . . . is placed within the precincts of a veritable Valhalla of monumental relics', built between the circles and the Cove as though to separate those pagan monstrosities.[29] Beyond the church three slabs, locally known as the Parson or Cook, the Bride and the Bridegroom are formed of dolomitic breccia suggesting that they were of a different period from the rings with their silicious breccia, sandstone and oolite.

The backstone has fallen outwards but the two sideslabs are erect and it can be seen that the three pieces came from a single block. The stone to the west stands like an inverted rudder, 3.1 m high but the top of the eastern is no more than 1.3 m above ground. In shape it would fit neatly under the southern corner of its partner. Were they to be reassembled they could be superimposed on the backstone which measures 4.4 m by 2.6 m, and which has a weathered fracture through it exactly matching the shapes of the others.

Late nineteenth-century probing and excavations by Dymond and Perfect found nothing prehistoric, only a mediaeval church tile and a few treasure-seekers' holes 60 cm to 1 m deep with bits of breccia and white sandstone in them.[30] A glazed recess leading to the roodloft inside the church preserves other fragments of mediaeval tiles found in the churchyard.

With a south-easterly bearing of about 147° and a declination of −30°.8 looking towards a gentle rise, this imitation of a Neolithic megalithic burial chamber may have been planned to face the major midsummer moonrise. But with sideslabs 3 m apart and no more than 2.6 m long[31] an observer standing by the backstone would have had a 'window' nearly 70° wide from 113°, ESE, to 181°, south. Any intended lunar orientation would have been of symbolic rather than of calendrical value.

HAUTEVILLE'S QUOIT

High on a ridge a third of a mile NNE of the rings lies Hautville's Quoit, a shattered and shamefully neglected stump behind a roadside hedge. When John Aubrey saw it in 1664, 'a great roundish stone, of the shape of a coyte', it was 3.2 m long, 2 m wide and 30 cm thick. John Wood agreed, 'a large flat Stone, called *Hakill's* or rather *Hakim's* Coit, now lying on the Brow of a Hill and . . . tho greatly delapidated, is still ten Feet long, six Feet broad, near two Feet thick'. Morgan analysed it as fine-grained cherty sandstone. Brentnall thought it almost pure silica with traces of iron like Avebury's local sarsen.[32]

It is now just over 2 m long, having lost over a metre since Aubrey's time. 'The wagon loads that have been broken from it at different times for the purpose of mending the roads have diminished its consequence as to bulk and appearance'.[33] Like the sandstone pillar of Long Meg outside a great ring near Penrith in Cumbria the Quoit may have acted as a 'signpost' on a Neolithic trackway, 'If those stones . . . were not set there for direction of the old Britons which way to come in this woody country, or where a ford of the river was, why might they not be stones dropped by the way in journeying to the temple?'.[34]

In 1969 Roger Mercer undertook a resistivity survey and a small excavation but did not locate any stonehole. The Quoit's proximity to a lynchet suggested that it had stood close to the Pensford–Chew Magna road which may have followed the line of a prehistoric ridgeway. Stukeley recorded a second, bigger stone nearer Chew Magna which may have been another trackway marker. In his later notes he confused it with the smaller Quoit. 'We measured that towards Pensford [the Quoit] 13 foot long, 8 broad and 4 thick [4 × 2.4 × 1.2 m] being a hard reddish stone', measurements contradicted by Aubrey's earlier and smaller dimensions.[35]

THE GEOLOGY

'It looks like a paste of flints, shells, crystals, and the like solid corpuscles crowded together and cemented, but infallibly by Nature's artifice'.[36] The bedrock in the immediate locality is a mixture of Triassic marl and sandstone which was available only if quarried, an infrequent practice in early prehistoric Britain. Instead, the stones came from farther away. They are mostly breccia of angular fragments of various shapes and sizes, embedded in a silicious matrix freely impregnated with iron, and with hollows of crystallised quartz. There is also dolomitic breccia with small fragments of limestone in a reddish matrix of iron and carbonate of lime, some oolitic limestone and occasional sandstones.

After examination Morgan, having first suggested a source near Dundry Hill to the west, hypothesised that it was probable that both the silicious and the dolomitic breccia came from a hill above West Harptree called Rudge or Ridge.[37]

Morgan's opinion was modified by Kellaway. The tracks of the stones 'have a strong west-east component'. There were local Triassic sandstones and hard Coal Measure outcrops within one and a half miles but neither were used in the rings. Some of the dolomitic conglomerates, could have come from Broadfield Down and Mendips; the Old Red sandstones from Wales or elsewhere but the Dundry Freestone (Inferior Oolite) must have come from the west end of Dundry Hill. 'The situation of the stones of Stanton Drew is entirely consistent with the possible site of a moraine upstream of the Chew Gorge at Pensford', one and a half miles to the east at ST 617 637. Some large tabular erratics, notably the dolomitic conglomerate of the Cove, could have 'been in the form of giant slabs which were later broken up, either by natural processes or by man'[38] – probably a combination of both as the three dissected blocks of the Cove imply, the natural fissures in a huge slab being split and detached for the two sideslabs and backstone.

TABLE 2. The Geology of Stanton Drew.

Sites	Indeterminate breccia	Silicious breccia	Dolomitic breccia	Old Red sandstone	Oolitic limestone
Great circle	12	6	1	2	2
Avenue	4	0	0	0	4
NE circle	6	2	0	0	0
Avenue	0	9	0	0	1
SSW circle	7	4	0	1	0
Cove	0	0	3	0	0
Hauteville's Quoit	0	0	0	1	0

With stones up to thirty tons in weight having to be transported over undulating countryside they may have been lashed onto sledges and dragged along moveable rails.

Even on gentle slopes gangs of four men per ton would be needed, a hundred-strong workforce comparable in size to the labourers required to erect the heavy blocks in their holes. For the thirty or more pillars of the central ring the organisation of hauliers, the digging of holes around the planned circumference and the erection of heavy blocks may have taken months, even years, autumn by autumn.

LEGENDS

The three rings are almost as rich in folklore as the Rollright Stones. The stories include petrifaction, giants and King Arthur. Best-known of all is the whimsy, probably emanating from seventeenth-century Puritan pulpits, of punishment for profanation on the Sabbath when an irreligious wedding party were turned to stone.

> That a Bride goeing to be maried, she and the rest of the company were metamorphis'd into these stones: but whether it were true or no they told me they could not tell. Why! Was not Lot's wife turn'd into a pillar of salt? I know that some will nauseate these old Fables; but I doe profess to regard them as the most considerable pieces of observable Antiquity.[39]

A few decades later the story had more substance. In Stukeley's words, the circles were 'vulgarly called the Weddings . . . that upon a time a couple were married on a Sunday; and the friends and guests were so prophane as to dance upon the green together, and by a divine judgement were thus converted into stones'. The avenues were fiddlers, the rings were maidens and the Cove was the bride, bridegroom and parson.[40]

Further elaboration changed the wedding day. At midnight on a Saturday a pious harper refused to continue playing. The excited bride swore that she was ready to go to Hell to find a musician whereupon an old piper appeared offering to play for the dancers. He began slowly but the music became faster and faster and only too late the merrymakers realised he was the Devil and that they were unable to stop dancing. When daylight came there was nothing to be seen but three rings of stone.[41] The devout harper survived and was discovered cowering in a hedge.

Sensibly, Stukeley mused:

> I have observed that this notion and appellation of Weddings, Brides, and the like, is not peculiar to this place, but applied to many other of these Celtic monuments about the kingdom . . . whence possibly one may conjecture, in very ancient times it was a custom here . . . to solemnise marriage and other holy rites in these ancient temples, perhaps before churches were built in little parishes . . . such names of these places may be derived from the mad, frolicksome and Bacchanalian ceremonies of the ancient Britons in their religious festivals.[42]

There were other legends. John Wood, the Bath architect, making a plan in 1740, was warned by villagers that the stones could not be counted. Those who tried 'were either struck dead upon the Spot, or with such an Illness as soon carried them off'. 'A storm accidentally arose just after, and blew down Part of a Great Tree near the Body of the Work, the People were then thoroughly satisfied that I had disturbed the Guardian Spirits of the metamorphosed Stones'.[43]

Even Hautville's Quoit was magical. '*Hakewell* stood upon the top of *Norton*-hill [Maes Knoll or Howe], about halfe a mile off where the Coyte now lies, and coyted it

Plate 21 The enormous central circle.

down to this place'.[44] As the hill overlooking Norton Malreward was a mile to the north and as the sandstone slab weighed many tons hurling it was more legendary than likely. Hauteville is also said to have thrown up the hill, a triangular Iron Age hillfort of some thirty acres, with a single spadeful of earth.

Sir John de Hauteville (1216–1272), whose dates of birth and death coincided exactly with the reign of Henry III, fought bravely in the seventh crusade of AD 1248–50. Being rewarded for his prowess with only an insignificant gift of land at Norton he is reputed to have resentfully renamed the village Norton Malreward. The story is probably fictitious.

A painted effigy, unusually of oak, purported to be of de Hauteville in St Andrew's church, Chew Magna, but anachronistically in plate armour rather than chain-mail, is probably that of John Wych who died in 1346. The statue may have been removed from a nearby chantry at the dissolution of the monasteries around 1540. The mistaken ascription below it is Victorian but the legend was alive as early as 1664 when Aubrey knew of Hauteville 'in Chew-church where he hath a Monument'.[45] John Strachey, being in holy orders, was sceptical about all the tales.

> As to ye idle Story that these were the Company of a Wedding promiscuously dancing on a Sunday with the Parson, fiddlers & Clerk all Turn'd into Stone I shall only observe that they are more Antient than Christianity itself in this Island & Consequently that such Sabaturian novelty [sic], but that as one great flat Stone here is Call'd Hautvil's Coyt so belonging to ye Monument at Avery [sic] & also at Stonehenge are ye Devills Coyts which last seem given by Christians perhaps in detestation to them as Altars belonging to Temples of Heathen gods.[46]

Other speculation about the stone circles was even more unlikely. According to Fergusson Stanton Drew was the site of Arthur's eleventh battle fought on the slopes of Maes Knoll. Misquoting the ninth-century *British History* of Nennius, Fergusson claimed that 'The eleventh was on the hill called Agned' adding with no justification apart from his own obsessive preoccupation with Arthur, 'in Somersetshire'. In justification he argued that strategically the site was in direct line of approach to the twelfth and final battle of Mount Badon.[47]

DATE, LAYOUT AND ASTRONOMY

Turning from fancy to deducible fact the circles, despite their ruinous state, provide persuasive evidence of numeracy, landscaping and an awareness of the sun and moon.

There have been no formal excavations. There is a seventeenth-century reference to an accidental find by a stone, 'one of which being lately fallen, in the Pitt, in which it stood, were found the crumbes of a man's bones and a round bell, like a large horse-bell, with a skrew as the stemme of it'.[48] In 1958 Grinsell and Kendal reported that probing had located missing stones in the avenues but they may have been geologically misled. In 1961 Professor Palmer undertook a resistivity survey and in spite of ill-health identified an underlying layer of hard ironpan 5 to 15 cm thick and about 30 cm down whose resistance to Strachey's sword and others' probes felt like buried stones.[49]

A likely sequence at Stanton Drew would be, first the outlying Quoit, a Neolithic standing stone on the ridge to the north, then the Cove, a Late Neolithic imitation of the chambers of earlier megalithic tombs.[50] Shortly afterwards the three rings would be raised: first the great circle around 2800 BC if its likeness to the rings at Avebury implies a date similar to theirs;[51] then the SSW ring; and, finally, the limited north-east ring unavoidably having to stand on cramped and sloping ground.

The megalithic group at Stanton Drew probably spanned a period from the earlier centuries of the third millennium BC into the very beginning of the Early Bronze Age when, apparently, they were abandoned, a lifetime of no more than a few hundred years. The site had been chosen as the centre of a fourteen mile wide ring of eleven chambered tombs in an area of 150 square miles, quite capable of sustaining a Late Neolithic population of many hundreds of men and women. The nearest tomb was the Fairy's Toot, 'the haunt of ghosts', five miles away at Butcombe. The distribution, as with other great circles, suggests that the rings at Stanton Drew were a Late Neolithic focus for clan gatherings, replacing the individual meetings at funerary shrines of families in previous generations.

If so, their function did not last. There are fewer than fifty round barrows in their vicinity, all at the outer limits of the seven-mile radius and a mere 10 per cent of those in the region. Stukeley noticed the discrepancy. 'I wondered that I observed no *tumuli*, or barrows, the burying-places of the people about it . . . and on Mendip hills, not far off, they are very numerous . . . Of Bronze Age round barrows there are scarcely any nearer than the Mendip Hills where they occur in their hundreds'.[52]

Altogether there were some 460 round barrows in North Somerset in a vast circle a score of miles across and today fringed by the cities of Bristol, Bath, Frome and Wells but the great majority were on the Mendips near the Priddy henges a few miles to the south-west of Stanton Drew. There, in a rectangle of no more than 50 square miles, were some 300 round barrows, 65 per cent of the total.[53] The well-drained brown earths of the Mendips and the development of east-west ridgeway trading routes in the

Early Bronze Age may have led to the change, a move from Stanton Drew to Priddy. It is noteworthy that a similar re-emphasis at a similar time occurred in Wiltshire where Avebury appears to have been abandoned at the time when the great sarsens of Stonehenge were being erected around 2600 BC.[54] Neither transition is likely to have been peaceful.

The stone circles at Stanton Drew were slighted, some stones toppled, the surrounding bank pushed back into the ditch that subsequently lay unknown until its rediscovery in 1997. It had certainly gone by 1664 when John Aubrey went to the barley-covered site. 'I could not percieve any trench about it as at Avebury, Stoneheng &c: It is in ploughed land and so easily worne out'.

It is unlikely that the bank was flattened and the ditch backfilled in mediaeval times. It was unnecessary. The 40 m wide causeway provided ample access for ox-drawn ploughs. Nor would the task have been easy. Even with a bank only 1 m high its 384 m circumference would have contained almost 2,300 m³ of earth, marls and clay. Allowing only a minimum weight of 3,900 lb per cubic metre the amount of material to be shovelled and dumped into the ditch was some 4,000 tons. It was wasteful toil whether for subjugated serfs or free yeomen but it was explicable if Stanton Drew had been desecrated in the Bronze Age, its place usurped by the henges of Priddy to the south, its power gone. With the bank and ditch obliterated, stones leaning or thrown down, little survived of its former grandeur.[55]

In their beginning, however, the circles had been wonders of design. Simple numeracy can be inferred from their numbers of stones: eight, twelve and a likely thirty-two, all multiples of four, a figure which is repeated in the diameters of the circles. All three seem to have been laid out by people using a unit of measurement of about 0.924 m, akin to a human pace. For the central circle a diameter of 114.6 m would fit 124 units very closely, a number which is again a multiple of 4. The same counting-base of 4 would account for the 32 units in the 29.6 m of the north-east ring and 48 for the 41.2 m of the ssw. For laying-out such huge rings the builders possibly found it convenient to use a rod of 3.696 m, four times longer than the yardstick, sixteen approximate lengths being required for the radius of the central ring, another multiple of 4. It is noteworthy but not puzzling that the bigger the ring the greater the divergence from precision, not astonishing when using long rods over uneven ground and long grass.

The layout of Stanton Drew is arcane and unique. It does not accord with the pattern of other multiple rings in south-western England. The centres are not in a straight line. The central ring is 40.5 m west of the line between the north-east and ssw. Nor are the circles evenly spaced, the ssw being three times farther than the north-east from the central circle. A multi-phase sequence of construction is likely.

It was John Wood in 1740 who noticed that a line from the centre of the north-east ring through the middle of the great circle pointed to the Cove.[56] Thus four great sites, two circles, a Cove and a church were set in a 430 m long, straight, ENE–WSW line and it is surprising that no ley-line enthusiast has celebrated this linear fusion of megalithic and ecclesiastical religious sites. Indeed, it is strange that this gigantic and sprawling site does not figure as a ley in the literature despite the more than a half mile long, very straight alignment from the Quoit to the ssw circle.

Wood observed that a second line from the ssw ring through the central was aligned on the distant Quoit.[57] This esoteric landscaping did explain why the circles were not

Plate 22 The heavy blocks of the north-east ring.

on a straight line but it did not account for the considerable difference in their spacing. An astronomical requirement caused that.

Unlike other settings of more than two sites, all of which form straight lines: Avebury with its two known and suspected third intended ring; Priddy's three southern henges; the three rings of the Hurlers; even the three Yorkshire henges at Thornborough, the line at Stanton Drew is bent. The centres of the north-east and central circles extend from 54° to 234°, north-east to south-west; but from the central to the ssw ring the angle veers 23° southwards to 21°–201°. Dowsers explained the bend by detecting an underground stream leading from the ssw to the central circle and continuing northwards whereas the unconnected north-east ring had an independent 'blind spring' that flowed into the River Chew.[58]

Anomalously, the spacing at Stanton Drew is both irregular and lengthy, variations unknown elsewhere. With the exception of the widely spaced Thornborough henges, 531 m and 547 m apart, the rings in other multiple complexes are closely grouped. At Avebury the distance between the south and north rings is 20 m. At Priddy in the Mendips the three southern henges are equidistantly spaced 59.4 m. On Dartmoor the two Grey Wethers are 6 m apart; the three Hurlers on Bodmin Moor 24.4 m and 27.4 m; the nearby pair on King Arthur's Down, 3 m; at Wendron near Land's End, c. 18 m; and Tregeseal c. 23 m. The average spacing for the ten gaps between the rings

Plate 23 The fallen stones of the north-eastern avenue.

is 18.1 m. Even the now-destroyed pair of rings at Bathampton on Claverdon Down, Bath, were close together.[59] But at Stanton Drew 43.3 m separates the north-east and central circles and 137.7 m lies between the central and ssw rings, more than twice the exceptional distances between the Priddy henges. The reasons for such divergence from the norm reveal the ritualistic needs of the people who had carefully arranged the rings.

Sir Norman Lockyer never went to Stanton Drew[60] but from a 'rough reading of the 25-inch [63.5 cm] Ordnance Survey map' and plans sent to him by Dymond he deduced that the middle of the great circle was the focal point for several celestial observations. From there, through the north-east ring, the orientation was to the midsummer sunrise. The direction of the avenue showed the rising of the May Day sun. An observer looking towards the Quoit would have seen the bright star Arcturus, α Böotis, rising in 1620 BC. A fourth alignment between the ssw and central circles indicated the appearance of the same star in 1420 BC. The dates are unlikely and the azimuths were in error by nearly 2°.[61]

Twenty years later Alfred Watkins proposed that a line from the north-east to the ssw ring brushed the eastern edge of the central circle.[62] This was not quite accurate. The 'sightline' between the circles passed 13 m inside the eastern arc of the central ring as Dymond's very accurate plan showed.[63]

Plate 24 The north-eastern avenue looking towards the River Chew.

The line is important because the angle subtended from centre to centre of the north-east and ssw rings is 211°.4. With a higher horizon of ±1°.7 the declination is −30°.9, that of the major southern setting of the midsummer moon.[64]

Thom considered that a line through the centres of the central and north-east rings had an azimuth of 52°.7 and a declination of +22°.9, the time of sunrise in early June. Being about a fortnight before the midsummer solstice it would give warning of that important calendrical event.[65] It is possible, but no more than speculation, that the alignment was intended to prepare people for midsummer ceremonies to be performed at the Cove or inside the ssw circle.

If the layout was deliberately planned it may be assumed that the central circle was the first of the three rings, erected on a broad stretch of level ground. The north-east ring was the last, uncomfortably built close to the great circle where the ground fell away to the east. Its position had been chosen for the two centres of the rings to be in line with the Cove. It demanded, however, that a second line from its centre to the ssw ring, 284 m away and 14 m higher had to pass between the outermost eastern stones of the ancient central circle if the midsummer lunar alignment were to be precise. The complications were considerable. The ssw circle contained not one but two sightlines, the lunar and the one to the Quoit. Had it been as close to the great circle as the north-east ring was the 31° to 211° alignment on the southern moonset between the outer rings would have been changed by more than a degree and lost. As it was, the development was a triumph of design.

Midsummer processions and ceremonies may be imagined, rituals by moonlight celebrated by hundreds of people from the countryside, assembling for considerations long forgotten but preserved silently in the stones themselves. It is a strange irony that William Stukeley, looking at the upheaval of the south-western ring, 'stones left upon the spot, but prostrate', termed the ring 'the Lunar Temple'.

Stanton Drew is as little likely to give up its secrets as Abury or Stonehenge, and we must not expect that it will ever be granted to any inhabitant of this present earth to unlock the riddle and interpret its dark sayings.

W. Long, *Arch J 15*, 1858, 210–11.

Plate 25 The Merry Maidens.

Chapter Four

A Cornish Quartet

ILLUSIONS AND TRANSFORMATIONS

William Borlase believed that 'Western Cornwall had evidently been one of the spots which the Druids particularly favoured; its stone circles were their temples, the outlying stones their idols, and their notables were buried beneath the capstones of its cromlechs or quoits'.

J. Michell, *Megalithomania*, 1982, 112.

At the end of the seventeenth century only one stone circle was generally known on the Land's End peninsula. Fifty years later the increasing curiosity about antiquities changed that. By 1754 the Cornish antiquarian, the Rev. William Borlase, was able to record that 'There are four Circles in the hundred of Penwith, Cornwall (the most distant two of which are not eight miles asunder)'. He was wrong. There were at least six and probably more. Today there are three and a half.[1]

The names Borlase gave for the rings were enchanting: Boscawen'uun, Rosmodereuy, Tregaseal, Boskednan. The rings themselves were very similar in size and number of stones. They had 'nineteen Stones each, a surprizing uniformity, expressing perhaps, the two principal divisions of the year, the twelve months, and the seven days of the week'.

They formed a scalene triangle of thirteen square miles. The Merry Maidens was at the south-east. From it a five and three-quarter mile long line led NNW to Boscawen-Un and Tregeseal. The fourth ring, Boskednan, was three and a half miles north-east of Tregeseal and almost seven miles north of Merry Maidens (Fig. 8).

The layout of the four rings is a nightmare for believers in megalithic landscaping, in astronomical orientations or in ley-lines. The triangle is not a right-angle, an equilateral or an isosceles. It is simply irregular and contains no sign of deliberate planning. Nor are its possible celestial alignments any more convincing. None of the angles from ring to ring points to important solar or lunar positions. The best, north-east from Tregeseal to Boskednan with a bearing of 59°, is fairly close to the minor northern moonrise, that obscure event, but misses it by over half a degree. The worst, from Boscawen-Un to Boskednan, is nearly 10° from any sightline to the sun or moon.

Enthusiasts for ley-lines will receive even less encouragement. Boscawen-Un is only 0.04 per cent from being precisely on the line between the Merry Maidens and Tregeseal but as that discrepancy represents a misalignment of 400 m for a ring no more than 24 m across the 'ley' must be discounted. Such negative results lead to the

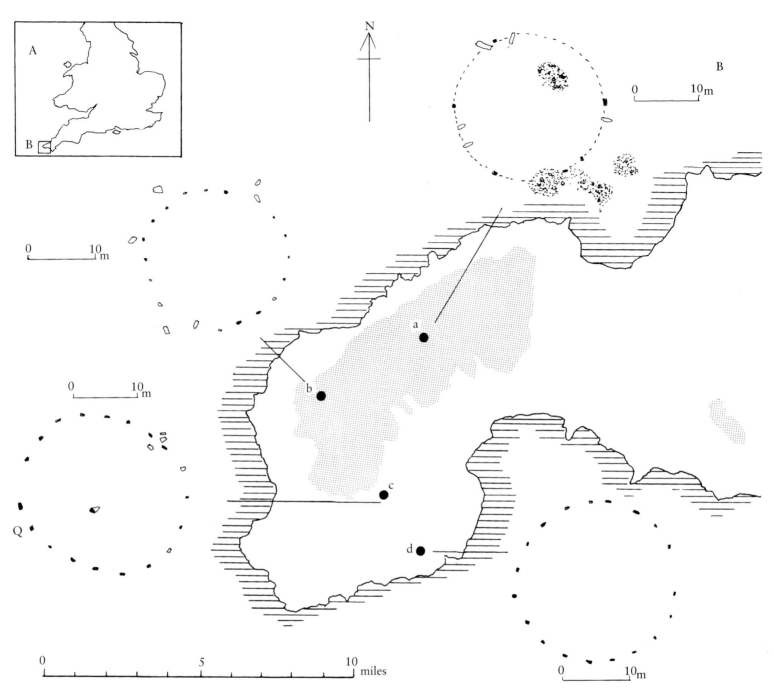

Fig. 8 Map and plans of four stone circles on Land's End, Cornwall. a. Boskednan; b. Tregeseal; c. Boscawen-Un; d. Merry Maidens.

prosaic conclusion that the builders of these circles were uninterested in anything but a location close to a convenient source of stones and a situation comfortably accessible in the community's territory. It was the mundane rather than the magical that determined the situations of the four rings.

They deceive. Delightful though the circles are what one sees today is not what their builders saw. Additions and losses have created an illusion of reality, of a permanence that the rings never knew. Theirs was a world of transformations.

The Merry Maidens stand in a field alongside a minor road near St Buryan. The nineteen stones are in an almost perfect circle about 24 m across with a wide space at the east, perhaps an original entrance. There is a suggestion that the pillars are graded in height.

Six and three-quarter miles to the north Boskednan is a wreck. The site is littered with the upheaval of tin-mining, seven stones erect or leaning, four down, vacant gaps at north-east and north-west, pits disfiguring the 22 m wide interior, a plundered round barrow slumped against the stones at the south-east. Also known as the Nine Maidens and Dans Maen, the 'stone dance' must have been a dizzily whirling reel from the present state of the participants. Tregeseal is better.

On Truthwell Common with the jagged rocks of Carn Kenidjack harsh against the north-eastern skyline the tidy ring, commonly called the Dancing Stones, is close to a field-wall. All but one of the nineteen stones are upright in a ring some 21 m in diameter. To the north are round barrows, two of them big and conspicuous, and not far away is a short row of standing stones with perforations through them.

Boscawen-Un, 'the dwelling by an elder tree on the downs', and another 'Nine Maidens', is three-and-a-half miles to the south-east at the end of a branch-tangled droveway. Low-lying, often shabby with undergrowth and bracken it has three distinctions, a possible entrance at the west, a white block of quartz at the south-west, and a long, leaning pillar near its centre. Pacing shows that the ring is not a circle but an irregular oval, about 24 m by 21 m with a long south-east/north-west axis.

Even such terse descriptions illustrate how remarkably alike the four rings are, all with folk-stories of girls turned to stone for impiously dancing on the Sabbath, all with nineteen or more stones, all of roughly the same size with diameters within the limits of 21 m to 24 m. The implication of a unified society with identical cultural bonds on the Land's End peninsula appears inescapable. That rings of some nineteen stones should consistently be called the Nine Maidens probably derived from Christian superstition, nine being a multiple of three, the triple Trinity.[2]

These are modern realities but they are also prehistoric distortions. Only in recent years have some of the misconceptions been clarified, revealing how each of the rings has changed over more than four thousand years.

THE MERRY MAIDENS

Three of the circles to be re-examined, The Merry Maidens, Boskednan and Tregeseal, did not become well-known until the mid-eighteenth century when William Borlase began searching for antiquities. This might seem particularly surprising in the case of the Merry Maidens which was alongside a road but the explanation lies in the state of the highways and lanes on the Land's End peninsula.

No roads had been laid in the Roman period and even by the seventeenth century travellers crossed from bridge to bridge along muddy, often uncared-for trackways. As late as 1538 Leland could write of 'a poore throughfare, a 4. Miles by morisch and no wood'. Nor were newcomers welcome. Sixty years after Leyland the cartographer, John Norden, with grim experience, remembered, 'A straunger traueler in those partes can hardlye finds contentement in ordinairie Inns in lodging or dyet'. His Cornish contemporary, Richard Carew, knew it to be true. 'Strangers occasioned to travel through the shire were wont, no less sharply than truly, to inveigh against the bad drink, coarse lodging and slack attendance which they found in those houses that went for inns'. Understandably travellers preferred to ride along the best-preserved highways, avoiding the almost impassable tracks between villages and hamlets.[3]

The Merry Maidens being in a field on the south side of a minor road, the modern B3315 from Penzance to Land's End via Treen, remained unnoticed. But in 1754 Borlase recorded a holed stone on the opposite side of the road, 'about 65 paces exactly North of Rosmodreuy', 'Mordred's roughland', a name that was to be distorted into 'Rosemodress'.[4]

The ring looks in excellent condition, circular, 23.4 m in diameter, its nineteen stones, 0.4 m to 1.4 m high, well-spaced, rather flat-topped and mostly with smoother inner faces. They appear to have been dressed before erection and carefully chocked to achieve almost perfect grading to the tallest pillar, 1.4 m high, in the wsw quadrant 'once again demonstrating the uniform importance of this orientation in the West Penwith circles'.[5]

The first revelation is that this 'beautifully-preserved' site has been partly and poorly restored. Borlase recorded only eighteen stones of which two at the southeast were prostrate. By 1862 one more had fallen but all three had been re-erected by 1869. Inspection of their heights and dispositions suggests that Stone 1 at the north is not original but added in the northernmost of two gaps 'to make the total tally with Borlase's inadvertent slip; he quoted 19 instead of 18 in his published work'. The other gap at the east may be an entrance. The reset Stone 6 at the southeast is correct but its partner, Stone 7, has been put up at right-angles to the circumference.[6]

It is just possible that there had been a formal approach to the ring. In 1905 that devotee of stone circles, A. L. Lewis, noticed that 15 m to the south of the circle there were two fallen stones about 4.9 m to 5.2 m apart which he wondered might have been the remains of an avenue. It is more probable that they are outcrops.[7]

Despite the reconstruction intended to restore the ring to perfection there were further attempts to remove the stones which were a nuisance to farmers. Around 1861 an old man saw two or three pushed over but they were upright again in the morning in a regeneration very reminiscent of the home-returning Rollright Stones. In the present century Sir Norman Lockyer was informed that Lord Falmouth would not allow the Merry Maidens' field to be ploughed 'and all antiquarians certainly owe him a debt of gratitude'. Later, during the First World War, it was patriotically intended to plough the field. It was a doomed project. Hardly had the men begun to uproot a stone 'when the lead horse suddenly dropped dead. The whole thing was called off, and everybody started crossing themselves'.[8]

More recently there was intentional vandalism. Chips were broken from a stone. In late June 1995 a group tried to dig up a stone but were disturbed by a member of the public. The stone was left tilted out of the ground. It was said that the offenders were born-again Christians depaganising a heathen stone circle. A letter to the *Cornishman* urged that the Merry Maidens should be protected with no vehicular access, the public footpath improved, and a discreet signboard set up for the benefit of the public.

Like many other stone circles the ring accreted layers of ignorance and superstition. An early supposition was that it was a memorial of a battle in AD 936 when Saxons defeated the Cornish 'Welshmen' at Boleigh – fancifully interpreted as 'the field of slaughter', but in reality 'the dwelling by the flat slab' – and put up the circle as 'a trophy to commemorate the victory'. A pair of tall outlying pillars, the Pipers, signified where the two leaders met to discuss peace terms.[9]

The Merry Maidens has had a variety of names including *Rosmoderet*, first recorded in 1201, a reference to the heath on which the ring was built, 'Mordred's rough land', Mordred or Medraud being the nephew of King Arthur, an unexpected Arthurian interpolation that does not occur anywhere else in the more than three hundred place-names at Land's End. The nearest geographical references to Mordred are 50 miles to the north-east at places like Slaughter Bridge near Camelford where the battle of Camlann was fought – unless it took place at Cadbury-Camelot in Somerset, Camlan in Merioneth or Camboglanna, a fort on Hadrian's Wall.[10]

Like other Land's End rings the Merry Maidens was supposed to be a petrified dance. 'In Cornwall there is a great number of these Circles . . . and the name they go by most commonly is, that of Dawns-Mên, that is, the Stone-Dance, "so called of the common people on no other account, that they are placed in a circular Order, and so make an area for Dancing" . . . ', mused Borlase. 'For the same reason, as I suppose . . . about eight miles West of Bath, a monument of this kind is called the Wedding'. The first record of Dauns Myne is at least as old as 1730 and it has been suggested that it was the disapproval of proto-Methodists who denounced the un-Christian stones and resulted in them being seen as the result of divine retribution.[11]

The story was explicit. Near the circle 'are two granite pillars, named the Pipers. One Sabbath evening some thoughtless maidens of the neighbouring village, instead of attending vespers, strayed into the fields, and two evil spirits, assuming the guise of pipers, began to play some dance tunes. The young people yielded to the temptation; and, forgetting the holy day, commenced dancing. The excitement increased with the exercise, and soon the music and the dance became extremely wild; when, lo! A flash of lightning from the clear sky, transfixed them all, the tempters and the tempted, and there in stone they stand'.[12]

The circle is surrounded by antiquities. Within a mile are no fewer than fifteen standing stones, several of them perforated, and a chambered tomb in a narrowly straggling north-east/south-west line with the ring almost at the centre. On the far side of the road is a perforated slab. The diligent Borlase saw it and explained why it was pierced. 'About 65 paces [*c.* 54 m] exactly North of Rosmodreuy Circle in Burien, Cornwall, is a flat Stone, six inches thick at a medium, two foot six wide, and five foot high [15 cm × 76 cm × 1.5 m]; 15 inches [38 cm] below the top, it has a hole six inches diameter [15 cm], quite through. In the adjoining hedge I perceived another, holed in the same manner; and in one wall of the village near by, a third of like make'. These 'were the detached Stones, to which the Ancients were wont to Tye their Victims, whilst the Priests were going through their preparatory Ceremonies, and making Supplications to the Gods to accept the ensuing Sacrifice'. In 1898 an old man told A. L. Lewis that the stone had been moved from a partner 60 m to the NNW. When the sun shone through both 'they called it Midsummer'.[13]

A quarter of a mile to the north-east are the Pipers, known locally as the Hurlers and used as a goal when 'country' played 'town' at that violent 'game'. An old stonebreaker recalled that a man dug against one of the Pipers and found a 'potfull of ashes'. If true it must have been before 11 March 1871, when William Copeland Borlase, great-great grandson of William, excavated there but 'on digging carefully around each of these stones nothing remarkable was found'.

They are the tallest stones in Cornwall. That to the north-east leans but was once 5.1 m tall. The second Piper 97 m up the ridge is 4.1 m high. An extension of their

Plate 26 The outlying Pipers beyond the Merry Maidens; the north-eastern stone is in the farther field on the right.

alignment would touch the western edge of the Merry Maidens and it is possible that they were put up as guidestones to the ring.[14] There are rumours of a third Piper. A 4 m long stone lies prostrate by the hedge to the north-east in line with the others and at the appropriate distance.

Alternatively if there was an eighteenth-century belief in a companion to the existing pair it could have been Goon Rith, 'Red Down' or the Longstone, although this did not stand in line with the others. This block, 3.3 m high, stands in a hedge 300 m ssw of the Pipers and 140 m wsw of the Merry Maidens. It is plainly visible from the ring. In 1871 Borlase recovered a worn beach pebble from its stonehole. Still farther to the south-west at Boscawen-Ros is a pair of two square pillars, 2.6 m and 2.4 m in height with a third low block beyond them.[15]

Down the hill, 200 m south-west of the Merry Maidens, is the Tregiffian entrance-tomb, half of its circular kerbed mound cut away in 1846 by road-makers. A rescue excavation in 1967–8 uncovered an eastern portal-stone covered with deep circular and oval cupmarks and grooves. Two other decorated slabs 'found loose' have disappeared. Under a scatter of human bone in the chamber were two pits. One with an intact collared urn contained charcoal dated to 1539 ± 59 bc (BM-935), some time in the years between 1950 and 1800 BC, showing that this Neolithic burial place had been re-used in the Early Bronze Age when the stone circle itself was already old.[16]

In addition to the manmade megalithic landscape around the stone circle there is a hint of prehistoric landscaping. From the ring the twin hills of Chapel Carn Brea and Bartinny rise in the distance four miles to the north-west 'appearing like the breasts of the Mother Goddess when viewed from the circle'. They were 'holy hills'.

Chapel Carn Brea, 'the first and last hill in Cornwall' had an extraordinary structure with an extraordinary history erected upon it, a multi-phase cairn containing an entrance-tomb and a semi-subterranean cist. In mediaeval times the tiny hermitage chapel of St Michael was built on the mound. It was demolished in 1816 only for a Second World War radar station to wreck the remnants of the prehistoric remains.

Bartinny, 'the hill of fires', was just as exceptional with a legend that no evil spirit could enter the nondescript enclosure on its summit. Midsummer bonfires in honour of the Celtic sun-god Belenus were lit there. With the increasing realisation that hills and mountains were vital elements of the Neolithic and Bronze Age world-picture this aspect of the horizon may have determined the choice of site for the Merry Maidens. The twin peaks of Carn Galva at Boskednan and the tor of Carn Kenidjack at Tregeseal still dominate the skyline of those rings.[17]

Astronomical alignments have been claimed for the circle. At Easter 1905, and again in January 1906 Sir Norman Lockyer visited the site. Using a multiplicity of alignments between barrows, menhirs, a fogou, stone crosses and the church at St Buryan he deduced sightlines to the midsummer solstitial sunset, to the May Day, August and November sunrises, the 'Celtic' festivals of Beltane, Lughnasa and Samain, and to the rising stars of Capella, α Aurigae, in 2160 BC, to the Pleiades, the Seven Sisters, in 1960 BC; to Arcturus, α Boötis, in 1640 BC, and to Antares, α Scorpii, in 1310 BC.[18]

Apart from the improbability of the chronology his proposed sightlines were wrong. Alexander Thom found no confirmation of them (1967, 100, S1/14). Nor did Barnatt in his own extensive fieldwork in Cornwall 'The relationship between Merry Maidens, visible menhirs and the horizon was investigated for solar and lunar alignments without success'. Lockyer's lines 'all could easily be chance . . . However, it is noticeable that many of the sites form a crude NE/SW band across the landscape, perhaps hinting at a processional route'.[19]

John Michell did deduce two leys that involved the circle but as they consisted of a similar mish-mash of targets like Lockyer's, a stone circle, standing stones, an Iron Age fogou, a subterranean structure of debatable purpose, and a Christian cross, lines that must have taken two thousand or more years to complete, they are unconvincing.[20]

The line of standing stones is not straight enough to form a classic ley but coincidence emerges from the conclusion of Alfred Watkins, the inventor of leys, that such lines were ancient trackways. The stones near the Merry Maidens do in fact follow contours that almost replicate the route of the modern road. The position of an important stone circle alongside an ancient ridgeway does make sense.

Although there has been no formal excavation at the Merry Maidens there have been both eccentric and unorthodox investigations. An idiosyncratic attempt to date the circle was made by the late Tom Lethbridge, 'one of the last of that invaluable band of dilettante scholars and skilled devoted amateurs' that have graced British archaeology. He believed that the age of the ring might be determined by counting the number of rotations made by the needle of a pendulum suspended over a stone. Ten years were allowed for each turn. On a fine day in 1970 he went to the circle, put his hand on a stone and set the pendulum swinging. After a multiplicity of gyrations a date of 2540 ± 10 BC was given. This might be fairly close to chronological reality but as a previous experiment by Lethbridge to date the bluestones of Stonehenge produced an age of 1870 ± 10 BC, an error of at least seven centuries as that stage of Stonehenge is now known to be within the bracket of 2850–2480 BC, the trial with the pendulum proved unreliable and needless.[21]

There have also been sensible if unorthodox attempts to test the circle for energy patterns. In 1991 dowsing detected that Stones 1 and 7 were wrong, something already observed by Barnatt in 1982. In 1977 the Dragon Project was founded to ascertain whether the stones held some form of energy. 'The circle has been checked on at least 4 separate occasions for anomalous radiation counts. Don Robins (1985) found an unexpected lower-than-background count inside the circle, and this was subsequently confirmed by a "Meyn Mamvro" geiger monitoring session in 1987 . . . The circle was checked again in 1988 when certain spots of lower radiation were found inside the circle, but no significant overall pattern; and again in 1991 by the local Earth Mysteries Group who found no significant lower readings . . . No significant ultrasound noises have been picked up'.[22]

Today's visitors to the Merry Maidens can see the circle, the stones, the entrance tomb but these are vestiges of antiquity, not the complete prehistoric landscape. There has been a transformation. What the visitor will not see is the companion to the Merry Maidens, the vanished stone circle of Boleigh once about 150 m to the south-west. Until the 1860s four stones stood and three were prostrate, the remnants of a ring about thirty paces or 27 m across, one of the biggest in this part of Cornwall. An old local man remembered that the circle was 'covered with furze' but 'never shown to antiquarians'. Later the field was ploughed and the circle was destroyed.

From Lockyer's account the ring should have been near SW 431 244. Cautionary words have been expressed about the accuracy of this reference but 'Crop marks of this circle were observed in the right place by someone who was not aware of its location or existence'.[23]

Multiple sites such as this, pairs, threes, even a projected four at the Priddy henges near Stanton Drew are a feature of south-western England and there has been much debate about the reason for these juxtapositions.[24] Thom thought that the angle formed between the centres of rings might have arranged astronomically so that an observer in one circle might have his eyes directed towards another and then to a position of the sun or moon. The results were unimpressive.

Nothing was found at Wendron, his site number S1/10. There was one improbable target and two unlikely dates of 1860 BC and 1800 BC at the Hurlers, S1/1, for the rising of the bright star Arcturus, an inaccurate alignment on the setting of the minor southern moon at the Grey Wethers, S2/1, and a sightline at Avebury, S5/3, to the setting of Deneb whose proposed declination of 36°.5 occurred in the years around 2000 BC, eight centuries too late.[25]

If astronomical considerations were not the cause then it might be thought that only guesswork remains, wondering whether the rings of these complexes had different functions, one for men, the other for women, or for calendrical assemblies at different times of the year, or for ceremonies associated with birth and death, or for other even more arcane possibilities. Fortunately, a careful inspection of the sites diminishes the problems.

Very often the conjoined rings are of different diameters, 43 m and 32.3 m at the Grey Wethers, 21 m and 16 m at Wendron. Their shapes vary, circular and oval both at King Arthur's Down and Tregeseal. Where there are three or more circles their centres do not lie in a straight line as though they had been laid out together. At the Hurlers the centre of the ssw ring at the end of the 125 m long line lies 8 m to the east of the alignment. At the three henges at Thornborough in North Yorkshire, 'almost in a straight line', the middle earthwork is 32 m to the east of the line between the NNW and SSE enclosures. At Priddy the centres of the three henges form a 475 m line from which the central henge deviates by 7.3 m to the west. Even more exaggeratedly the unfinished fourth henge is a full 67 m away from the line.[26]

Nowhere is this lack of cohesion in size and layout more obvious than at Stanton Drew where the north-east circle is 29.6 m in diameter, the central 114.6 m and the ssw ring 44.2 m. The spacing is grossly different with 43.3 m separating the north-east from the central circle, 137.7 m from the central to the ssw. The line is grotesquely bent. The orientation from the north-east to the central circle has an azimuth of 234° whereas that from the central to the ssw is 201°.

The accumulated data implies that rather than being contemporaries the assemblages were composites to replace a desecrated original or to permit more elaborate ceremonies. This sequence becomes obvious at the two Llandegai henges near Bangor in North Wales. A fire-pit near the middle of the north-east henge contained charcoal from which an assay of 2790 ± 150 bc (NPL-220) was obtained. A cremation deposit outside the one entrance gave a determination of 2530 ± 145 bc (NPL-2240), the two radiocarbon 'dates' converting into a bracket of about 3700–3050 BC in real years.

A dedicatory cremation pit outside the south-western of two entrances in the second henge 165 m to the south-west yielded a determination of 1790 ± 145 bc (NPL-222), a range of some 2400–2000 BC in real years. At their very closest, subtracting 145 years from 2530 bc and adding 145 years to 1790 bc, 2385 bc and 1935 bc, the equivalent of 3050 BC and 2450 BC, the second henge was at least six centuries later than the first.[27]

It appears that multiple sites are aggregates that developed over many years. The problem at the Merry Maidens is that we cannot yet tell which of the two circles came first.

BOSKEDNAN

On a flat and windswept moorland almost seven miles due north of Merry Maidens are the surviving stones of the Boskednan stone circle. What transformation occurred here did not come from superstition or neglect but from industrial indifference to antiquities.

First written as *Boskennen* in 1310 the name has been variously interpreted as *Bos + kenen*, 'the dwelling by the reeds', or + *conyn*, 'near rabbits'. By 1700 it had also become *mein yn dans*, the 'stone dance', and, inevitably, the Nine Maidens.[28]

The ring is less than half a mile from the enigmatic Men-an-Tol. It exists on a ridge north of the onomatopoeic Ding Dong tin mine, now long since silent, one of the oldest in Cornwall and a landmark for miles. Its abandoned engine-house overlooks the tatters of a circle of stones that stagger rather than stand, unfortunately situated within a plunderous half-mile wide semi-circle of mine-shafts from east to south to west, the ring pitted by trial quarries for the lodes of tin ore, stones savagely broken

for re-use in mine-buildings, a few surviving like half-burnt candles of a birthday cake.

When Borlase sketched the circle in 1754 thirteen stones were standing, the tallest at the north, and six were prostrate. By 1825 only six stones were erect. Two others were slumping and three were down. Eight had disappeared. By 1864 miners had dug an ugly pit inside the north-east quadrant. A stone at the west had holes drilled into it for it to be split and carted to the mines. Other stones had been taken away intact. In consequence, much of the northern half of the ring has gone.

At the ssw a ruined barrow, about 8 m across and 1.2 m high appears to intrude into the circle but the spread is actually upcast dumped by prospectors onto the inner edge of the barrow.[29] In the mound are the remains of a cist. In 1848 it was dug into by labourers who found, broke and discarded a Middle Bronze Age ribbon-handled Trevisker urn.

On 26 July 1872 William Copeland Borlase re-examined the barrow, his two excavation trenches still visible today. He found the sideslabs of the paved cist and just to the west there was a dense patch of burnt wood. Less than a metre farther away were fragments of the urn with its unperforated lugs, decorated inside and out with impressed twisted-cord chevrons. Borlase noted the absence of bones and ashes, remarking that 'it may reasonably be supposed that the vessel, originally interred in

Plate 27 Boskednan from the south-west; the ruined barrow can be seen on the right.

the kist had been broken by the workmen who discovered it, and the pieces careless-
ly thrown aside'.[30]

In the beginning Boskednan had been an accurate circle 21.9 m in diameter whose
circumference had been almost exactly 33 of Alexander Thom's Megalithic Rods of
2.07 m. The regular spacing between the stones suggests an original number of 22 to
23. The bleached stones of local granite with their chosen flat inner faces are 1.1 m to
1.4 m high but an outstanding pillar at the NNW is 2 m tall. A bulky block lying against
it to the west may have formed a 2.5 m wide entrance that framed the prominent rise
of Carn Galva or Carn Galver, the 'lookout tor', a mile to the NNE. The tor has an
enclosure on it, possibly a Neolithic settlement like Carn Brea. Other isolated hut-cir-
cles and a settlement have been recorded on the oddly-named Hannibal's Carn just to
the east.[31]

Perhaps by coincidence a sightline to the eastern side of the western entrance stone
has an azimuth of 319°. With the lower slopes of Carn Galva 0°.2 above the stone
circle the combination of azimuth and altitude at the latitude of 50°.6 produces the
declination of 28°.6, that of the setting of the northern midwinter moon.

A tall outlier once about 1.7 m high some 36 m to the north-west of the ring has
been cut and reduced to a stump. On a rise to the north-west is a large kerbed round
barrow, 10.7 m across with large slanting uprights like a neglected coronet. The outlier and a number of round barrows stray north-eastwards towards the hill and the
'number of barrows and a menhir strengthen the impression of a "processional way"
from settlement to circle and beyond to Carn Galva'.[32]

There is little solemnity in the mournful condition of the ring today.

TREGESEAL

Less than four miles south-west of Boskednan is the Tregeseal stone circle, recorded
as *tregathihael*, in 1284, 'Catihael's farm'. It is a flattened ring of nineteen stones.
Within a radius of a mile and a half is a diverse concentration of prehistoric monuments: chambered tombs, cairn-cemeteries, a hut-circle, enclosures, field-systems and
standing stones.

An oval, kerbed entrance-tomb lies to the WSW. Excavated by Borlase in 1879 it
contained cremated bones, sherds and a small perforated whetstone. In a later cist
was an intact inverted large Middle Bronze Age urn covering burnt bones.[33] Many
barrows are on the moor to the north-east of the ring, one of them a kerbed oval barrow 15 cm high, perhaps another entrance-tomb. The Soldier's Croft field-system is
350 m to the north.[34]

To the north-west of the stone circle are five holed stones, three of them and an
unperforated block in a WSW-ENE alignment. To the north-east is a fourth holed stone
and a fifth stands to the north-west. Both outliers have fractured and repaired tops.
All the stones had been uprooted and removed, broken, then cemented and returned
approximately to their places.[35]

On the far horizon the 2.6 m high Boswens pillar has been described as a May Day
sunrise marker but it is hardly visible. It is also 10° off the proposed sightline.

As well as these existing sites there is a possible 'lost' stone circle at Kenython Hill
to the west where some sixteen circle-like stones lie in a cottage garden. Other rings
have been claimed. In his *St Just – A Statistical Account* of 1842 Buller wrote that at

Plate 28 Tregeseal with Carn Kenidjack in the background.

Gol Voel half a mile north-west of the Tregeseal ring were two stone circles, the larger north of the other. They were protean in their mutations. On an 1876 map they were shown not as adjacent but as concentric rings. Thirty years later another map portrayed the stones as the remains of a burial chamber. Finally the 1981 Ordnance Survey 6 in map reduced them to a mundane cattle enclosure.[36] Ignoring this kaleidoscopic site the genuine stone circle at Tregeseal is the most spectacular of the complex.

Properly called Tregeseal East it was entitled Botallack by Thom, his site S1/16.[37] Predictably the ring is also known as the 'Dancing Stones', and the 'Nine Maidens'. Half-edged by a crescent of summer bracken to its south the circle stands on the open flatness of Truthwell Common with the sudden ridge of Carn Kenidjack to its north, its humps resembling the outline of a stegosaurus rising from a swamp. The tor is misnamed. The nineteenth-century tautological 'Carn' was an unnecessary addition because 'Kenidjack' is a corruption of 'carn eedgack' 'or hooting tor' 'from the sound of the wind blowing through its weird shapes'.[38]

In the mid-eighteenth century William Borlase saw twenty stones of which seventeen stood but seventy years later in 1825 there were only seventeen, five of them fallen. At some time between 1861 and 1869 the already-disturbed ring was further disrupted by a small quarry that burrowed away an untidy $50\,m^2$ of the western side.

Two standing stones and four more prostrate were removed. By 1902 three more had fallen and the entire western half of the ring had collapsed. In 1932 several stones were re-erected and others brought in by persons unknown but the results were rather ridiculous with two of the new stones set up in the trench of the quarry.

Today's circle is an extensive restoration with nineteen stones, one of them lying at the south. There were probably twenty-one originally. The circle is not perfect. It is flattened to the NNE and is markedly ovoid, 21.3 × 20.1 m, it has stones of local granite 0.8 m to 1.4 m high, regularly spaced and graded to the south-west.[39] Six stones are claimed to be cupmarked, one at the north-east, the others in the western half.[40] It is an impressively isolated ring. What cannot be seen is its partner to the west (Fig. 9).

When Borlase saw Tregeseal Central there were ten stones standing and four fallen of a possible eighteen–nineteen in a ring about 23.8 m in diameter. In the early nineteenth century it had been enclosed in the corner of a field. By 1879 only five of its stones were erect. Six were down. The site was even more badly wrecked shortly before 1905 when all the remaining stones were cleared away with three standing and one supine lodged in a hedge-wall. Today only one is visible. Everything was finally destroyed in 1961 because they were 'in the way' when the land was cleared and ploughed.[41]

A recent discovery has added to the transformation. Aerial photography has recorded the site of a third ring to the west on the same axis and equidistantly spaced. It is arguable that the markings may have been signs of a hut settlement but it is more probable that once there had been three stone circles in an east-west 110 m line, each about 20 m across and 35 m apart, the reconstructed Tregeseal East being the sole survivor of a multiphase complex like the Hurlers on Bodmin Moor. Standing almost exactly east–west they may have been intentionally arranged toward the equinoxes.

The territory of two square miles would be capable of supporting thirty pastoralists, even more if theirs was a mixed economy.[42] Allowing 5 m² for each person in the ring and setting aside half the interior for the leader or priest a congregation of

Fig. 9 An etching by the Rev. W. Cotton, 1826, of the destroyed stone circle of Tregeseal Centre.

about thirty-six participants could have been accommodated, a number quite adequate to provide work-gangs of seven or eight to raise the heaviest stones which weigh no more than about two tons.

Plate 29 Boscawen Un from the south-west; the quartz slab is the fourth from the left in the foreground.

BOSCAWEN-UN

Three and a half miles to the south-east of Tregeseal and hardly two miles north-west of the Merry Maidens Boscawen-Un is remarkably similar to that ring in its number of stones and entrance but remarkably dissimilar from it in shape and in its quartz block and an off-centre pillar. Called *boscawenwoen* in 1319 the name means the 'dwelling by the elder tree', an ominous association with that unlucky tree, Judas and evil like the witchcraft legend at the Rollright Stones. Unsurprisingly, the ring is also known as the Nine Maidens.

Despite the repeated Land's End stories of dancing girls turned to stone it would be optimistic for visitors to the ring to anticipate visions of lovely young maids in fetching nudity treading moonlight measures inside the circles. Such fortune is given to few. When the late Peter Pool, student of linguistics and amateur archaeologist, was 'making his annual cut of the pathways' with his secateurs to the Boscawen-Un ring he was taken aback to see naked women dancing and chanting inside the stones. He coughed discreetly. Unavailingly. Only when the rites were completed to the party's unclad satisfaction did the celebrants disperse, allowing Peter Pool to return to his shears. For most of us, however, cold stones rather than delectable Salomes will be the customary experience.[43]

Unlike the Merry Maidens by its minor lane Boscawen-Un was already known in the seventeenth century because it stood within 500 m of a major road, today's A30, from Penzance to Land's End where the many tin-mines needed firm trackways for the carts carrying ore to ports and towns.[44]

As early as 1586 Camden knew of it although not of its makers. 'Giants in times past Inhabited this country . . . Neere unto this, in a place which they call *Biscaw Woune*, are to bee seene nineteene stones set in a round circle, distant every one about twelve foote from the other, and in the very center there is one pitched far higher and greater than the rest'.[45]

John Aubrey had not seen the ring but deduced that it was not a memorial or cenotaph. 'Not a trophy. I presume this also to have been a Temple'. Nor had Stukeley been to Cornwall. It was from the Cornish antiquarian, John Anstis, that he learned of the ring which he believed had been built by a colony of Phoenicians led by Hercules shortly after Noah's Flood. The circle was 'call'd *Biscawoon*, consisting of 19 pillars in a circle and a central *kebla*. The entrance is made of 2 some-what larger stones, than the rest: not improbably one of the *Herculean* labours'. He knew that the central pillar was leaning, its base probably loosened by treasure-seekers.[46]

There was an even stronger reason for Boscawen-Un being known so early. It had a unique history of continuity from the late Neolithic to historic times. Until AD 926 when the Saxon king, Athelstan, overcame the Cornish leader, Hywel, it had been an important meeting place or moot for the people of the kingdom of West Wales.

As an historic aside the year is also interesting for yet another revelation of the links between ancient ritual centres and the persistence of pagan customs. Also in AD 926 when 'fiery rays of light appeared in the northern sky' Athelstan defeated 'all the kings in this island . . . and they confirmed peace with pledges and with oaths in a place which is called Rivers' Meeting [Eamont Bridge near Penrith] on 12 July, and they forbade all devil-worship', perhaps referring to continuing abominable practices at the adjacent henges of Mayburgh and King Arthur's Round Table.

To return to Boscawen-Un after this brief Saxon exegesis, in a Welsh triad the circle was honoured as one of three prestigiously ancient choirs or gorsedds. The Triads, verses with subjects grouped in threes, were ancient chronicles dating back to the sixth or seventh centuries AD. Boscawen-Un was mentioned in them.[47]

> The three principal Gorsedds of the Isle of Britain:
> The Gorsedd of Meriw Hill,
> The Gorsedd of Beiscawen,
> The Gorsedd of Bryn Gwyddon.

The verse is not contained in the accepted canon edited by Rachel Bromwich but came from another source, 'The Triads of the Bards – the Triads of Privilege and Usage', recorded by Llewllyn Sion, fl. *c.* 1516–1600, in a Welsh manuscript in the library of the Earl of Pembroke, Raglan Castle, and destroyed during the Civil War. It

Plate 30 Boscawen-Un, the leaning central pillar.

was copied during the seventeenth century by the Rev. John Williams and there is no reason to doubt its authenticity.

Whether by genuine research or inventive forgery an eighteenth-century bard, Iolw Morganw, who purported to have discovered some forgotten triads, drew a plan of a 'traditional' gorsedd as a ring of nineteen stones with a central pillar. Boscawen-Un was an ideal example. Such an ancestry led the Cornish College of Bards to hold their inaugural ceremony inside the ring, 'the most noteworthy stone circle in Cornwall'. On 21 September 1928, modern druids in local blue robes passed reverently down the 'grass-grown lane', led by the Penzance Silver Band. In 1978 on the fiftieth anniversary of that first modern gorsedd their successors went to Boscawen-Un again, going also to the Merry Maidens.[48]

The circle had baffled people before them. 'Neither does tradition offer to leave any part of their history upon record; as whether it was a trophy, or a monument of burial, or an altar for worship, or what else; so that all that can be learn'd of them is that here they are: the parish where they stand is call'd Boscawone', wrote Daniel Defoe. Modern research has removed some of the despair.

The ring stands on a gentle slope down to the ssw with limited views to north or east. The south-east skyline is visible. The south is obscured by a hedge. Today there are nineteen stones and four hundred years ago Camden also stated nineteen so that a recent suggestion that there had been twenty seems misguided. Borlase saw eighteen standing and one fallen confirming the number. By 1825 two more were down.

The circle was restored in 1862 when a wall, a 'cornish hedge', across the site was removed and the three stones re-erected, one at the north, one at the east and the third at the south-east. About that time Miss Elizabeth Carne had a small trench dug across the ring but nothing was found. Two years later the Penzance Natural History Antiquarian Society dug down to the base of the central pillar 'and found that it was carefully placed in its leaning position',[49] a very improbable deduction.

The flattened ring, 24.9 × 21.9 m, has a long axis lying approximately 122°.5–302°.5, very vaguely in line with the most northerly setting of the minor moon. The round-topped stones, 0.9 m to 1.3 m high, with flat inner faces are subtly graded to the west. The only stones to spoil the pattern are the three restored, their heights and disposition distorting the careful layout.

There is other interference. 'In the entrance-way are the two halves of another block which in 1826 lay outside the circle and at right-angles to it'. The partly buried slabs, each about a metre long, are perhaps the broken halves of a large capstone of a cist, 'part of a Cromlêh to be seen on the Skirts of Boscawen-un Circle'.[50]

A 'central pillar', 2.7 m south-west of the middle of the circle, is 2.6 m long, tilted 30° from the vertical, leaning to the NNE. Its tip is now only 2 m above ground but once it stood 2.6 m high. 'Dr Stukeley's supposition was that it originally stood upright and that "somebody digging by it to find treasure disturbed it". Two controversial axe-carvings have been noticed near the bottom of the stone, supposedly detectable only at midsummer sunrise.[51]

Eighteen of the stones are local granite but there is a substantial block of white quartz at the wsw, 1.2 m high, 0.9 m wide and 0.6 m thick, weighing well over two tons, one of the largest stones in the circle. Lockyer, who went to the ring on 'a pouring day', calculated that from its 'post of honour' the May Day sun would rise over the centre of the site. An alternative interpretation is that the obviously important boulder was intended to indicate the Candlemas sunset, the 'Celtic' festival of Imbolc.[52]

Lockyer proposed further alignments. Using a medley of foresights, six standing stones and a cross he listed sightlines to the May, November and midsummer sunrises, to the rising of the Pleiades, Alcyone η Tauri, in September 2120 BC and in May 1480 BC, and to the rising of Capella, α Aurigae, in 2250 BC. He was enthusiastic but in error. Thom could find nothing convincing. Nor could Barnatt. 'No astronomical orientations to outliers, [long or short] axes, grading or horizon features were found. . . . Astronomical alignments claimed by Lockyer are not convincing: a tall menhir a short distance to the north-east was claimed to align with Capella in 2250 BC; other features are more distant and not visible'.[53]

The absence of finds leaves the age of Boscawen-Un inferential. Even 2250 BC seems very late. Artefacts and urns have been discovered in two adjacent barrows. In one were two cremations and bronze fragments, and in the other two pots, the larger lost. The smaller is a typical Cornish biconical urn of the Trevisker style. With it was a broken saddle quern. The circle itself was probably ancient when such Middle Bronze Age material was left near it.

The situation and shape of the Boscawen-Un ring becomes explicable through a consideration of its off-centre pillar. There was a multitude of standing stones in the West Penwith area of Land's End, three-quarters of them within a mile of a stone circle. In 1982 Barnatt estimated that up to forty-four still existed and another forty-five destroyed. Since that year more have been discovered by local field-workers. A study by Frances Peters of nearly a hundred stones, some known only by documents or by field-names, concluded that there were two major groups in the region, a northern and a southern, all very conspicuous on the higher slopes. In seventy-three cases 'stones that seemed intervisible on the maps could be seen from one another on the ground'. They had been 'purposely positioned along contours, possibly marking the boundary of one type of land or land use' and the fact that some could be seen from as far as a mile away 'suggests a more than local significance. The lines were far from straight.[54]

In contrast, John Michell considered that many stones at Land's End were arranged in planned alignments, including a very straight line of six, incorporating Boscawen-Un, to the sea six miles away. 'the nucleus of a greater megalithic structure extending across the whole southern area of the Land's End peninsula'.[55] He listed twenty-two alignments from fifty-three sites, with an average width of only 1 m but despite his claim the components of the lines were not homogeneous, sometimes being no more than a free-lying boulder, even an outcrop.

There has been extensive criticism of his selection, amongst it the observation that he had chosen West Penwith because of its profusion of megaliths, stating that he had chosen only menhirs, stone circles and dolmens for consistency whereas, in reality, his leys were a mixture: a majority of standing stones, not all certainly prehistoric, four stone circles, five portal-dolmens, seven crosses, the Men-an-Tol and some rubbing-stones, one in an Iron Age pound. Other stones, it was said, were ignored by Michell because they were in the wrong place.[56]

It is in this context that Boscawen-Un should be assessed. The wandering line of standing stones to the north and south of its central pillar follow the contours of the modern A30. The meandering row begins a mile and a half to the north-east of the

Plate 31 The Blind Fiddler near the Penzance–Lands End road.

circle at the pair of stones at Higher Drift, SW 437 283. A mile to their wsw, SW 425 282, stands the Blind Fiddler, a quartz-speckled pillar of granite, 3.6 m high, hidden in a field behind a high hedge. Legend says that the musician was petrified for playing on the Sabbath. Some years before 1872 a labourer dug at its foot and came upon 'bone chips and ashes'.[57]

Visible to its south at SW 417 277, is the 2.3 m tall triangular Hedge Stone. Another block lies on the opposite side of the lane. Just to the south-west and only 366 m from Boscawen-Un are two more stones, one upright, its partner fallen at SW 414 276.

The pillar inside Boscawen-Un should be seen as a member of these trackway markers leading from the Penzance area towards Land's End. To the circle's south-west at SW 404 272 and SW 403 271 were two more stones that were thrown down and dragged away early in 1980, the fate of many of these impediments to agriculture. Today the line ends at a block miserably dumped in a hedge near Trevear, SW 368 260, a couple of miles from Land's End, the toppled survivor of a long mutilated line of stones that guided travellers along the easiest slopes of the uncharted countryside.

It is arguable that the pillar inside Boscawen-Un stood long before the ring was arranged around it. There are many instances of such enhancement. Outliers to stone circles such as the red sandstone pillar of Long Meg outside the grey, glacial boulders of a ring near Penrith, the King Stone outside the Rollright Stones, probably the Heel Stone to the north-east of Stonehenge may be instances of circles being erected alongside a long-venerated pillar. The central stone at Callanish in the Outer Hebrides can be confidently interpreted as an original navigational marker for seafarers like other isolated tall stones along the coastline such as Clach an Tursa at the bay of Loch Carloway or the 5.8 m high Clach an Thrushel stone by the west coast, both the pillars 'stones of mourning'. Such an interpretation would explain why not a single megalithic ring with an undoubted internal stone is circular.

Alexander Thom planned eight of these 'central' stone sites. Four were his flattened type A, one was type B, another type D, there was an egg-shape and a complex ring but there was no true circle.[58] Whether one accepts his geometrical analyses for these designs is irrelevant. The absence of any circle is not.

If men laid out a ring swinging a rope from the base of an ancient standing stone the first half of the perimeter would be a perfect semi-circle but as the rope was extended to each side of the pillar the arcs would become shorter and shorter until they began to pull in on themselves. Where that occurred the two places would be marked and the points connected producing a ring with a straightened side, one of Thom's flattened circles.

CONCLUSIONS

Visitors to Land's End marvel at the stone circles there but what they see are interrupted echoes of the past. Roads, hedges and fields distort the prehistoric landscape. Stones of the circles are weathered by fifty centuries of winter. Many have been replaced, some of them wrongly. There are lost rings at Tregeseal and the Merry Maidens. There is a tumbled entrance, vanished stones and tin-mining damage at Boskednan. Boscawen-Un is likely to be a monument of two distinct phases. Standing stones have disappeared. The sites are reminders that many of today's enticing stone circles are modern illusions, historic transformations of the sacred centres of prehistoric life.

Plate 32 A general view of Woodhenge.

Chapter Five

Woodhenge, Wiltshire

DIMENSIONS, DEPOSITS AND DEATH

*A few hundred yards to the right of the Cursus is Woodhenge, a circular earthwork
... surrounding what was probably a roofed building ... There are no clues to the
purpose of the building.*

J. Wilcock, *A Guide to Occult Britain*, 1977, 90.

*The extraordinary accuracy of the geometry of Woodhenge has attracted a good
deal of attention and various attempts have been made to find the principles on
which it was laid out.*

J. Michell, *The View Over Atlantis*, 1973, 119.

Blandly anonymous, visually uninteresting in its bureaucratic reconstruction
Woodhenge is an archaeological paradox, cut grass and dull concrete yet holding vivid
glimpses of its strange prehistoric world. The messages are not casually apparent.
They shimmer like fading ghosts at the very edges of our perception. But they exist.
And it is not of life but of death that they signal.

'And death shall have no dominion', wrote Dylan Thomas. At Woodhenge it did
dominate. It was a domination surrounded by paradoxes and contradictions that
emphasise the frailties of the evidence left from the prehistoric past. Woodhenge, just
north-east of Stonehenge's colossal sarsens, was made of timber, earth and chalk (Fig.
10). That was the first contradiction.

A dozen miles south-west of Stonehenge, seven miles closer to it than that circle's
sarsens from the Marlborough Downs and nearly 200 miles nearer than its Preseli
bluestones from south-west Wales, is the little hamlet of Chilmark. One of its lovely
lanes leads down to the Chilmark Ravine, an ancient quarry with a cavernous man-
hollowed vault up to 30 m high. From it came hundreds of thousands of tons of finely
grained sandy limestone, perhaps first extracted by the Romans but certainly taken
for the mediaeval cathedrals of Chichester, Rochester and Salisbury. But not for
Stonehenge or Woodhenge.[1]

For bulky objects: encircling banks, sturdy wooden pillars, standing stones,
Neolithic people used easily-obtained local material, soil, trees, glacial erratics lying
on the ground. They did not quarry for anything large. There are no stone circles and
very few megalithic tombs on the chalks and clays of Kent or Lincolnshire or the
Yorkshire Wolds. Stonehenge is a contradiction because it is built of stones brought
from considerable distances.

Woodhenge is not. The chalk from its ditch was used to pile up its bank. The timber for its posts came from the dense oak forests along the banks of the nearby River
Avon. The puzzle of Woodhenge is not what it was made of but what it was made for
and, even more demanding, the contradiction of its contents, useless artefacts of chalk,

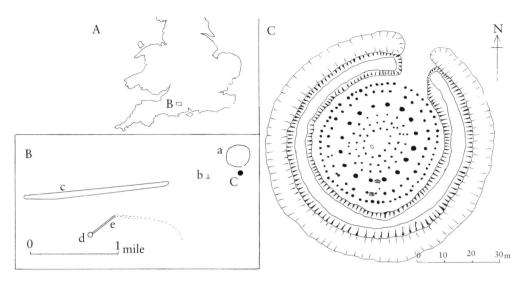

Fig. 10 Map and plan of Woodhenge, Wiltshire. a. Durrington Walls; b. Cuckoo Stone; c. Cursus; d. Stonehenge; e. Avenue.

and animal teeth and bones that were not thrown away or dumped in the river but buried reverently in carefully calculated positions.

It has even been seen as the inspiration for Stonehenge. 'It is suggested that Woodhenge was the prototype and forerunner of Stonehenge. It had been conjectured on purely technical grounds that Stonehenge must have had a wooden prototype, or at least that its builders were familiar with working in wood'.[2] Recent radiocarbon assays from Stonehenge reject Woodhenge as its predecessor.

Since the early nineteenth century its earthwork has been 'thought to be that of a very large disc barrow', 'the mutilated remains of an enormous Druid barrow'.[3] The site consists of a small, irregular henge with a single entrance at the NNE. Inside its central plateau of some 1,850 m² are six sub-circular settings of posts.

THE EXCAVATIONS

In December 1925 the dark marks of postholes inside the slightly domed interior of this worn-down, earthwork just south of the sprawling settlement of Durrington Walls were noticed from the air by Squadron-Leader Insall. From 1926 to 1928 the Wiltshire archaeologist, Maud Cunnington, and her husband Benjamin, great-grandson of Sir Richard Colt Hoare's colleague, William, excavated both sides of the entrance, drove trenches across the ditch at east, ESE, south and west and emptied every one of the 156 postholes.[4]

In the first year when the tops of the postholes were appearing below the stripped turf the anonymous site was called 'Wood-henge' in a jocular comparison to the nearby Stonehenge. The 'jest' has induced no more smiles than the local village name of the 'dough cover' that likened the central area to an upturned saucer. Agriculture had flattened the bank but

> the only way to plough this small circular field [the interior of the henge], surrounded on all sides by a ditch too deep to allow the plough oxen to be turned at the end of each furrow, would have to plough round it. The centre part could have been worked in straight furrows, and the part towards the edge of the ditch in a round-about way, like headland is now ploughed in a direction contrary to the rest of the field.[5]

The henge is now flat – like the jokes.

Today Woodhenge is quiet and unexpressive, as visually unimposing as its *doppelgänger* of the Sanctuary near Avebury, fenced, mown, with low concrete cylinders standing where posts once rose, the modern pillars varying in width to show the different sizes of those posts. They are polychromatic. With untypical flair English Heritage has had the tops of each ring painted in different colours to make it visually distinct from the others. Despite this the site is unspectacular. Yet it contains the challenge of a tragedy and deep revelations of the beliefs of its builders.

The henge and the rings of posts inside it fit uneasily together. The NNE causewayed entrance across the ditch and the north-east end of the axis of the elliptical rings do not coincide but are a full 12 m apart. The shapes also vary. In plan the bank and ditch form an oblong with rounded corners resembling a squat brandy bottle with the henge's entrance at its neck. The rings, in contrast, are almost perfectly elliptical, subtly narrowing into egg-shapes at their north-east. Radio-carbon assays of 1805 ± 54 bc (BM-678) and 1867 ± 74 bc (BM-677), from antler and bone at the bottom of the ditch suggest that the earthwork was thrown up some time in the centuries between about 2400 and 2100 BC when users of grooved ware pottery were occupying Durrington Walls. This was confirmed by the discovery of grooved ware sherds deep in the ditch and below the bank of Woodhenge itself, and by the contents of two pits outside the entrance with culturally characteristic deposits of animal bones, burnt

Plate 33 The flint-covered grave near the centre of Woodhenge, from the south-west.

Plate 34 An aerial view of Woodhenge; the outlines of ring-barrows can be seen in the field beyond.

flints, charcoal and potsherds, a collection of 'rubbish' that in fact was the very antithesis of that to the dualistically-minded people who buried it, spiritual precursors of the mediaeval Cathars of the Languedoc in France, believers in the association of opposing elements and the struggle between the goodness of the spirit, and the evil of physical matter.

Although Cunnington's six ditch sections, two at the entrance, were limited in extent over fifty grooved ware sherds were found lying on the old land surface beneath the bank and therefore predating it and the ditch from which its chalk came. Nearly a score more of rims and pieces came from the ditch-terminals on either side of the entrance, sixteen to the east, three to the west as though most of the workers were right-handed, throwing their bits of pot into the newly-dug ditch at the end of a day's work.[6]

In contrast, only a few sherds together with some beaker fragments came from the postholes, the majority from the deep, broad pits of Ring C, amongst their packing or fairly high up suggesting that they had been débris that had slipped into the holes as the posts rotted.[7]

The date of the rings is unknown. The posts could have been set up after the henge by different people, beaker users, who slighted the bank, shovelling some of its earth and chalk back into the ditch. This wide and deep trench had quickly eroded from its rim, depositing a thick layer of silt that had been followed by more gradual weathering 'finally so slow that a thick band of turf clothed the surface' which settled almost a metre above the original base. Two more were created above it as ploughs in historic times churned earth into the weed-filled ditch.[8]

The entrances offer a clue to the sequence of construction. The average spacing between the sixty posts of the outer ring is about 2 m whereas the gap of the entrance is almost twice that width. Had the post-ring been primary it would be expected that its entrance would have been on one of its four axes at the north-east, ESE, south-west or WNW. Instead, it is at the NNE in line with the henge's causeway, respecting the earlier earthwork. Artefactual evidence supports the architectural inference, beaker pottery from the post-rings being later than grooved ware found in the ditch.

It was just below the earliest turf layer that sherds of an AOC beaker were found. Elsewhere there were broken W/MR and 'European' beakers dumped there decades after the henge had been constructed.[9] Such evidence offers the possibility of a peaceful takeover but more probably the annexation of an alien ritual centre.

UNITS OF MEASUREMENT

Of the six settings of posts the outermost, Ring A, 43.9 by about 40.8 m, was composed of light poles set only 60 cm into the ground, perhaps supporting the light hurdles of an enclosing outer palisade fencing the interior from the outside world. Inside it was the controversy of either a roofed structure or the alternative of five freestanding ellipses of one or more phases, open to the sky like the framework of a large and unfinished house.

The first ring to be erected was the third from the outside, Cunnington's Ring C, with a long diameter of 29.3 m and a short of some 26 m. It consisted of sixteen metre-thick, five-ton oak trunks dragged from the nearby forests. The setting was constructed in two stages. At the south-west the long, sloping ramps 'or sloping racks cut to about half the depth of the hole to aid in the erection of the uprights' were all on the outside showing that the posts had been hauled upright from inside the uncluttered interior, twenty or thirty men straining at the ropes and levers until the timbers were vertical, their tops towering some 7 m above the ground.[10]

In contrast, every one of the north-eastern ramps was inside the oval indicating that theirs had been a secondary phase of the operation to be completed only when the southern posts were in place. Blocks of chalk were rammed and packed deeply into the pits, jammed against the posts to keep them stable.

It was after the completion of this great enclosure that the two inner Rings, F and E, of more slender posts were constructed, followed by Ring D whose holes were measured off from E just as rings A and B had been similarly laid off outside C. Whether all these rings were contemporaries is unknown. If not, C, B and A were arguably earlier than D, E and F.

Their shapes have caused uncertainty. Cunnington believed that the rings had been scribed out as circles and then changed into ovals by bringing in the sides, a process that inevitably created inaccuracies. She did not ask why such shapes were required. In contrast, Alexander Thom considered that they were geometrically designed to have perimeters that were multiples of 20 of his Megalithic Yard of 0.829 m, respectively 40, 60, 80, 100, 140 and 160. His dimensions, however, were based on a survey of the modern concrete markers and differed from Cunnington's lengths, his long diameter for Ring F being a full metre shorter. For Ring A his diameter was 44.2 m long against Cunnington's 43.9 m; for Ring B 39.4 m against 38.1 m; and consecutively: C, 28.7 m against 29.3 m; D, 23.4 m and 23.4 m; E, 17.7 m against 17.6 m; and, F, 12.7 m against 11.7 m. As Mrs Cunnington had made a point of commending her nephew, Lt-Col. R. H. Cunnington of the Royal Engineers who 'surveyed and made all the measurements' on the exposed postholes themselves rather than on their later substitutes, it seems wise to accept her figures.[11]

The rings are not true ellipses but ovates whose north-eastern apices are narrower than those at the south-west, a design that owes nothing to structural demands whether the rings were roofed or open to the sky. The design can be explained. First their dimensions must be considered.

With an unorthodox insight, anticipating Thom by more than thirty years, Cunnington suggested that a unit of measurement, a 'Short Foot' of $11\frac{1}{2}$ inches (29.2 cm) had been used, so that the modern Imperial lengths had been prehistoric multiples of 10 Short Feet: 40 Short Feet (S.F.) for Ring F; 60 S.F. for E; 80 for D; 100 for C; 130 for B and 150 for A.

This was an appealing idea implying as it did at least semi-numeracy and mathematical planning on the part of the designers but the decimalisation of the lengths conflicts with the numbers of posts in the ellipses. Only Ring A contained an integer of 10. Ring F had 12 posts, E, 18, D, 18, C, 16, B, 32 and F, 60. Nor are Cunnington's multiples as perfect as she reckoned (Table 3).

TABLE 3. A comparison of possible units of measurement used at Woodhenge.

RINGS	A	B	C	D	E	F
Long diameters in metres	43.9	38.1	29.3	23.4	17.6	11.7
'Short Feet'	150.3	130.5	100.2	80.2	60.1	40.1
Megalithic Yards	52.9	46.0	35.3	28.2	21.2	14.1
Beaker Yards	60.0	52.0	40.0	32.0	24.0	16.0
Number of posts	60	32	16	18	18	12
Divided by 4	15	8	4	$4\frac{1}{2}$	$4\frac{1}{2}$	3

Years later Alexander Thom replanned the rings: 'Fig. 4 is a reduced copy of an accurate survey of the concrete pillars which have been erected to mark the post holes in the underlying chalk. The survey was made by theodolite and steel tape and so may be taken as accurate. The azimuths were determined astronomically to ±2 minutes of arc'. He believed that the rings were egg-shaped and had been laid out by the use of a right-angled triangle of $12^2 + 35^2 = 37^2$. 'At first sight it seems unlikely (but not impossible) that it was known and used'.[12]

Both Cunnington and Thom were slightly in error. A counting-base of 4 would fit better than 10 and if instead of the Short Foot of $11\frac{1}{2}$ inches (29.2 cm) or the Megalithic Yard of 2.72 ft (0.829 m) the unit of measurement had been a 'Beaker Yard' of 2 ft $4^{3/4}$ inches (73.2 cm), then both the units used in the diameters and the numbers of posts would be whole or half-multiples of 4.[13]

According to Cunnington the rings were spaced 9 feet 7 inches (2.9 m) apart, very significantly the exact equivalent of four Beaker Yards, yet another appearance of the number 4. The short diameters, less well recorded, may also be quadruple multiples of the Beaker Yard, approximately but not invariably close to it: 56, 48, 36, 28, 20 (a poor fit) and 12 respectively.

A counting-system based on 4 would have been easy to use for small sums, 5 being reckoned as 4 + 1, and 11 as 4 + 4 + 1 + 1 + 1 but it was a clumsy method for any total of more than 20. There is clear evidence that errors did occur when prehistoric people attempted anything more ambitious. Counting-bases of 4, 5 and 6 have been deduced for structures in prehistoric Britain but, rather surprisingly, there is no support for a radix or counting base of 3.[14]

ASTRONOMY

At Woodhenge one probable reason for the non-circular shapes was the wish to have a long axis that would act as an astronomical sightline. It was a method often used by people laying out stone 'circles' such as Cultoon on Islay where the axis was directed towards the midwinter sunset. 'The 55-mile long alignment makes it one of the most accurate sun observatories known'.[15]

A simple but ingenious sighting-device was incorporated into Woodhenge. Having noted where the midsummer sun rose on the skyline eight miles to the north-east men set up two slender posts, 27 m apart as a practical sightline, Cunnington's 'a' at the north-east and 'b' at the south-west, in line with that sunrise. The long diameters of the rings were arranged around these to form an extended but restricted 'window' that was as accurate as a gunsight. At the south-west end of the outer ring an observer would look between posts A8 and A9 to the centimetres-wide gap formed between sighting-post 'b' and post B9. Beyond it the alignment passed by C3 to one side and D3 on the other, then E3 to the west and F3 to the east, over the centre of Woodhenge, through the slit of the distant sighting-post 'a' and E12, out to A39 and A40 and the exact point on the horizon of the summer solstitial rising. It was economical, clever and precise.[16]

Nor was this all. Another post was erected at the north, and a second at the west where the 'equinoctial' sun would set behind the distant 'Cuckoo' or, more suggestively, Cuckold Stone as it was moralistically known in the eighteenth century. Woodhenge, however, was not an observatory for astronomer-priests wishing to make a scientific study of the celestial mechanics of heavenly bodies.

BURIALS

Close to the centre of the rings a small grave was found, flint-covered, 'lying on the line of midsummer sunrise and at right-angles to it'. In it was the skeleton of a $3\frac{1}{2}$ year-old child, probably a girl, lying on its right side facing the sunrise. Her skull lay in two halves, 'cleft before burial', one of the clearest examples of human sacrifice in prehistoric Britain and one which suggests that the child may have been killed in a ceremony of re-dedication. The eastern side of the henge's entrance at 39° had been raised in line with the most northerly rising of the moon. Now, just as at Stonehenge, the monument had been transformed from a lunar temple into a sanctuary of the sun.[17]

In 1934 the child's skull was sent for further examination to the Royal College of Surgeons in London only to be destroyed by fire during an air raid in the Second World War. Another skeleton, presumably also female, from the Sanctuary near Avebury, was lost at the same time.[18]

DEPOSITS

The communities that used Woodhenge left revealing evidence of their beliefs. In the postholes they had placed scraps of animal bones as well as flints, some worked, some burnt and an analysis of the 'rubbish' produced interesting patterns. Scores of ox and pig teeth were recovered, most of them in the holes of the two outer rings, those of the ox mainly in the north-east and south-west quadrants, those of the pig in the north-west and south-east. Jaws of these animals were closer to the centre.

Such systematic distributions have been recognised as cultural traits amongst grooved ware users. As Julian Thomas has stated, 'At Woodhenge the pattern is all the more emphatic: not only are the bones of wild animals restricted to the outer ditch, but the ratio of pig to cattle changes between each of the six concentric rings of postholes, pig dominating the outer holes, cattle the inner. It has long been recognised that Grooved Ware is rarely to be found associated with funerary monuments or burials . . . The sporadic finds of human bones on henges with Grooved Ware associations are thus all the more interesting for they correspond precisely to the locations from which the bones of undomesticated animals have been recovered'.[19]

Thomas pointed to the unusual contrasts and comparisons noticed in grooved ware deposits: inside and out, tame and wild, culture and nature as though bringing the world into balance through the relationships between opposites. At Woodhenge flints and pottery were kept separate, 'flints as "natural", pottery as "cultural"'. Flint flakes, scrapers and burnt flints were concentrated around the two outer rings, mostly to the south of the grave and with the flints, animal bone occurred in hole after hole. Heavier meat-bones, including part of a pig's skull, lay nearer the centre.

Pollard elaborated. To the east of the long axis pig bones were peripheral whereas a third of all cattle bones were discovered in the centre of the monument. 'Possibly a process of clockwise procession was intended along the 4 m wide corridor between rings B and C'. The entrance with its human remains was given special treatment, 'ascribed significance through the deposition of either joints of meat or the residue of such prime cuts'.[20]

In this manner the juxtaposition of similarities and the isolation of disparates formed contrasts between darkness and light, between life and death, good and evil, stabilised the instability of an existence subjected to unpredictable drought, storm and pestilence. The interment of chosen offerings at Woodhenge created a centre in which nature itself could be manipulated.

Woodhenge with its solar alignment was not an abattoir for the inhabitants of the adjacent Durrington Walls. More probably it was a place where the corpses of the newly-dead were taken, a symbolic mortuary house, open to the sky and sun, sanctified by the burial of magical objects in magical positions, protected from scavenging animals by the outer stockade, mourners performing rituals around the bodies, feasts held in their honour, their possessions by their sides during the weeks or months before the fleshless remains were carried away.

Human bones have been found inside Woodhenge. As well as the skeleton in the ditch and a cremation in Ring B a human radius lay at the bottom of the ditch, and pieces of human skull and some teeth were recovered high up in posthole C13. Fragments of a child's jaw and some milk teeth lay a metre deep at the entrance, and the bones of a very young infant were discovered nearby just above the lowest of the three turf-lines. It may be, that as at Stonehenge and other ritual centres, these were the remains of sacrifices to protect the entrance to a ritual centre.[21]

ROOFED OR UNROOFED?

Such an interpretation would resolve an argument as to whether the rings of posts had ever been roofed. Despite Musson's architectural opinion it has generally been accepted that Piggott was correct that the rings had been pennanular, covered except for an open space at the centre. There are reasons for disbelieving this. The excavation had revealed no signs of drip-runnels made by rain falling from the roof either outside the building or from the innermost edge of the roof.

Helpful comparisons can be made between the plan of Woodhenge and the two circular structures at Durrington Walls whose postholes were recovered during the excavations of 1966–8. The northernmost was interpreted as a roofed structure of two concentric rings, about 14.5 m across. The southern had two phases, the first of three roofed rings, 23 m in diameter, the second a more elaborate setting somewhat akin to Woodhenge of five rings, 41 m in size with an open central space. There were structural and spatial problems with these hypothetical models and Musson's conclusion was that 'the best hope of an all-embracing explanation may lie in the idea of ritual or symbolic settings of free-standing posts controlled by some numerical, dimensional or geometrical logic', particularly if those rings were lintelled and if 'some of the less deeply embedded rings [represented a] line of enclosing fences'.[22]

Geometrical analysis has shown that the rings are ovate. There was no architecturally physical necessity for this but there was a social one. It may have been at the wider south-western end that participants gathered to watch rites performed by officiants at the far side at the time of the midsummer rising sun. If so, a roofed building would have prevented the view. Free-standing rings of posts, probably lintelled to ensure stability, are more likely.

Elsewhere in Britain there were comparable settings. At the henge of Balfarg in Fife there were as many as six concentric timber rings associated with grooved ware. They were succeeded by two concentric stone circles with a central pit containing a cremation with a handled beaker. There are multiple stone rings surrounding burials on Dartmoor. Other timber rings existed at Croft Moraig and Moncreiffe, Perthshire. Only eighteen miles north of Woodhenge the upright posts of the Sanctuary near Avebury, were uprooted and replaced by two sarsen rings. Neatly at the east the body of a young girl with a 'Barbed-Wire' beaker was buried under a sarsen slab. In Powys a timber ring at Sarn y Bryn Caled surrounded a cremation, perhaps a sacrifice. These were houses of the dead. The absence of a roof and walls mattered no more than the absence of scenery in a classical Greek play. The symbol of the house was more powerful than the uncovered reality of rings of timber.[23]

The ritual nature of Woodhenge cannot be doubted. Cardinal and calendrical orientations were integrated into the plan. Special deposits were buried in postholes on these alignments, probably before the posts were set up, objects made of friable chalk and of no practical value: 'cups', plaques or discs, and axes.

It has been inferred that the axe, whether of durable stone or fragile chalk, was the token of a guardian of the dead just as the crucifix is the embodiment of the Crucifixion. Two chalk axes were discovered inside Woodhenge. With one was a crude disc of perforated chalk in a posthole of the outer ring. A second rested at the bottom of B21.

The association of the axe with the sun and with death was widespread amongst primitive societies in western Europe and the chalk axes at Woodhenge are reminders of an axe-cult in Neolithic and Bronze Age Britain. A fragment of a chalk axe was discovered in a barrow at Westbury in Wiltshire and 'does not make sense unless votive' and 'the small size and soft material [limestone] of the little axe from Hengistbury Head likewise suggest a votive purpose'.[24]

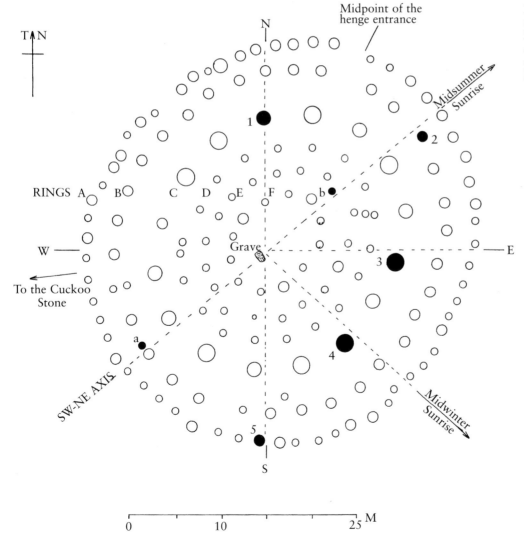

Fig. 11 Astronomical alignments and ritual deposits at Woodhenge. 1. the only cremation; 2. chalk axe and worked chalk; 3. chalk 'cup' and worked chalk; 4. chalk 'cup' and worked chalk; 5 chalk axe and worked chalk. a. and b. sighting-posts.

Other 'axes' specially made as ritual objects have been found with burials. An axe, believed to be of pottery, came from the passage-tomb of Tara in Ireland. At Brownstone Farm near Kingswear in Devon a miniature axe of jadeite had been left in a cist with two cremations. The chalk axes, the 'cups', the perforated discs, all esoteric, all linked with death, the human bones, the arcane deposits of opposites, they combine in a statement that Woodhenge had mysteries that can be sensed, imagined but never understood.

In posthole C9 a chalk 'cup' was found. Such objects, hand-sized blocks with a shallow depression on their upper surface and known from other Neolithic ritual sites, are too small to have been cups or lamps for oil. Their scooped hollow, no deeper than a thumb-mark, offers an explanation. Frequently associated with chalk phalli, these 'cups' may have been the female counterpart of the male organ, talismen of fertility, life-giving and appropriate for a house of the dead. In Ring C a second 'cup' lay in Hole 7 (Fig. 11).

'Cups' of chalk have been found in Neolithic causewayed enclosures and flint-mines as well as in ritual centres such as Stonehenge, Woodhenge and Maumbury Rings in Dorset. 'We prefer to consider them not primarily as lamps but as belonging to the same class of votive or ritualistic objects as the phallic carvings, the ladles and spoons, fabricators, mace-heads and those other unexplained things with which Neolithic tribesmen attempted to make their corn grow, their cattle multiply, and their trade thrive'.[25]

The ditches of Windmill Hill near Avebury were repositories of totems, fecundity charms and ju-jus: six 'cups' intermingled with holed discs and carved phalli. Thirty chalk balls there, usually lying in pairs, can plausibly be identified as representations of testicles. There were even two putative representations of figurines.[26]

With the second 'cup' at Woodhenge there was a palm-sized rectangle of chalk with a hole bored through it. These perforated plaques or discs, like the phalli and 'cups', are also associated with the Neolithic dead. A similar holed disc was found with a chalk ball in the ditch at Stonehenge. A further link with that circle was provided by a second disc at Woodhenge, its perforation only half-finished. With it in Hole 16 of Ring A was a chalk axe like the one found by Hawley in the ramp of Stone 56, the tallest sarsen in Stonehenge. Close to the next sarsen was a chalk phallus.[27]

Coarsely-fashioned discs have constantly been found with the dead. Two were recovered from the sealed forecourt of the Cairnholy chambered tomb in Scotland. Small enough to fit into the hand their edges were roughly flaked but their surfaces were beautifully smoothed. One had a delicate cupmark no bigger than a baby's fingernail, not big enough to hold anything solid or liquid unless a raindrop. Other discs have been left with burials: in West Kennet long barrow; at the multi-phase megalithic tomb of Ty-Isaf in Powys and at Pant-y-Saer on Anglesey. Not far from Cairnholy a sherd and a tiny stone disc lay beside the blue-grey stains of bodies in the Clyde tomb of Brackley on the Kintyre peninsula.

The discs puzzle. Of slate, sandstone, sarsen, quartz, a few centimetres across, discovered in tombs, cists, round barrows, stone circles, in the ditches of causewayed enclosures and henges, with inhumations and cremations, their symbolism remains obscure. Found as far north as Stenness in the Orkneys they are ubiquitous but always it is death that is their companion. Like the axes, the phalli, the 'cups' at Woodhenge, their presence is redolent not only of death but of fecundity and revival.[28]

The disposition of these extraordinary objects was selective. Maud Cunnington emptied every one of the 156 postholes but it was only in the five cardinal or calendrical pits that the unique deposits of chalk discs, axes and 'lamps' were found. That they had been purposefully concealed is unquestionable. Cunnington herself remarked that 'these chalk objects if exposed to a hard frost would go to pieces in a single night, and they must therefore have been buried intentionally . . . very soon after they were made'.[29]

The cardinal points of north, east, west and south were emphasised. The sole cremation at Woodhenge lay in the northernmost hole of Ring C. In C9 east was recorded by a chalk 'cup', probably a symbol of female sexuality and fertility. A piece of worked chalk was deposited on the same line. Beyond it the skeleton of a young man was buried in the ditch of the henge on the identical alignment. A chalk axe lay at the south in A16 near which a hollow may once have held a large sarsen like an altar. West was marked. 'A line drawn from the centre of the rings between the hole "c" [an 'extra' small hole on the perimeter of Ring D] and D1, prolonged beyond the enclosure cuts the rough sarsen stone lying on the down a quarter of a mile away, known as the "Cuckoo Stone"'. It was an approximate alignment on the 'equinoctial sunset'.[30]

It is easy to understand the wish to record the sun at its equinoctial positions of east and west but the reasons for establishing orientations to north and south are elusive. It may be that there was a desire to establish those positions midway between the sun's risings and settings, the extreme 'edges' of the celestial world.

> At the round earth's imagin'd corners, blow
> Your trumpets, Angells, and arise, arise
> From death, you numberlesse infinities
> Of souls . . .
>
> John Donne, *Holy Sonnets*, VII

It has been noticed that the Stonehenge Cursus, the Cuckoo Stone and Woodhenge form a line towards a notable bend in the River Avon and the midpoint between the midsummer and midwinter sunrises.[31] It must also be noted that as well as the cardinal points there were calendrical alignments to the sun at Woodhenge. A chalk axe from B21 was on the summer solstice alignment. A broken greenstone axe from Cornwall had been put in C11 on the same line. A chalk 'cup' in C7 was on the orientation of the midwinter sunrise. It is the repetition of deposits in these important situations and, just as important, their entire absence elsewhere, never in the innermost three rings, D, E and F, that confirms the interpretation of Woodhenge as a ritual centre.

It is demanding too much of coincidence to question the astronomical interests of the Woodhenge people when every one of the carved chalk objects discovered there was in a posthole related to a solar or cardinal alignment. Drab though Woodhenge may appear today its design and contents provide intriguing illuminations about the thinking and needs of our distant ancestors.

It is a paradox of prehistoric archaeology that a place so unappealing to the eye should have so much to tell us of the minds of people four millennia ago, whose faiths and values were as alien to us as those of inter-galactic travellers. Their systems of beliefs will always elude our final understanding. But Woodhenge through the excavations of the Cunningtons, the analyses of Thom, the reconstructions by Musson, the researches of Thomas and Pollard, is a glow in the darkness.

Tis opportune to look back upon old times, and contemplate our Forefathers. Sir T. Browne, *Hydriotaphia*, 1658, 94[32]

PART TWO

Stonehenge

Plate 35 *(previous pages)* Stonehenge in Winter, from the west.

Plate 36 *(above)* Stonehenge, entrance.

Chapter Six

Stonehenge, Wiltshire

AN INTRODUCTION

Stonehenge is the world's most well-known stone circle. It is also the most discussed and the most enigmatic with many individual features unexplained or the subjects of sharp argument.

Even the name has caused controversy. It first appeared early in the twelfth century in Henry of Huntingdon's *Historia Anglorum*, 'The History of the English'. His *stanenges* can be translated as 'the hanging stones' because the five trilithons inside the circle were like the lintelled mediaeval gibbets used for multiple executions. In 1740 the psychically perceptive William Stukeley agreed. 'The ancient *Britons* call'd it *choir-gaur*, which the *Monks* latiniz'd into chorea gigantum, the giants dance . . . *Rode-hengenn* is Saxon hanging-rod or pole, and *Stonehenge* is a stone gallows, called so from the hanging post'.[1]

Although the most famous stone circle it is the least characteristic being an atypical ring of idiosyncratic design built by native woodworkers on Salisbury Plain. Nor was this all. Until very recently even the builders and the chronology were unclear as the minor poet, Walter Pope, puzzled in 1676.

> I will not forget, the stones that are set
> In a round, on Salisbury plaines,
> Though who put 'em there, 'tis hard to declare,
> The Romans, or Merlin, or Danes.

The Romans began by maltreating it. Early post-conquest coins found in the ring suggest the wrecking of a centre of druidical resistance when those priests and law-givers and their followers had been massacred on Anglesey in AD 60, the year in which Boudicca's rebellion erupted. It may have been then that the Great Trilithon and Altar Stone were toppled and smaller stones pushed over or physically removed to deface and emasculate the monument.[2]

By the usual inconstancy of human behaviour centuries later the ruin became a Roman tourist attraction. Bronze coins from the years around AD 400, used and worn, have been discovered mixed with personal objects such as a hairpin, 'a toilet or manicure instrument', pottery, brooches, pins, oyster shells from toga-clad picnics, 'all items that could have been lost by casual visitors'. As early as 1724 Stukeley had employed Richard Hayns, an old man from Amesbury, to dig in barrows near the circle and the man also found 'some little, worn-out *Roman* coins at Stonehenge, among the earth rooted up by the rabbets'.[3]

But nothing was recorded. For two thousand years from its abandonment in the Late Bronze Age around 1000 BC to post-Norman Conquest decades not a word has survived. After some brief and minor Romano-British settlements in the vicinity the ring was deserted and ignored. Anglo-Saxon and early mediaeval farmers cultivated the sheltered valleys with sporadic grazing on the downs. The gaunt stones were things of wonder only to the few literate monks and clerics passing by.

In his *Historia Anglorum* of about 1129 AD Henry, archdeacon of Huntingdon, termed Stonehenge the Second Wonder of Britain.

Henry's first Wonder was the Peak Cavern in the Peak District, Derbyshire from which swirling winds howled. The Third was the tunnel of Wookey Hole in Cheddar Caves, Somerset whose end no one could discover. But the Fourth Wonder would be no surprise to today's stone circle enthusiasts: 'The Fourth is that in some parts of the country, the rain is seen to gather about the tops of the hills, and forthwith to fall on the plains'. Anyone who has gone to a stone circle exposed on the open moors will have experienced rain gathering around the hills and falling upon the ground beneath.

These were all natural phenomena. Stonehenge was a manmade amazement. 'where stones of extraordinary dimensions are raised as columns, and others fixed above, like lintels of immense portals; and no one has been able to discover by what mechanism such vast masses of stone were elevated, nor for what purpose they were designed'. It was secondhand garble presumably told to an uninformed East Anglian clergyman by a colleague who had seen the monument.

The rickety description by Henry was followed by the Arthurian fantasy of Geoffrey of Monmouth, *c.* 1138, in his *Historia Regum Britanniae*, 'The History of the Kings of Britain', in which the magician, Merlin, magically transported the stones of a ring built by giants in Ireland, using them for a cenotaph to British warriors treacherously slain by Saxons.

A few years later Geoffrey's stately Latin prose was enlivened in the poetical Anglo-Norman transcription of the *History* by Wace of Jersey whose *Le Roman de Brut* of 1155 remarked on the name. 'This circle of stones was called by the Britons in their own tongue "The Giant's Carol" [Dance], but in English it bears the name of Stonehenge'. And 'Stonehenge' it has remained.[4]

It was the beginning of a library of conjecture about the sarsen ring. In 1901 Jerome Harrison was able to list more than forty books published between 1655 and 1900 dedicated solely to the monument and this did not include the scores, perhaps hundreds of more general studies in books, articles and letters to newspapers that debated the techniques of the builders, the age of the stones, their function, druids, sacrifices, astronomy, and a myriad of improbable theories such as Edmund Bolton's in his *Nero Caesar, or Monarchie Depraved* of 1624 in which he affirmed that Stonehenge had been the honoured burial place of Boudicca.

Harrison was not just a chronicler. As a professional geologist he was perceptive enough to observe that 'the so-called "greenstones", "blue-stones" or "foreign" rocks

Plate 37 The title-page of William Charleton's *Stone-Heng*.

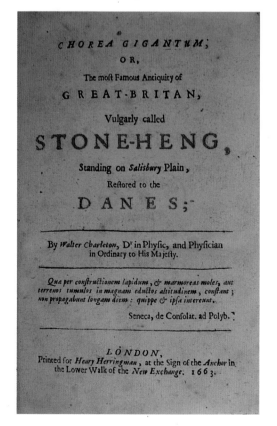

. . . may have been brought from Wales', half-anticipating by forty years Thomas's conclusion that the stones had come from the Welsh Preselis.[5]

Since 1900 there have been many more books about the circle and even a meticulously detailed Bibliography of 1997 omitted several sensible publications.[6] Gleaning sense from a haystack of ignorance, wild speculation and escapism the most valuable contributions chronologically have been Inigo Jones's recognition in the early 1620s that the sarsens of Stonehenge had come from the Marlborough Downs, eighteen miles to the north. Forty years later John Aubrey deduced that the circle was British and prehistoric. He was the first to record the existence of the Heel Stone. In the hot and dry summer of 1666 his acute eyes made out the faint depressions of the Aubrey Holes. In July and August of 1723 his fine successor at Stonehenge, William Stukeley, discerned the avenue, the distant Cursus, and devised the term, 'trilithon', for the lintelled archways inside the ring.[7]

In 1740 the architect, John Wood, made the first accurate plan of the circle and its earthwork, the sight of his triangulated surveying stakes causing Lady Frances Hanbury Williams 'much amusement'. Thirty years later a frustrated inoculator against the smallpox, John Smith, noticed that the Heel Stone stood in line with the midsummer sunrise.[8]

Then came the second great silence. During virtually the entire nineteenth century there was an almost complete lack of enquiry, commentators being satisfied with romantic horrors of Druidical sacrifice and barbarous festivals. It was a void ended by the meticulous surveys of Flinders Petrie first in 1874 and then in 1877 with 'a new pattern of chain, expressly for accurate work'. He recorded the measurements of stones and devised the numbering system that is still in use.[9]

Rather surprisingly, except for the occasional and usually ill-performed interference by treasure-seekers there had been little excavation in the ring but this lacuna was deleted by the investigations of William Hawley, often helped by Robert Newall, at the beginning of the 1920s. His trenches showed that the primary north-east entrance had been widened. Across it were fifty-three inexplicable postholes in six meandering lines. Pottery, stone artefacts and human remains were discovered. Over half of the fifty-six Aubrey Holes were emptied. The evidence of prehistoric sherds and artefacts demonstrated an early date for Stonehenge.[10]

While the excavations were proceeding there was an important discovery about the stones themselves. Inigo Jones had realised that the sarsens were relatively local. In 1923 the geologist, Herbert Thomas, analysed the mineralogy of the varied bluestones and concluded that their most likely source was the Carn Meini ridge of the Preseli mountains in south-west Wales, 200 sea- and land-miles away.[11]

A well-written and scholarly synthesis of these advances appeared in Richard Atkinson's *Stonehenge* of 1956. Having excavated parts of the ring with Stuart Piggott and J. F. S. 'Marcus' Stone he constructed a persuasive sequence of three phases for Stonehenge, the first for the Late Neolithic henge and Aubrey Holes, the second for the concentric bluestone circles, and a third for the Early Bronze Age sarsen ring and the Middle Bronze Age Y and Z Holes. He suggested feasible working practices, engineering techniques, routes and means of transportation, and, almost as a climax to these explanations, in July 1953 he made the first discovery of axe and dagger carvings on the sarsens. A pioneering radiocarbon assay of 1848 ± 275 bc (C-602), from charcoal in Aubrey Hole 32 offered an exciting but very broad calibrated bracket of *c.* 2600 to 1850 BC for an early period of the site.

Atkinson's splendid book proved seminal to further studies and generated an out-pouring of debate about diverse aspects of Stonehenge, its astronomy, its geometrical design and the use of a standardised yardstick, the nature of its society and the origins of the ring. In 1962 'Peter' Newham claimed lunar as well as solar alignments in the circle and the Four Stations rectangle around it, and in 1972 he brilliantly analysed the 'inexplicable' postholes across the north-eastern entrance as a series of sighting-devices for marking the progress of the moon on its 18.61 year cycle towards its most northerly rising.[12]

Four years later the present writer in a comprehensive study of stone circles was able to place Stonehenge in the general context of megalithic rings emphasising that 'To begin a book about stone circles by mentioning Stonehenge is like starting a discussion about birds by talking about the Dodo. Neither is a typical example of its class. Both are above average in size, of peculiar construction, and both represent a dead-end in development.[13]

In *Antiquity 50*, 1976, Thatcher pointed out that the rectangle of the Four Stations around Stonehenge had not been laid out as an expected square but as an oblong so that its SE–NW diagonal would form a neat alignment on the May Day sunrise, the pre-historic festival of Beltane, 'the shining one'.[14]

The 1980s saw yet more developments: Chippindale's *Stonehenge Complete* of 1983 was a delightful – and scholarly – social history of the circle from the time of Henry of Huntingdon to the present day, serious, amusing, very well-informed and containing delectable chapters on 'Wessex to Mycenae and back', 'Alternative visions' and 'A delusion of Druids'. It was revised and enlarged in 1994.

In 1987 came the astonishment of two books with the identical title of *The Stonehenge People*, one by this author which amongst other considerations detailed the evidence for an early timber building inside the henge. The other volume by Castleden provided information about the carvings and debated Roman vandalism. In his later *The Meaning of Stonehenge*, 1993, by the ingenious superimposing of two resistivity and geo-magnetometer plans, he inferred that the earthen avenue to Stonehenge had once been lined with standing stones.[15]

In 1995 arrived a *pièce de resistance* in terms of raw data about the results of the finds from excavations. It included a new series of radio-carbon determinations. In *Stonehenge in its Landscape* Rosamund Cleal, her co-editors and colleagues produced a thesaurus of information. Atkinson's three-phase chronology was reconsidered and a tentatively revised sequence was put forward based upon the large series of C-14 assays: Phase I for the henge, 3500–2910 BC; II for the silted ditch of 3300–2140 BC; 2580–1890 BC for the avenue; Phase III for the sarsen circle of 2850–2200 BC; for the inner bluestone circle and horseshoe of 2480–1940 BC; and, last of all, for the Y and Z Holes around the circle, 2030–1520 BC.[16]

Yet, despite all these endeavours, many questions remain unanswered about little-considered but important aspects of the site. It has never been wondered whether the outlying Heel Stone might have been the first feature on the site, pre-dating even the henge, an isolated pillar perhaps acting as a territorial marker, or a megalithic 'signpost' on a trackway, or a statement that the land was occupied. Other outliers can be explained in this way: Long Meg in Cumbria, a tall and thin needle of red sand-stone, quite different from the bulbous grey boulders of the lower-positioned stone cir-cle, standing conspicuously on a ridge above the River Eden to its south; or the King Stone at the Rollright Stones in Oxfordshire, again standing on a ridgeway and very visible from the slopes below it from which the stone circle is out of sight. The possibility that the Heel Stone performed a similar directional purpose remains to be considered.

It is questions like these that are the subjects of the succeeding chapters: whether the bluestones at Stonehenge were transported by men or by glaciation; whether the Heel Stone really was a midsummer sunrise marker; whether it is possible to decide which of the fallen sarsens the original Friar's Heel was; if the non-sacrificial function of the Slaughter Stone can be recovered today; and why there should have been an unusual rectangle of four stones around the circle, why the setting of five trilithons inside the circle should be arranged in a horseshoe, and why the carvings on Stonehenge are utterly unlike the known repertoire of British megalithic art.

Stonehenge will continue to be a perpetual puzzle. But with the insights of investigators from Inigo Jones to the present day research has moved steadily although slowly towards answers. Knowledge has advanced far beyond Henry of Huntingdon's 'no one has been able to discover by what mechanism such vast masses of stone were elevated, nor for what purpose they were designed'. As long as human curiosity exists erosion of the tantalus will continue.

Plate 38 The stones and dentals of the outer circle.

Chapter Seven

Transportation or Glaciation?

*If you want to grace the burial-place of these men with some lasting monument',
replied Merlin, 'send for the Giants' Ring which is on Mount Killaraus in Ireland. In
that place there is a stone construction which no man of this period could ever erect,
unless he combined great skill and artistry. The stones are enormous and there is no
one alive strong enough to move them.*
        Geoffrey of Monmouth, *The History of the Kings of Britain, c.* 1139, 172–3.

Stonehenge is composed of two types of stone, a consistent group of heavy sarsens
from the Avebury region eighteen miles to the north; and an inconsistent muddle of
much smaller dolerites and different stones from the Preseli mountains of south-west
Wales 140 miles directly to the west. There is continuing controversy about the
method by which the bluestones reached Salisbury Plain. There is almost none about
the sarsens.

In terms of prehistoric man's movement of raw materials over long distances
there was an understandable distinction between the willingness to carry small, easily packaged items and a reluctance to drag tediously heavy loads. Weight and size
were always limitations. There is an important qualification. To make their ritual
monuments more attractive communities were quite prepared to import coloured
pieces of stone and pebbles from considerable distances. Some Yorkshire round
barrows were composed of selected varieties of waterworn pebbles brought from
remote parts. One contained $4\,m^3$ of sand blanched as white as snow from at least
seven miles away.[1] The burdens were no heavier than was convenient. Porters could
always return for more. Such manageable fragments were easily loaded and floated
along rivers as cargoes in boats or shouldered in manageable amounts on men's
backs.

Conversely, work-gangs were seldom prepared to search far for ponderous blocks
of ordinary, functional stone. The greatest distance known for the moving of heavy
loads was less than twenty miles and even that was exceptional. In Ireland the great
standing stones of Counties Carlow and Kildare were all of local granite. The six tons
of the Longstone at Mullaghmast demanded the most strenuous effort, coming from
a source some five miles away. The even taller and heavier pillars at Craddockstown
West, Longstone Rath and Punchestown came from areas much closer to their
erection.[2]

This was true everywhere. Anything more than a fraction of a ton came from the
locality of its monument. Back-breaking boulders, cumbersome slabs were left unconsidered unless they were nearby with no river, obstructive marsh or precipitous valley

between. Stonehenge, ever the maverick, breached this practical rule-of-thumb with its sarsens. It did not with its bluestones.

SARSENS: THEIR SHORTAGE ON SALISBURY PLAIN

It has seldom been questioned that in Neolithic and Bronze Age times sarsens were scarce on Salisbury Plain and that they had been brought to Stonehenge by human intervention. Bartenstein and Fletcher did consider that the late eighteenth-century geologist, de Luc, had seen many there 'in terms of the occurrence of sarsen material on Salisbury Plain as a result of natural (silcrete) formation or glacial transport' but this appears to have been a misinterpretation. De Luc, had referred not to Wiltshire but to counties to its west and north and separated from it by Gloucestershire, Oxfordshire and Berkshire.[3]

The Stonehenge sarsens are blocks of New Red Sandstone averaging some $5.5 \times 2.1 \times 1.1$ m, and weighing about thirty tons. They were densely littered on the Marlborough Downs but always rare on Salisbury Plain.[4] Just two standing near the New King barrow group east of Stonehenge were shown in Hassell's sketch of the 'North Prospect' of Stonehenge in the second edition of Jones's *Stone-Heng*, 1725. In the same decade Stukeley saw others. 'I have found several of these kind of large stones, either travelling to *Stonehenge* or from it. One as big as any at *Stonehenge*, lies about three miles off northward in *Durington* fields'. This was the Cuckoo or Cuckold Stone near Woodhenge,[5] a sarsen about 1.8 m long, 1.2 m wide and 0.3 m thick. Stukeley continued, 'Another in the water at *Milford* [Milston], another at *Fighelden*' and others at Amesbury, at Bulford and at Preshute near Marlborough.[6] The fact that in ten square miles near Stonehenge he could find only five sarsens, all close to the River Avon, with a sixth at Preshute a few miles from Avebury, shows how uncommon sarsens were away from the Marlborough Downs.

The paucity persuaded early writers that the Stonehenge sarsens must have come from the Downs where they were plentiful. Inigo Jones recorded the abundance, 'especially about *Aibury* in North-*Wiltshire*'. John Aubrey dismissed the fable that Merlin had brought the sarsens from Ireland, like Jones preferring an origin on the Marlborough Downs. 'They are of the very same kind of Stones with the Grey-Weathers about fourteen miles off'. William Stukeley was dogmatic. 'The stones of which *Stonehenge* is compos'd, beyond any controversy, came from those called the gray weathers upon *Marlborough* downs near *Abury*'.[7]

Celia Fiennes was even more positive about the 'prodigeous stones' of the circle. Living at Newton Tony less than six miles east of Stonehenge, she observed that 'no such sort of stone is seen in the country nearer than 20 mile'. A century later Sir Richard Colt Hoare agreed. Only three sarsens were noticeable near Stonehenge, all lying in the direction of Marlborough, one near Durrington, 'another in Bulford river; and another in Bulford field' but 'they are particularly numerous between Abury and Marlborough. In 1910 Herbert Stone waded waist-deep in the River Avon to locate the Bulford stone which was a mere 84 cm long, 76 cm wide and 60 cm thick, 'of no great size'. More recent research has confirmed that 'sarsen blocks in apparently natural context are present with a frequency of approximately $1/30 \text{ km}^2$ over the whole of south Wiltshire, and there is no concentration of more than two or three blocks'.[8]

SARSENS: MEGALITHIC TOMBS AND EARTHEN LONG BARROWS

It cannot be argued that the shortage around Stonehenge was the result of prehistoric people removing a glut of convenient slabs for the construction of megalithic burial monuments. The reason for the lack was not Neolithic depredation but geological morphology. There were no stone-built chambers in the long barrows near Stonehenge. The report of a long mound, now destroyed, (Amesbury 104) 'with a cist at one end' is more likely to have referred to a 'simple pit or grave dug into the sub-soil', quite possibly 'the circular feature visible in an aerial photograph', rather than a megalithic chamber. In the early nineteenth century Hoare and Cunnington may have dug into it and come upon 'a circular cist like a little well', devoid of anything. They had found similar burial pits in many earthen long barrows on Salisbury Plain.[9]

Free-lying stones were rare on Salisbury Plain. On that spacious upland there are the remains of over fifty earthen long barrows but no more than three of them, all some miles to the west of Stonehenge, contain substantial stones. One was inside Arn Hill (Warminster 1) sixteen miles away, where a 1.5 m high sarsen stood alongside three skeletons under the mound. At Corton (Boyton 1), a conspicuous barrow two miles south-east of Boles Barrow, Cunnington came upon a slab resting on a heap of flints. It 'took the strength of three men to lift out'. There was also the block, unexpectedly of bluestone, mixed with other stones in the long mound of Boles Barrow (Heytesbury 1) twelve miles west of Stonehenge.[10]

These were isolated stones and not the remains of collapsed tombs. The nearest megalithic barrow was a full fifteen miles north-east of Stonehenge, the sarsen-built Tidcombe Down (Tidcombe & Fosbury 1). The long mound of that barrow was laboriously delved into by gold-seeking villagers throughout the summer of 1750 finding only 'three prodigious big stones . . . These stood up perpendicular, having two others of like sort laid on the tops of them, and thereby making a sepulchre, for under them was deposited one human skeleton' adding, significantly, that the stones were of the same size as those at Stonehenge 'and probably brought, as those were, from Marlborough Downs'.[11]

This tomb with its simple chamber is at the far northern edge of Salisbury Plain but very close to the Marlborough Downs where there are other long barrows with single chambers composed of sideslabs, a backstone and capstone: Adam's Grave, the Devil's Den, Manton Down, Millbarrow and the Shelving Stones amongst them. Showing how under normal conditions prehistoric people were reluctant to go far for heavily awkward slabs each of these tombs contained just one economical cell. Transepted barrows like West Kennet with five chambers were uncommon.[12]

In contrast to those sturdy burial-places of sarsen the chambers of long barrows on Salisbury Plain were built of perishable wood from the adjacent glades and forests. There is evidence from at least thirteen sites, including Winterbourne Stoke (Winterbourne Stoke 53) just west of Stonehenge, of tumbled heaps of flint that once covered sloping timber mortuary structures like pitched tents. Inside Fussells Lodge (Clarendon Park 4a), less than eight miles south-east of Stonehenge, the shape of the mass of débris suggested that it was the fallen remains of a ridged enclosure of oak that had been supported by hefty vertical posts, everything eventually collapsing under the weight of the overlying layers of dirty chalk and weathered flint nodules.[13]

Beneath the mound at Corton (Boyton 1) was 'a pyramid of loose flints, marl stones &c. which became wider near the bottom, where the base of the ridge measured more than twenty feet in length and about ten feet in width' [6 × 3 m]. Again, at Boles Barrow (Heytesbury 1) there was no megalithic chamber, only 'a ridge of large stones and flints which extended wider as the men worked downwards . . . Afterwards this pile (in form like the ridge of a house) was covered with marl' [chalk]. It was during Cunnington's excavation at the western end of the mound that the revealing bluestone was recognised.[14]

With the obvious availability of timber and the equal absence of suitable stone it might be asked why it was that Stonehenge was constructed of sarsens. One wonders why the ring was not erected in durable oak like the mortuary chambers of the preceding long barrows and the contemporary neighbouring structures of Coneybury henge, Woodhenge and Durrington Walls.[15]

Overseas influence may have caused the infidelity. The sarsens of Stonehenge were shaped in carpentry techniques by the woodworking natives of stoneless Salisbury Plain. If, as suggested the ring was partly Breton in design, incomers from the granitic Armorican peninsula may have preferred stone to unfamiliar timber.[16]

The dearth of sarsens and megalithic tombs on Salisbury Plain suggests that the stones of the final phase of Stonehenge arrived there by human intervention, dragged on sledges and moveable rails by men or oxen. Geology suggests that this is an unlikely explanation for the presence of the Welsh bluestones at Stonehenge.

BLUESTONES: SOURCE

> There can be no question of the stones having been carried even part of the way towards southern England by ice during the Pleistocene period, and their appearance at Stonehenge can only be explained as the result of deliberate transport by man'.
> R. J. C. Atkinson, 1979, 105.

The 'bluestones' were much smaller than the sarsens. An average block was about 2.4 m long, 0.6 m wide and 0.6 m thick, weighing, because of the different rock types, mainly dolerite but including tuffs, sandstones and others, anywhere between three and six tons. Unlike the sarsens whose Marlborough provenance had been recognised early in the seventeenth century their source remained a matter of controversy until 1923 when H. H. Thomas, identified it as the Preseli ridge, Pembrokeshire, at the south-western tip of Wales.[17]

BLUESTONES: TRANSPORTATION OR GLACIATION

Since that time it has been popularly accepted that the stones could only have reached Salisbury Plain by human effort.[18] Despite cogent arguments favouring glaciation the majority of geologists have been firm that this was impossible even though erratics from West Wales have been identified two-thirds of the way from the Preselis to

Plate 39 Tumbled bluestones in the Preseli mountains.

Salisbury Plain at a site near Cardiff, at another on Flatholme and Steep Holme islands in the Bristol Channel less than sixty miles west of Stonehenge.[19]

Archaeologists have been even firmer in their support for a belief in an almost superhuman feat of men transferring some eighty heavy slabs and blocks by sea and land from south-west Wales to Wiltshire, a tortuous distance of over 200 miles.

The belief is almost as fanatical as the fanaticism of the prehistoric carriers who supposedly performed that task. Nowhere else in Britain, Ireland or Brittany were such heavy stones moved so far. The recumbent stones of circles in north-eastern Scotland were never brought from more than six miles away. On Jersey the great passage-tomb of La Hougue Bie was composed of stones from distant parts of the island but seldom farther than five miles. The colossal menhir of the Grand Menhir Brisé in Brittany was composed of granite from a source no more than two and a half miles away, and quite possibly much closer. Even the obsessive haulage of the Stonehenge sarsens from the Marlborough Downs involved a distance of only nineteen miles, less than a tenth of the hypothetical Welsh odyssey and much easier because the journey was all across dry land.[20]

Data from standing stones, circles and tombs reveal that prehistoric societies did not fetch demandingly massive blocks from any great distance. Where there was convenient stone they used stone. Where there was not they used timber or earth. Such mundane considerations make the bluestone enterprise more romantic than realistic.

Nevertheless, Thomas's identification of the Preseli source caused archaeological excitement. The very next year E. H. Stone recalled the fable of the early twelfth-century chronicler, Geoffrey of Monmouth, in which the magician, Merlin, had carried the Stonehenge pillars from Ireland. To archaeologists the legend was enticingly explicable as a warped folk-memory of Late Neolithic Beaker metal-smiths from Wessex prospecting for copper ores in the Wicklow mountains of eastern Ireland and, returning across the Irish Sea to western Wales, steering towards the awesome and numinous landmark of the Preselis.

There was an amusing numismatic gloss to Merlin's theft of the Stonehenge pillars. It reported that the magician saw the huge stones in a backyard of an old woman in Ireland. Cunningly, he employed the Devil who dressed up as a gentleman and generously offered the woman a big bag of odd coins, $4^1/_2$d, 9d, $13^1/_2$d, which he said that she could keep if she could count them while he removed the stones. She happily accepted the silly bargain. But hardly had she counted one coin than the stones had disappeared, magically transported by Satan. And that is how Stonehenge was transported.

Turning from the ludicrous to the likely until recently it seemed entirely credible that it had been Beaker Folk rather than Beelzebub who had brought the bluestones to Stonehenge. That Beaker prospectors should remove stones from a sacred place seemed plausible because until the 1970s it was popularly believed that Beaker Folk were the builders of British stone circles such as Avebury and the Rollright Stones.

Wishing to believe is credulity but it is not proof. The archaeology is out-of-date. The once-fashionable, warlike 'Beaker Folk' are now more prosaically thought to be simply people using beaker pots. They certainly were not the innovators of stone circles which existed in Britain and Ireland long before the introduction of beakers.[21] This, however, is the slightest of objections to the theory of transportation. People other than 'Beaker Folk' could have moved the bluestones.

> It appears probable that the blue stones before they were transported to the Stonehenge site had been set up as a stone circle. . . . According to an old tradition these stones were believed to possess magical and medicinal properties. We may suppose that the fame of the mystic attributes of the stones was a matter of common belief in western Britain, and that on an occasion of a tribal war, in which the Salisbury Plain people were the victors, the stones of the sacred circle were carried off as a trophy to be re-erected at Stonehenge.[22]

The possibility of an earlier stone circle, possibly lintelled, in the vicinity of the Preselis and transferred in its entirety to Wessex has been revived in a very balanced and objective discussion of the transportation/glaciation dispute.[23]

Referring to battle-axes made from Preseli stone an authority on Stonehenge, Richard Atkinson, noted that they would have 'had a significance in prehistoric times beyond that of mere efficiency or utility. Like Excalibur, they possessed symbolic and magical qualities'. Was it 'this [Preseli] rock, from the cloud-capped crest of the sacred mountain far to the west that was chosen in preference to all others?'[24]

There are six poignant objections to human transportation: (i) E. H. Stone was mistaken about the bluestones being considered medicinal. (ii) Conditions at sea and overland would have made the venture almost suicidal. (iii) The claim that 'magical' stones were specifically and exclusively chosen is wrong. (iv) Geoffrey of Monmouth did not write about bluestones. (v) The stones themselves are evidence of indifferent selection. Finally, (vi) there were bluestones on Salisbury Plain long before Stonehenge.

BLUESTONES: MEDICINAL STONES

In general it was the resistant sarsens that visitors chipped for amulets. Geoffrey of Monmouth's mediaeval legend, the origin of the myth, made it clear that giants poured water over the sarsens, not the bluestones, for a potion that would heal their wounds. As late as the eighteenth century the Rev. James Brome remarked that if the sarsens 'be rubbed or scraped, and water thrown upon the scrapings, they will (some say) heal any green wound, or old sore'. There was nothing therapeutical about the pimply, spotted dolerites.[25]

BLUESTONES: THE JOURNEY FROM WALES

In the mid-1950s Professor Atkinson showed that 4 schoolboys and a simple raft were equal to the task of moving a two-ton bluestone by river. The largest bluestones are twice this size and the men who transported them on the heavy tides of the Bristol Channel must have had seaworthy craft, nerves of iron and a liking for the blue-grey rock which bordered on insanity R. Muir, *Riddles in the British Landscape*, 1981, 70.

The actuality was of even less consequence. The four boys did no more than float a lightweight concrete block in imitation of a bluestone on three linked punt-shaped canoes, the entire load of boats, boys and blocks weighing no more than one and a half tons rather than a more realistic five or six tons. Muir's criticism was valid.[26]

Disappointingly, there has been little serious consideration about the logistics involved in the hypothetical journey from Wales to Wiltshire (Fig. 12). The most meticulous was by Atkinson. Having brought the stones from the Preselis by land and river to Milford Haven 'the next and longest stage of the journey must have been coastwise along the shores of South Wales to the estuary of the Severn . . . leaving to human effort only the task of keeping the vessels far enough off-shore to avoid submerged rocks and the more violent currents and eddies round the headlands'. Then the stones were taken by rivers and land-portage up to Stonehenge.[27]

Fig. 12 Route of the bluestones from the Preseli mountains, south-west Wales, to Salisbury Plain. a. Preseli; b. Milford Haven; c. Carmarthen Bay; d. Tusker Rock; e. Severn Estuary; f. Bristol Avon; g. River Wylye; h. Christchurch Avon.

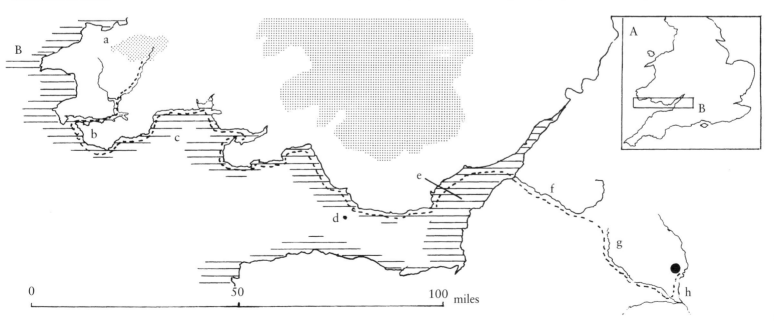

Other explanations were more facile. 'The stones were then transported by sea up the Bristol Channel, and then on river-craft along the Bristol Avon ... All that remained was their hauling in triumphal procession up the Stonehenge Avenue to the temple itself'. 'Then they were no doubt taken by some form of craft (or hung between two or more) around the coast of south Wales and across the mouth of the Severn to the Bristol Avon', a throwaway description reducing the appalling journey to a casual outing of 240 miles by water and land, a cruise hardly more arduous than children in a paddleboat on a boating lake.[28]

Gerald Hawkins, however, calculated that the undertaking demanded nearly 210,000 man-hours of labour, moving some eighty bluestones, about four tons each, twenty-four miles overland, paddling them along the coast and up rivers for over 216 miles. He was entirely justified in his observation that 'nothing like this astonishing feat of transportation was ever attempted by any other people anywhere else in prehistoric Europe'.[29]

Atkinson suggested the use of a pine raft manoeuvred by a crew of twelve. A modification of his description would envisage a tree-trunk platform about 6 m square, constructed for buoyancy in three layers, each of twenty logs 6 m long and 0.3 m thick. With a dry weight of 35 lb per $0.03 \, m^3$ the logs would have weighed about twenty tons and the entire cargo of wood, stone and men over thirty tons.[30] Whether this unwieldy craft was seaworthy and capable of being manoeuvred during the day and beached night after night by the limited amount of man-power is doubtful.

Words are easily read and can just as easily mislead. There are many reasons for claiming that the project never occurred, one of the most compelling being a consideration of the perils and obstacles that confronted the hauliers. Contrasted with entirely feasible voyages for copper prospectors or stone-axe traders travelling in manoeuvrable, easily-beached canoes the endeavours of crews attempting to steer a heavily-laden, clumsy raft along the seas of the Welsh coast were almost commitments to suicide.

On a floating platform without sails, with propulsion dependent on paddles and poles, with little control over steering, affected by every capricious current of the Atlantic Ocean and Bristol Channel, the kamikaze crews faced daunting challenges. Once out of the shelter of Milford Haven the voyage was a sequence of hazards, exposed not only to the vicissitudes of weather but to a recurring series of threats along the coastline of southern Wales. Almost immediately the voyagers would have encountered strong tides and undertows across the dangerous waters surging southwards near Freshwater West. Tidal flows of three to five knots streamed at Whitford Sands on the east side of Carmarthen Bay and, once beyond them, there were treacherous sandbanks at Cefn Sidon Sands, always menacing when winds blew shorewards. Between Carmarthen and Swansea Bays heavy currents swirled at every headland, often too great to be resisted by craft moved only by human muscles; savage races off Ogmore-by-Sea where, a mile from the coast, lay the terrifying reef of Tusker Rock on which in later millennia many mechanically-powered ships foundered.[31]

Even when the mouth of the Severn was reached the struggle was not done. The river could pour seawards at up to ten knots, there were submerged mudbanks, the highest rise and fall of tides anywhere in the British Isles, all this before the Bristol Avon was reached at Portishead. At that point the raft would have to be left and the stone transferred to something more suitable for travel along narrow and winding rivers, maybe a 7m long trimaran, at least 5m across to accommodate anything as long and large as the Altar Stone.

Further miles against the current took the vessel to Frome and a permanent staging-point where everything again had to be disembarked for a portage that required sledges, rails and an attendant work-gang of at least ten men to drag the stone across eight or nine miles, perhaps following the line of the modern A362, the land rising gently but persistently and exhaustingly, across the central four miles from the east of Rodden Hill, 84m O.D., through Corsley Heath, 137m O.D., up to Picket Post Gate, 183m O.D., while the crew, having rested, shouldered the unlinked boats across to Warminster, where the cargo was replaced in the reassembled craft for the last up-river crawl along the twisting Wylye, the 'tricky or treacherous stream', then northwards up the Christchurch Avon towards West Amesbury. Once again it had to be unloaded and hauled up the chalk slopes of Salisbury Plain to Stonehenge. On the most recent assessment of the number of stones involved this unprecedented undertaking had to be repeated almost eighty times and possibly for as many years.[32]

BLUESTONES: MAGICAL PROPERTIES

Justification for a belief in human manpower is that the spotted dolerites of the Preselis were magical ingredients of a sacred landscape. For this to be believable only those would have been chosen for Stonehenge. They were not. They merely formed the greater part of an indifferent mixture. All the stones, moreover, should have come from the mountains. They did not. The heaviest and biggest of these Welsh pillars, the Altar Stone, a 4.9m long, 1.1m wide and 0.5m thick column of fine-grained sandstone weighing some seven tons, came from the Cosheston Beds by the River Cleddau at the mouth of Milford Haven a full twenty miles ssw of the Preseli mountains.[33]

It is also manifest that the natives of south-western Wales did not consider spotted dolerite of special value. Of twenty-seven megalithic monuments inspected in the neighbourhood of the Preselis only one, the Gors Fawr stone circle, was composed entirely of spotted together with unspotted dolerite. And that ring stands on a common littered with blocks of dolerite.[34]

Spotted dolerite is not special. Except for Gors Fawr no other nearby circle was built solely of it. The stones at Dyffryn Syfynwy were ten or more rhyolites, one unspotted dolerite and some internal quartz boulders. Waun-Mawn consisted of unspotted dolerite. Of the remaining blocks at the ruined Meini-gwyr one was plain dolerite and the other had one inconspicuous spot. Nor had any of the rings lintels, pegs or grooves like those at Stonehenge. They were simple circles made of what stones lay locally. And it is unbelievable that a 'magical' bluestone would be so dishonoured as to be merely one of a great, indiscriminate dump of slabs, blocks and boulders of sarsens and flints forming the body of the Boles long barrow on Salisbury Plain.[35]

BLUESTONES: GEOFFREY OF MONMOUTH

Geoffrey of Monmouth's story has been misunderstood. It was about the sarsens, not the bluestones. The early mediaeval chronicler deliberately emphasised how gigantic the stones were, massive pillars like those still standing near Naas in County Kildare, entirely dissimilar to the unobtrusive bluestones.[36] 'The stones are enormous and there is no one alive strong enough to move them', said Merlin. Geoffrey of Monmouth also specifically referred to Mount Killaraus *in Ireland*. Although Welsh he never mentioned Wales. The solution to the enigma is simple and begins with the location of Mount Killaraus where the Giants' Ring stood.

Early investigators suggested the hill to be in the Irish county of Kildare, a region that twelfth-century English clerics would know because of its rich monastery of St Brigid. It possessed one of the finest illuminated manuscripts in western Europe. Gerald of Wales saw it in 1183 and declared 'Among all the wonders of Kildare nothing seems to me more miraculous than that wonderful book'.[37]

There was nothing unusual about a Welsh archdeacon visiting the monastery. Anglo-Norman churchmen had been travelling to Ireland since Lanfranc asserted the authority of the Church of Rome over Celtic christianity in 1074 and 1085. The natural landing-place from England and Wales was Dublin and from there the wayfarer would skirt the Wicklow mountains and pass through Naas ten miles from Kildare.

That area had been one of the most potent in prehistoric times. The Curragh with its henges, earthwork and barrows was immediately east of Kildare. There were also scattered, startlingly high pillars. Gerald of Wales noticed them. 'There was in ancient times in Ireland a remarkable pile of stones which was called the Giants' Dance because giants . . . erected it . . . near the castle of Naas, employing truly remarkable skill and ability. It is amazing how so many great stones were ever brought together or erected in one place, and with skill upon such great and high stones others no less great were placed' quite obviously imagining a partly-dismantled, monstrous ring with lintels like Stonehenge.[38]

Some still stand. These famous pillars of Wicklow granite are amongst the tallest stones in Britain and Ireland. They are concentrated in the counties of Carlow and Kildare. Aghade, 1.8 m high; Mullaghmast, 2.1 m; Ardristan, 2.7 m are only a few miles south of Kildare. The very highest are even closer. Craddockstown West, 4.4 m high; Longstone Rath, an elegant 5.3 m tall pillar; Punchestown, only 3 miles from Kildare, no less than 6 m high, is the second highest stone in the British Isles.[39]

These towering pillars were the great stones, similar in size and appearance to the sarsens of Stonehenge, that were remarked upon by the visiting clerics. It is easy to imagine Gerald of Wales and others visualising them as the remnants of a once-enormous stone circle, the handiwork of giants, that had been decimated by Merlin who 'put the stones up in a circle . . . in exactly the same way as they had been arranged on Mount Killaraus'.[40] The folk-story is a myth. It had nothing to do with the bluestones.

AXE-FACTORIES AND WORKERS IN STONE

There is a positive objection to the selective ferrying of special stones to Stonehenge. They would have been transported by experienced mineralogists. Bronze Age societies with their flint and stone tools inherited centuries of expertise in differentiating between good and bad material. They would certainly have rejected poor quality volcanic ashes like those discovered at Stonehenge.

There were Early Bronze Age axe-factories (Groups XIII, XXIII) on the Preselis and St David's Head just to the west, producing both plain axes and shaft-hole mace-heads, battle-axes and axe hammers, their makers using only the hardest igneous rock for pecking and smoothing and drilling.[41] It was a tedious but skilled process demanding discrimination in the recognition of the most suitable stone.

The tools and regalia have a rather unbalanced distribution, mostly in Wales but with a small concentration in Wessex where, amongst other Preselite artefacts, a carefully made battle-axe and an axe-hammer have been found. Their similarity makes it possible that they had been shaped by the same smith from bluestone fragments glaciated to Salisbury.[42] R. S. Newall, who assisted Hawley in the excavations at Stonehenge, possessed a largish piece of Welsh tuff that he had found on the site. 'Mr Newall was convinced that this weathered stone had been trimmed on one edge in a fruitless attempt to make an artefact and had therefore been rejected. It is inconceivable that such a stone would have been carried two to three hundred miles by Neolithic man only to be thrown away on Salisbury Plain; like other poor quality weathered rocks this must have been found locally'.[43]

There were other, more splendid articles from Wales. A magnificent axe-hammer of spotted dolerite, weighing 5 lb 2 oz, was discovered at Fifield Bavant twelve miles ssw of Stonehenge. A good battle-axe came from Wilsford G54, a round barrow in the Lake group within sight of the circle. With its skeleton were three barbed-and-tanged flint arrowheads, a three-rivetted bronze dagger and sherds of E, AOC and W/MR beakers. The assemblage is unlikely to be much earlier than 2200 BC.[44]

Axe-factory miners in the Preselis had a preference for spotted dolerite, ignoring the coarser-textured slabs and blocks lying amongst them. No such discrimination exists in the motley of Welsh stones at Stonehenge. Those so-called 'bluestones' are not homogeneous. They are a rag-bag. Of the stones 62 per cent were of the hard spotted dolerite, but some 10 per cent were of softer altered volcanic ash all of which were rapidly reduced to stumps. Plain dolerite and rhyolite each represented 7 per cent, both rhyolitic tuffs and sandstone formed not quite 5 per cent. In addition to this mineralogical farrago there were individual blocks of calcareous ash, a stump, and the greenish sandstone of the Altar Stone.[45] Such proportions at Stonehenge may reflect the natural ratios of the different types of outcropping stones at the Preselis. Should this prove to be true it would make the likelihood of glaciation all the more probable.

Of the soft, erodible, altered volcanic ash, rhyolitic tuff and calcareous ash some were so friable that they survived only under ground. 'Owing, however, to their fissile nature, and the ease with which they succumb to weathering agencies, all seem to have disappeared except a stump which was discovered by Mr H. Cunnington in 1881'. It is now known that there are at least nine buried lumps of shale or volcanic ash.[46]

Just as unexpectedly, the stones had not been roughly shaped at source to lighten them but had been 'transported' as they had been found. 'Is it conceivable', asked Judd, ' that these skilful builders would have transported such blocks of stone *in their rough state* over mountains, hills and rivers (and possibly over seas) in order to shape them at the point of erection when the rough-hewing of the blocks at the place where they were found would have so greatly diminished their weight and the difficulties of their transport?', pointing out that the sarsens had been sensibly half-shaped on the Downs, their handlers leaving 'only the final dressing to be done after their transport, and to have reduced their weight as far as possible before removal'.[47]

That dressing was done on site is revealed by the $3^1/_2$: 1 ratio of bluestone to sarsen chippings at Stonehenge[48] even though in bulk the forty lintelled sarsen circle-stones and trilithons, c. 2,100m^3 outmassed the eighty bluestones, c. 240m^3, almost ninefold.

THE BLUESTONE IN BOLES BARROW

There are unsubstantiated reports of a bluestone known as the 'Devil's Whet Stone' in the Summerham Brook near Seend sixteen miles north-west of Stonehenge. More reliably, four miles to the south Preselitic stones may have been used for statuary in Edington church just east of Westbury. 'Before the levelling of the chancel pavement, there used to be, on the south side, near the modern door, a large blue stone with sockets of a figure and shields . . . Some other large blue-stones with marks of brasses were likewise removed'.[49] Edington church is no more than four miles north of Boles Barrow in which an indisputable bluestone was found.

The most compelling evidence for the glaciation of the bluestones is that at least one substantial block was on Salisbury Plain centuries before the construction of Stonehenge. It lay in the Neolithic Boles long barrow which had been blocked up and abandoned long before the time of the theoretical human transportation of the blue-stones to Stonehenge. In his excavation of early July 1801, 'making a section of con-siderable width and depth across the Barrow near the East end'[50] William Cunnington recognised it amongst the large stones in the mound.[51]

In a letter of 18 July 1801, to a friend, H. P. Wyndham, M.P. for Wiltshire, a few days after his four labourers had toiled with pickaxes and spades for three days he mentioned the dangerously 'large stones continually rolling down upon the labourers' adding that the heavy boulders were 'of the same species as the very large stones at Stonehenge, which the Country people call Sarcens'. They weighed up to 200lb. In a postscript he added 'Since writing the above I discovered amongst them the Blue hard Stone, ye same as the upright Stones in ye inner Circle at Stonehenge'.[52]

This may well have been on the final day and such an afterthought about the bluestone is entirely explicable when the excavation method and the composition of the barrow are considered. Cunnington wrote of a 1.4m thick capping of white chalk, quarried from the mound's side-ditches, that covered a 1.8m high pile of stones and flints 'in form like the ridge of a house' whose blocks and boulders understandably increased in bulk the deeper the workmen quarried. With its size and its weight of 12.04cwt, which was established by a test in 1990,[53] the bluestone may well have been found in the very bottom layers explaining Cunnington's late discovery of it.

His bluestone would not have been an object as small as an axe from the Preseli fac-tory. The majority of them belong to a period late in stone-axe production years after the closing of long barrows. Nor are they big. One of the heaviest, the impressive axe-hammer from Fifield Bavant, was only 22cm long and 10cm wide. The truth appears to be that a considerable bluestone had been incorporated in an earthen long barrow a few miles to the west of Stonehenge several hundred years before the circle was thought of. The stone was given to the Salisbury and South Wiltshire Museum by Siegfried Sassoon in 1934 (accession no: 68/1934).

For his period Cunnington was a competent geologist, well able to distinguish between sarsen and dolerite. He described the sarsens as 'fine-grained sandstones' possibly deriving from the Bagshot Beds or the 'Northern Drift' gravels.[54] He speculated on the source of the entirely differently composed bluestones, first suggesting Frome, later Devon or Cornwall, consulting his friend, the distinguished botanist and geologist, James Sowerby, on the problem. He also received the opinion of the eminent geologist, William Smith, about the composition of the sarsens and the bluestones.

There are three compelling reasons for believing that the stone in Salisbury Museum came from Boles Barrow[55] rather than from Stonehenge: the distance from Stonehenge to Heytesbury; the size of the block; and Cunnington's unequivocal testimony to which he added a telling sentence that should demolish the controversy.

Common sense, a deceitful guide but relevant in terms of early nineteenth-century transport, suggests that the slab came from the barrow rather than the sarsen circle. Simple logistics make it probable. The barrow was less than three miles from Cunnington's home in Heytesbury whereas Stonehenge was twelve miles away. And, as will be seen, beyond common sense there is also Cunnington's own statement.

Secondly, the stone was of hard spotted dolerite, almost impervious to weathering unlike the softer volcanic ashes and rhyolites. Yet in bulk, $0.21\,\mathrm{m}^3$, it was less than a quarter of the $0.86\,\mathrm{m}^3$ average bluestone pillar of Stonehenge, and in length less than one third, $0.76\,\mathrm{m}$: $2.4\,\mathrm{m}$. Nor are any of the Stonehenge bluestones as light. They weigh between three and six tons. The museum block is barely one-seventh of their average. Its size militates against Stonehenge as its source.

Vandalism was unlikely. The block had not been chipped and truncated by visitors wishing to take away an amulet or a keepsake. Dolerite was even less susceptible to brute force than sarsen and sarsen was deterrent enough. 'The stone is so exceeding hard', wrote John Evelyn in 1654, 'that all my strength with a hammer could not break a fragment'.[56] Although there is a horrifying late eighteenth-century engraving of a man hammering at a fallen bluestone, probably futilely, most tourists hacked at the sarsens even though they were 'almost impenetrable to the chisel and mallet'.[57]

Cunnington knew Stonehenge. He had already excavated there in 1798. His words show that he was able to distinguish between the tall sarsens of the outer ring and the circle of slighter bluestones inside them. It is also significant that he referred to a stone, not an axe, similar to the stones at Stonehenge and presumably more comparable in size to those of the bluestone circle than to an axe.

He was so taken with the massive stones and their mixture in the barrow that he told Wyndham, 'I have brought away Ten [from Boles] to my house . . .'.[58] 'I have brought away Ten'. It is strangely overlooked but essential information. It would push opponents of glaciation to the point of prejudice to believe that Cunnington went to the bother of having ten heavy stones carted all the way from Boles Barrow to Heytesbury without including the unique bluestone, maybe even bluestone/s, amongst them. The distinctive blocks were arranged in a circle around a tree on the lawn outside his home.

His record of having stones from the barrow taken to Heytesbury was reinforced a year later in a letter of 8 November 1802 to his friend, John Britton. 'I think I showed you a great variety of the stones found in a large oblong barrow [Boles] near this place that are of the same kind with several of those at Stonehenge'.[59] 'Great variety' demands emphasis. Sarsens do not vary. They are all the same. Cunnington may have been referring not just to the bluestone but to other different types of Preseli stone recognised at Stonehenge such as the sandstones and tuffs.

Despite these indisputable statements some researchers have suggested that the stone in the museum is not the one that Cunnington removed from the barrow for his garden and that it is therefore irrelevant to the question of glaciation. They are mistaken for two reasons. The first is that such a debate about the provenance of the museum bluestone is a geological red herring because the incontrovertible fact, recorded by the excavator within days of his discovery, is that he had recognised a bluestone amongst the other stones forming the body of that long barrow. Where that stone is now, in the museum or elsewhere, has no bearing on Cunnington's unequivocal statement.

THE BLUESTONE CAME FROM BOLES BARROW, NOT FROM STONEHENGE

Cunnington's bluestone stone, however, did come from Boles Barrow, not from Stonehenge, and there is virtually no doubt that it is the block in the museum. To deny this is to contradict a positive statement of Flinders Petrie. Following his punctilious survey of Stonehenge in 1877 in which 'no distinction is made . . . between perfect stones and mere stumps of which the upper part is removed' he was able to assert entirely confidently' that 'No stones are missing since Wood's plan in 1747'.[60] Cunnington could not have removed it in 1801.

John Wood had made the first really accurate plan of Stonehenge. As befitted the architect who designed the elegant Royal Crescent at Bath he was fastidious in his recording of the size and position of every stone. His survey of August 1740, was so detailed that by hatching, cross-hatching and dotting he distinguished between 'the erect Stones in the Body of the Work, together with those in a Leaning Position, and such as are buried in the Ground from those that lye flat on the Surface of the Earth, or on the Surface of other Stones'.[61] It is an unambiguous sentence.

Flinders Petrie, later to become a famous Egyptologist, was equally conscientious, checking Wood's plans minutely. Wood is unlikely to have left a largish bluestone of two-thirds of a ton unplanned in 1740, especially as he had gone to the extent of plotting stone 32 at the east of the bluestone circle, a stump no bigger than Cunnington's. It is still there. In 1877 Petrie was just as unlikely to have overlooked the absence of Cunnington's bluestone from Wood's plan. Scrutiny of the two plans shows that Petrie was right. No stone is missing.[62] As Cunnington found his bluestone in 1801 it could not have come from Stonehenge.

Belief that it had been taken from the circle, now proved to be impossible, was encouraged by its appearance. Benjamin Cunnington who examined it in 1923 decided that 'it certainly has been dressed on its faces, and is not a rough block as quarried'. Such assurance led Green to write that 'Its dimensions and shape are consistent with its having been part of a stone in the bluestone horseshoe at Stonehenge and this is a possibility that could be explored more fully'.

It is unnecessary both because of Petrie's survey and because of the confident conclusions of Richard Atkinson, doyen of Stonehenge studies, who with colleagues spent several seasons, planning and excavating at the site. He agreed that the surfaces of the bluestones have a rounded smoothness suggestive of deliberate tooling. However, a more critical inspection, combined with a close comparison with the stones of the bluestone horseshoe (all of which have undoubtedly been tooled) makes it quite clear that this impression is false. With . . . two exceptions **all** the bluestones of the circle are in their natural state and none shows any sign of deliberate tooling or dressing. Their columnar shapes and their relatively smooth surfaces are the product of natural fracture and weathering.

It makes it probable that Benjamin Cunnington had been misled by the seemingly artificial condition of the Boles Barrow bluestone.[63]

THE BLUESTONE IN SALISBURY MUSEUM

William Cunnington took the stone from Boles Barrow to his house in Heytesbury. The stone is now in the museum at Salisbury. A letter from Eliza Cunnington, his grand-daughter, in 1864 said that 'A circle of blocks of stones from Boles barrow, near Imber, was placed round a weeping ash at the end of the lawn' in front of Cunnington's house, which today is number 108, Heytesbury, almost opposite Heytesbury House. The letter strengthens the connection between Boles Barrow and the seminal bluestone. It was the 'Stonehenge Stone' but not a stone from Stonehenge.

In 1923 the aunt of Lord Heytesbury, the Hon. Mrs Hamersley, who had lived at Heytesbury House, wrote that 'the stone was removed from the late Mr Wm. Cunnington's garden at Heytesbury to its present site at Heytesbury House before 1860. It was called the "Stonehenge Stone" and was placed under the beech tree where it now is'.

Benjamin Cunnington, great-grandson of Eliza, visited Heytesbury House in 1923 and inspected the 'missing' bluestone, 76 cm high, 67 cm wide, 41 cm thick, a sizeable block of 0.21 m^3 but a dwarf in contrast to the bluestones of Stonehenge itself. A substantial triangular fragment had been broken from one corner. The dimensions cited by Cunnington, moreover, are exactly those of the museum block and his sketches show the same broken corner (Fig. 13). Not stating its provenance Cunnington sent a flake to the geologist, H. H. Thomas, who confirmed its origin. 'There is no doubt at all that the specimen you sent me is of the spotted Prescelly type and identical with the spotted Blue stones of Stonehenge'.

The evidence is clear-cut. Cunnington noticed an unexpected bluestone in Boles Barrow. He had ten stones from the barrow taken to his house. It is unbelievable that the bluestone was not among them. The bluestone was later taken across the road to Heytesbury House. It is now in Salisbury Museum. As Benjamin Cunnington himself wrote, 'There can be little doubt that the stone now standing in the grounds of Heytesbury House is the one found by William Cunnington in Boles Barrow'.[64]

LONG BARROWS AND STONE CIRCLES

The archaeological evidence indicates that the stone had been incorporated in the barrow as many as a thousand years before the bluestone phase of Stonehenge. The earliest bluestones of the ring had stood in the Q and R Holes, assigned to Phase II of the monument by Atkinson but now of disputed chronology.[65] Two undiagnostic beaker sherds and a lack of reliable organic material made the holes' place in the sequence of construction uncertain. Accepted as a genuine and independent feature they could have formed a concentric semi-circle, even a three-sided setting. 'There is no need to see the setting as unfinished, or it may be that there were modifications begun but not finished'.[66]

They were succeeded by the bluestone circle some of whose holes had cut into the earlier ones. Radio-carbon assays obtained from a variety of organic material: charcoal, antler, antler pick, animal bone, a bone chisel and a human femur suggested that the first bluestones were brought to Stonehenge after Phase 2 ended around 2900 BC and the earliest period of Phase 3, *c.* 2600–2300 BC but before the construction of the bluestone circle, *c.* 2200 BC. Two bluestone circle assays produced three determinations of 1915 ± 50 bc (OxA-4900); 1790 ± 40 bc (OxA-4878); and 1745 ± 55 bc (OxA-4877), a span of 1965–1690 bc, *c.* 2450–2090 BC, with a mid-point around 2200 BC. Assays from a different source produced a similar chronology: the sarsen ring, *c.* 2655–2485 BC; and the bluestone circle, *c.* 2270–1930 BC.[67]

Whichever set is preferred the bluestones were erected centuries after the blocking of Boles Barrow. In Britain the majority of long barrows had been abandoned by 2500 bc, *c.* 3200 BC. Even a late one, Alfriston, Sussex, with an assay of 2360 ± 110 bc, *c.* 3000–2900 BC, would not have been deserted much later than about 2700 BC. The likelihood is that the bluestone was in the body of Boles Barrow by 2900 BC at the very latest.

The Group XIII and XXIII factories, however, were not being exploited until around 2000 bc, around 2500 BC. As the date of the bluestones at Stonehenge is no longer certain to belong to Atkinson's Phase II and could be 'close in time to the Sarsen

Plate 40 The bluestone in Salisbury Museum.

Fig. 13 Sketches of the block of bluestone in Salisbury Museum (*WAM 42*, 1924).

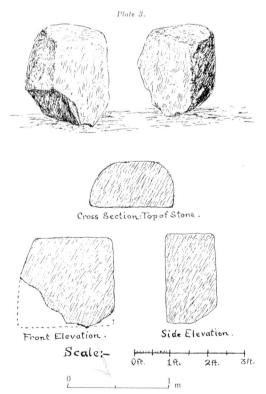

Circle and Trilithons',[68] it makes the Boles Barrow find even more significant and the enthusiasm for human transportation over a distance of more than 200 miles a far-fetched long shot.

CONCLUSIONS

The accumulated evidence does not support belief in human transportation of the bluestones from south-west Wales. The stones were not considered magical. Local Welsh circles were not built of spotted dolerite. Nor were they lintelled. Geoffrey of Monmouth's tale is both fantastic and misunderstood. Transportation by land and sea would have been so hazardous as to be improbable. At least one bluestone was on Salisbury Plain centuries before the relevant phase of Stonehenge. William Cunnington, John Wood and Flinders Petrie provide literary testimony to this. Even if Cunnington's 'Blue hard Stone' had been a fragment, which clearly it was not, it was still a piece of dolerite deeply embedded in the mound of Boles Barrow centuries before the 'bluestones' were brought to Stonehenge.

Geologists may quite properly reply that no other stone has 'ever been described from a natural context on Salisbury Plain, or even more telling[ly], in the river gravels that are the sweepings of this area . . . The answer is simple. No natural agency has ever brought these rocks into Wessex'.[69]

Few answers are simple. All the evidence that actually exists: the legends, the Welsh stone circles, the archaeological radiocarbon assays, the bluestone in Boles Barrow, Wood's and Petrie's surveys, argues against long-distance human transportation. Instead, a mixed collection of unshaped stones, little and big, including dolerites, was probably dragged to Stonehenge from no more than ten or twelve miles to the west in the vicinity of Heytesbury. To the question of why no other fragment of bluestone has been found lying naturally on Salisbury Plain one must correctly reply, 'absence of evidence is not evidence of absence'.

There is a final observation. 'One thing about "glacial solutions" has always puzzled me: The glaciers seem to have brought just enough stones to make the monument. If one asks what happened to the others, large and small, the answer given is that they disappeared long ago'.[70] There is another explanation. They may never have existed.

If the solution lies with glaciation then a miscellany of stones from the Preselis: dolerites, sandstones, tuffs and other types, some half- or almost completely buried, lay within a few miles of Stonehenge. Their discoverers may ambitiously have planned a concentric circle for which the eighty-two Q and R holes were intended, arranged in thirty-eight pairs with an additional six at the north-eastern entrance. But when the last bluestone was unearthed and the countryside scoured no more were to be found. In frustration, the scheme was modified into a less impressive single circle of about fifty-seven stones enclosing an elegant horseshoe of nineteen pillars.[71] Even in the golden age of prehistory there could be blunders. Stonehenge was no exception.

All our Druid temples are built, where these sort of stones from the surface can be had at reasonable distances . . . It was a matter of much labour to draw them hither, 16 miles. William Stukeley, 1740, 6.

Plate 41 The Heel Stone at dawn.

Chapter Eight

The Heel Stone

A STUDY IN MISFORTUNES

The Friar's Heel, the Heel-Stone, Sun-stone or Index-stone. By means of this huge unwrought rock the temple is set to the rising sun at the summer solstice.
E. Barclay, *Stonehenge and its Earthworks*, 1895, 11.

Its original purpose is totally unknown, though conjecture has not been idle in ascribing various uses to it.
Sir R. C. Hoare, *The Ancient History of South Wiltshire*, 1812, 143.

It is doubtful whether any prehistoric standing stone has experienced as many changes of name and interpretation, most of them wrong, as Stone 96, the famous pillar standing to the north-east outside Stonehenge. As an example, there are two major errors in Barclay's statement quoted above. The name is wrong and so is the solar alignment. One might also wonder why it was that, despite the work of earlier investigators such as John Aubrey and William Stukeley, it was not until 1770 that the stone was claimed to be an astronomical marker. The mistakes and the problems can be explained.

The outlier is an eroded block of sarsen about 77.3 m from the centre of the sarsen circle. It leans towards the south-west at an angle almost 27° from the vertical[1] and its tip is now 4.7 m above ground.[2] Upright it would have been 5.2 m high, the difference of 0.5 m making a considerable difference to its popular association with the midsummer sunrise. Its base is 1.2 m below ground level.[3] Crudely cylindrical, with a tapering top, 2.4 m thick and with an overall girth of about 7.6 m the stone weighs well over 35 tons and would have demanded the strength of more than 150 men to haul it upright.[4]

Excavation of 'secondary' beaker sherds in the ditch around the stone seemed to show that the Heel belonged to the first phase of Stonehenge[5] when the site was a simple earthwork henge with two entrances, the wider at the north-east and a less well-known, narrower causeway at the south. This is uncertain and reconsideration has suggested 'only that the Heelstone [sic] was erected either within, or prior to, phase 3', the late stage in the history of Stonehenge.[6] From the known changes in the width of the north-east entrance the present writer favours the earlier date when there was probably a massive timber structure inside the henge.[7]

The megalithic outlier was the only stone in that monument.

THE NAME

Turning from fancy to fact, the word Hele, from which the stone takes its name, is possibly derived from the Anglo-Saxon verb helan = 'to conceal', and is so applied to the stone because it conceals the sun at rising on the day of the Summer Solstice. Nor must the Greek word, 'Helios' = 'The Sun' be overlooked. F. Stevens, 1929, 29.

The outlying sarsen has been known variously through the years as the Friar's Heel, *Crwm Leche* or the Bowing Stone, the Marker Stone, the Pointer Stone, the Index Stone, the Sun Stone and the Hele Stone. It is only in recent decades that its name has generally been accepted as the Heel Stone or, more eccentrically, as the Heelstone. To understand how such an improbable mélange came about it is necessary to look back from the present day to the seventeenth century.

The most whimsical of the titles has been the 'Hele' Stone, so called from a belief that 'Heel' was a corruption of the Old English *helan*, 'to hide', because the block was believed, entirely wrongly, to conceal the rising of the sun at the summer solstice. A variation on this solar theme was that 'Hele' came from the Greek ηλιοζ or *helios*, 'the sun'. This faulty reasoning led to the renaming of the pillar as the Sunstone.[8]

Cunnington, dubious about 'Hele' whether Old English or classical Greek, offered a Celtic option, *Freas heol*, an abbreviation of what he thought might have been the stone's full title, *cloch na freas heol*, or 'stone of the rising sun'.[9] This was etymologically optimistic. The more accurate translation of 'fresh sun' is celestially meaningless.

'Hele' happily never became popular and had a lifespan of barely fifty years. It can be found in F. Stevens and Gowland, the latter adopting it from its apparent inventor, Lady Antrobus, wife of the owner of Stonehenge.

In her book, *A Sentimental and Practical Guide to Amesbury and Stonehenge* she wrote, 'The stone is also named the "Pointer" because from the middle of the Altar Stone the sun is seen at the summer solstice (21st of June) to rise immediately above it. The Hele Stone is the true name, "Hele" meaning "to hide", from Heol or Haul or Geol or Jul, all names for the sun which this stone seems to hide'.[10]

This reference appears to be the earliest appearance of 'Hele' and one can be grateful that it was a solecism that did not endure. It made one late but notable recurrence. 'The axis . . . of Stonehenge is aligned approximately on the point of midsummer sunrise though not . . . on the Hele Stone'.[11] Professor Atkinson then promptly dropped the term when he published his seminal book *Stonehenge* the very next year.

In the late nineteenth century interest in the theoretical solar alignment at Stonehenge increased. In his comprehensive bibliography of Avebury and Stonehenge Harrison listed articles by authors such as Bacon, 'the grandest annual sun-register' in Europe, and Maurice, 'a stupendous solar temple', who discussed the accuracy of the outlier's orientation. People often referred to it as the Pointer Stone because of its supposed directional properties. Fidler calculated that the chances were 1:1,400 against the solar alignment being fortuitous.[12]

In 1880 the Heel Stone was included in the definitive numbering system for Stonehenge. Following his meticulous survey of 1877 Petrie rejected previous schemes by John Wood, John Smith, and Colt Hoare, preferring his own more logical and flexible method, each stone being given a number from 1 to 96 for the standing stones and 101a to 160a for the lintels. The outlier, Petrie's 'Friar's Heel' was Stone 96.[13]

The 'Friar's Heel' remained the most popular name for the stone from the seventeenth to the late nineteenth century despite a solitary attempt to follow Stukeley in calling it 'the *Crwm Leche* or bowing stone'. Sir Richard Colt Hoare wrote of the 'Friar's heel'. So did Wansey and John Smith.[14]

It was Smith who introduced the misconception that the stone had been a marker for the midsummer sunrise. His creation of the greatest archaeo-astronomical fallacy of prehistoric Europe will be considered later.

Paradoxically, although he wrote with complete assurance that 'the apex of the stone number 1 points directly to the place' of the solstitial sunrise he had earlier disclaimed any understanding of the function of the outlier. 'The use of it I can't certainly tell: but I am inclined to think, that, as part of the religious worship, in old patriarchal times, consisted in a solemn adoration, or three silent bowings; the first bowing might be performed at this stone, just without the ditch'.[15]

The contradiction between the two statements arose from Smith's unscholarly reluctance to admit that Stukeley had anticipated him by almost fifty years in the question of Stonehenge's astronomy. As early as 1723, Stukeley had speculated that the ancient Britons had set Stonehenge's entrance 'to the N.E. loc. that is the Suns utmost elongation in somer Solstice when they held a grand festival'.[16] Smith's quotation above about the bowing-stone had been copied word for word from Stukeley's *Stonehenge* and much of Smith's account of the circle was plagiarised directly from the book. He was unaware of Stukeley's 1723 manuscript but Stukeley's published references to the midsummer sunrise although not to the Heel Stone were never acknowledged by Smith.[17]

Depressingly, to this ingratitude and astronomical misapprehension must be added that Smith was also in error about the identification of the Heel Stone. It was he alone who was responsible for transferring the title of the Friar's Heel from the correct, fallen stone at the far side of Stonehenge to the previously anonymous outlier at the north-east. 'As the spectator advances, from the valley, up the grand avenue to the temple, the first stone, that offers to his view, is called the Friar's heel, and stands two hundred and ten feet from the body of the structure'.[18]

He was wrong. Smith had read the earlier descriptions of Stonehenge by John Wood and William Stukeley but neither of them had specified the whereabouts of the Friar's Heel. Indeed, Stukeley never mentioned it. Smith had to guess. In so doing and unluckily choosing the outlier he misled almost every future student of Stonehenge.

A few years before Smith John Wood made the first accurate plan of the site. In his book John Wood repeated a legend recorded by Geoffrey of Monmouth in the early twelfth century but embellished by a later mediaeval recension that brought the Devil into the story.

According to this, Merlin the magician employed the Devil to transport huge stones from Ireland to Salisbury Plain for the construction of Stonehenge. When he had completed the ring the Devil was so pleased with his handiwork that he boasted that no one would ever know how the enormous circle had been built.

> A friar who had lain all the Night concealed near the Building, hearing the Devil's Declaration, replied to it by saying, 'That is more than thee canst tell'; which put Satan in such a Passion, that he snatched up a Pillar and hurled it at the Friar with an Intention to bruise him to Dirt; but he running for his Life, the Stone in its fall, only reached his Heel, and struck him in it, the Mark of which appears in that Pillar even unto this day.[19]

What is significant in this account is that Wood never thought of today's Heel Stone and his own Friar's Heel, which presumably had fallen flat, as one and the same although he referred to the outlier, his Stone R, many times in his book. Even when discussing the etymology of the word *Heil* and claiming it as 'the *British*' name of the 'SUN' he never attached it to the outlier. Clearly, in his time the Heel Stone was not linked with the sun, and no such term as 'Heel Stone' existed.[20]

Plate 42 The Heel Stone. The fallen Slaughter Stone can just be made out between it and Stonehenge.

Similarly, Stukeley whose *Stonehenge* had been published seven years before Wood's book never referred to a Heel Stone or even a Friar's Heel. Instead, he called the outlier 'a *Crwm leche* still standing in its original position and place in the avenue . . . The use of it I can't certainly tell'.[21]

Which of the Stonehenge sarsens the Friar's Heel had been is still a matter of conjecture although from John Aubrey's manuscript it is clear that it could not have been the Heel Stone.

Sixty years before Stukeley Aubrey distinguished unambiguously between the modern Heel Stone standing at the north-east and the Friar's Heel which was prostrate somewhere in the western arc of the circle. The outlier, he wrote was 'a good way off northeastward from the circularish bank, of which there hath not been any notice taken'. He thought the stone to be a survivor of an avenue that had led up to Stonehenge. That it was erect in his day there is no doubt. He showed it as standing and he described it: 'The great one answereth to fig. 7th in the Walke or Avenue. The other two [Station Stone 91 at the ese and number 93 at the wnw] are but about six foot high'.[22] The plan can be seen in its entirely in Long where all the stones are shown.[23]

To Aubrey the Friar's Heel was a different stone. 'One of the great Stones that lies downe, on the west side, hath a cavity something resembling the print of a man's foot; concerning which the Shepherds and countrey people have a Tradition (wch many of them doe stedfastly believe) that when Merlin conveyed these Stones from Ireland by Art Magick, the Devill hitt him in the heele with that stone, and so left the print there'.[24]

If it should be wondered why later investigators so readily accepted Smith's blunder and the substitution of a friar for Merlin it should be remembered that the three parts of Aubrey's *Monumenta Britannica* with its details of Stonehenge were not published until 1980 and 1982 and access to it, even awareness of it, in the eighteenth century cannot be assumed. It was only in the nineteenth century when the manuscript was available in the Bodleian Library, Oxford, that lengthy extracts were copied and printed.[25]

Indeed, by the nineteenth century the acceptance of the outlier as the Heel Stone was so established that E. T. Stevens actually questioned whether Aubrey had not blundered. 'Aubrey . . . appears to have mistaken the "slaughtering stone" for the "Friar's Heel" stone', and quoting Aubrey's 'One of the great stones that *lies downe* on the west side . . .', Stevens queried whether the direction should not have been 'north-east' where the Slaughter Stone lay. He was unaware that that slab had been erect in Aubrey's time and therefore ineligible as the Friar's Heel. Thus fable becomes fact.[26]

Surprisingly, given the increased seventeenth-century interest in Stonehenge, the outlier was never mentioned before Aubrey's brief notes although it is shown standing in a Tudor sketch of 1575 signed 'R.F.'. There is no reference to it in Camden's *Britain* of 1610 nor in Inigo Jones's *Stone-Heng* who persuaded himself, but few others, 'that Roman architects had designed the great temple of the ancient god, Coelus'. Despite visiting Stonehenge and digging inside the circle Jones completely ignored the outlier.[27]

Which stone was the real Friar's Heel is questionable. As a 'great stone' it must have been a sarsen rather than one of the much smaller bluestones, and if it was in the south-western quadrant there are only two eligible prostrate blocks, Petrie's 12 and 14 (Fig. 14). When John Wood made his plan in 1740 Stones 8 and 9 were also down but both were badly broken. It is probable, moreover, that in Aubrey's time Stone 9 was standing. Of the two intact fallen sarsens Atkinson favoured no. 14 'on which such a natural "footprint" can still be seen. A trial fitting suggests that the Friar's right foot was considerably bigger than my own!'.[28]

There are problems. Stone 14 is not at the west but at the south-west though this is not a major objection. More pertinent is the fact that eighty years after Aubrey John Wood stated that the stone was still half-leaning. 'The Stone number ten leans against

Fig. 14 Plan of Stonehenge showing Petrie's Stones 12 and 14 and the lunar and solar alignments through the north-east entrance.

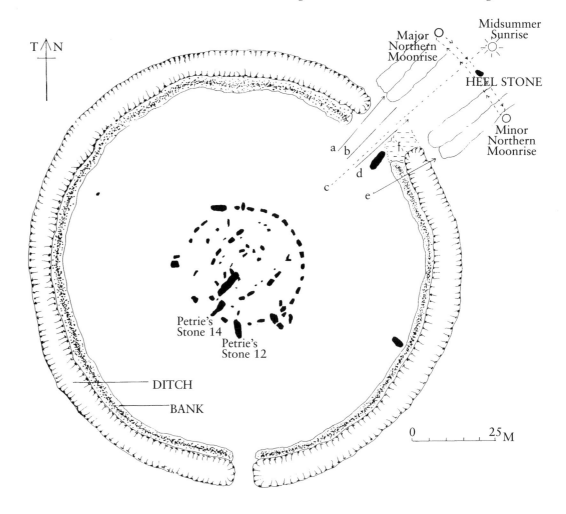

the Stone number twenty four, his numbers corresponding to Petrie's 14 and 38. Stone 12 to the east of 14 was flat'.[29]

Twenty years after Wood John Smith confirmed this. 'Number 8 [14] leans on the same number [38] of the inner circle'. A century later Flinders Petrie recorded that Stone 14 had fallen farther forward, half-displacing the lower stone on which it rested. Its present, near-prostrate position is therefore misleading.[30]

It is possible, even so, to accept that this was the sarsen to which Aubrey had referred. In the early eighteenth century Stukeley's sketch showed it leaning badly, almost touching the broken trilithon 55. Aubrey's own schematic plan distinguishes between upright and fallen stones and apparently depicts Stone 14 as down.[31]

Against this is the fact that he also showed Stone 12 supine and that this pillar of the outer sarsen circle was certainly flat on the ground when Wood made his 1740 plan. The ravaged upper surface of the stone had several cavities that the credulous might perceive as the imprint of a heel. We may never know the truth. The genuine Friar's Heel may for ever remain tantalisingly elusive.

As an aside the friar – or Merlin or both – were particularly unlucky in being hit by the Devil. Whether in Britain or in Brittany the incompetent Devil was continually throwing angry stones at people and places and just as continually missing them whether his target was the church at Rudston or the entire town of Aldborough. His aim there was so bad that he fell short of the settlement by a mile not once but four or five times, his shower of missiles embedding themselves in the fields west of Boroughbridge where they became known as the Devil's Arrows.[32]

THE ASTRONOMY

> An eclipse of the moon or sun *always* occurred when the winter moon – that is, the full moon nearest the winter solstice – rose over the heel stone. G. Hawkins, 1966, 139.

On Salisbury Plain the sun reaches its extreme north-easterly rising near 50° from True North on 21 June. For four days it seems to rise in the same place on the skyline, its 'solstice' or 'sun standstill'. Then on 25 June it begins its six-month long journey southwards towards its midwinter sunrise at the south-east before once again metronomically returning to its midsummer rising.

The first person to believe that Stonehenge had an astronomical alignment built into it was William Stukeley. 'The Avenue . . . answers, as we have said before, to the principal line of the whole work, the north-east, where abouts the sun rises, when the days are longest'. It is noticeable that Stukeley was referring not to the Heel Stone but to the SW–NE axis and avenue of Stonehenge thereby anticipating Lockyer by almost two hundred years.[33]

'The intent of the founders of *Stonehenge* was to set the entrance full north east, being the point where the sun rises, or nearly, at the summer solstice'.[34] It is a pity that his 'or nearly' was not considered more conscientiously by subsequent proponents of a solar alignment.

Stukeley, however, did not regard the outlying Heel Stone as an astronomical marker. That was left to John Wood. Referring to the pillar he said that in the same way as at the Stanton Drew stone circles in Somerset 'the great Pillar before the Front of STONEHENGE is situated North Eastward from that Edifice; and in each Work [referring again to Stanton Drew] a Phase of the new Moon is pointed out'. This was the first astronomical attribution given to the outlier and, ironically, it was a lunar one. According to Wood the Heel Stone was 'in a Line to that Quarter of the Heavens where the new Moon first appears on that Day of her Age when the Druids began their Times and Festivals'.

Unfortunately, Wood's interpretation was based on an error in orientation of almost 10°. It was soon superseded by the seemingly more thorough astronomical survey of Dr John Smith undertaken in 1770 when that lethal inoculator against smallpox was driven from his Wiltshire practice by antagonistic villagers. As a diversion he made many visits to Stonehenge from his empty surgery at Boscombe six miles away.[35]

He conceived Stonehenge 'to be an Astronomical Temple'. His procedure was not reassuring. 'Without an Instrument, or any assistance whatever, but White's *Ephemeris*, I began my survey. I suspected the Stone, called the Friar's Heel, to be the Index that would disclose the uses of this Structure; nor was I deceived'. It was a statement as confident as Hawkins's two hundred years later. 'There can be no doubt that Stonehenge was an observatory; the impartial mathematics of probability and the celestial sphere are on my side'.[36]

Smith was convinced that the Heel Stone stood on a solar alignment.

The stone number 1 [the Heel] in the middle of the grand avenue to the Temple is the Key or Gnomon, by which I propose to unlock this Ambre, or Repository of Druidical Secrets . . . At the summer solstice, when the days are longest, he [the sun] enters the sign Cancer, and seems to rise in the same point of the horizon, three days together. The Arch-Druid standing against his stall, and looking down the right line of the temple, over the stones II and I [Smith's stone II was the Slaughter Stone, by then fallen] his eye is bounded by Durrington field (a charming horizon about two miles distant), he there sees the sun rise from behind the hill; the apex of the stone number 1, points directly to the place'.

This was the first solar interpretation and it has been accepted ever since by the majority of writers such as Wansey. 'On the top of that stone the Sun is supposed to make its first appearance on the longest day of the year'. Others concurred. Even in the late twentieth century the inaccuracy has persisted.[37]

Even when the more precise lunar alignments are acknowledged there is resistance. 'The lunar connections are weak by comparison with the strong solar alignment, and the confused nature of the evidence of both post-holes and cremations opens up these conclusions to serious doubt'.[38] Confusion is correct.

It emphasises the strength of popular tradition. The solar interpretation has endured obstinately, uncritically, even though it has been known beyond question that the orientation of the Heel Stone towards the midsummer sunrise is inexact. Unprejudiced surveyor after surveyor has emphasised this. Unavailingly.

Sir Norman Lockyer: 'In this investigation the so-called Friar's Heel was used only as a convenient point for reference and verification in measurement, and no theory was formed as to its purpose. It is placed at some distance . . . to the south of the axis so that . . . the Sun must have completely risen before it was vertically over the summit of the stone'.

E. H. Stone: 'Midsummer sunrise . . . has never yet taken place over the Heel Stone, and will not do so until more than 1,000 years have passed away'.

F. Niel: 'If the top of the Heel Stone marked the direction in which the sun rose above the horizon at the summer solstice, the sun ought to rise to the right of the top of the Heel Stone on the morning of June 21 in our time. But it does not: it rises a foot and half to the left'.

R. J. C. Atkinson: 'The Heel Stone is the subject of one of the most popular and persistent misconceptions concerning Stonehenge, namely that it marks the point of sunrise on Midsummer Day for an observer stationed at the centre of Stonehenge, or on the Altar Stone. Actually, it does nothing of the sort'.[39]

This vigorous and unequivocal statement by Atkinson was ignored by his publishers. For the second edition of his *Stonehenge* they wilfully used a photograph by Dr Georg Gerster for the book's front cover. It showed the sun poised dramatically above the Heel Stone but only because the photographer had elected to stand away from the centre of the circle. 'The many photographs . . . which seem to show half the sun's disc sitting neatly on top of the Heel Stone are all "adjusted": as the sun begins to come up, the photographer moves to one side – a foot or two is ample – to align the sun over the Heel Stone, and stands up straighter or crouches a little to get them exactly into the vertical relation he wants'.[40] So much for the 'strong solar alignment'.

There is no mystery, only ignorance and bigotry, about the astronomical rôle of the Heel Stone.

When, around 3200 BC, the henge earthwork was thrown up at Stonehenge the north-eastern causeway across the ditch was only 10.7 m wide. From the centre of the monument the SW–NE axis through the midpoint of the entrance had a bearing of 46°33' (Fig. 15). The Heel Stone was set up in line with the right-hand, eastern, side of the gap. This custom of directing an alignment not to the unmarked centre of an entrance but to one of its well-defined sides was a common and practical prehistoric custom. It can be found in the stone circles of Long Meg and Her Daughters, at Swinside, at the Druids' Circle and at the Rollright Stones.[41]

In the years when the ditch and bank at Stonehenge were constructed midsummer sunrise on Salisbury Plain occurred close to +50° from True North. The Heel Stone, however, was erected at +51° 18', over a degree and nearly 2 m from the correct position if it had been intended as a solar foresight. By the same reckoning it was barely 40 cm from a lunar alignment.

An illuminating insight by the late 'Peter' Newham, demonstrated that the builders had laid out an orientation towards the moon. Evidence from six lines of postholes across the causeway that Hawley had uncovered in 1922 and 1923 suggested to Newham that the posts had been temporary sighting devices for recording the moon's northerly risings from its minor at the ENE, 61°, to its major at the NNE, 41°, and back over its 18.61 year cycle with the Heel Stone standing at 51°, the midpoint between those extreme risings.

Understandably Newham's theory has been criticised. Heggie thought the explanation poor 'for it would imply that the holes should be more thickly distributed on the left, near the standstill position, than on the right, whereas they are not'. Cleal believed that 'the postholes form a very restricted entrance to the monument, possibly consisting of two narrow corridors barely 1 m wide and flanked by at least two lines on each other side and by three in the middle'.[42]

There is, however, plausible and independent confirmation of Newham's idea. Beyond the entrance Hawley came upon a line of four deep postholes in 1924. These 'A' Holes were twice as wide as those across the causeway and parallel with them.

The Heel Stone neatly placed halfway along the moon's swing would have warned observers that once the full moon rose to the left, northern side it would reach its most

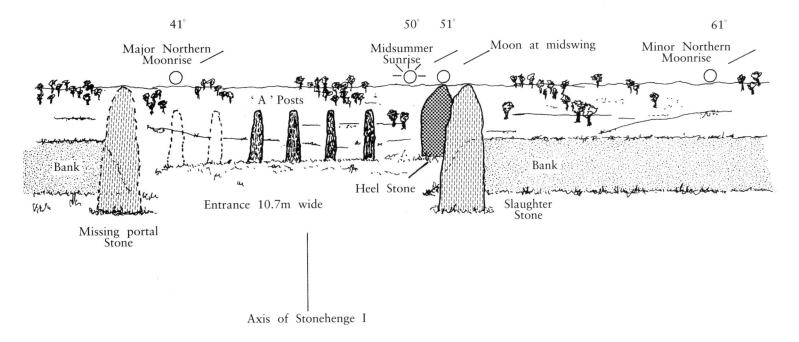

41°   50° 51°   61°

Major Northern Moonrise   Midsummer Sunrise   Moon at midswing   Minor Northern Moonrise

'A' Posts

Bank   Heel Stone   Bank

Missing portal Stone   Entrance 10.7m wide   Slaughter Stone

Axis of Stonehenge I

Fig. 15 The narrow north-east entrance of the early Stonehenge.

northerly rising four years later, something that John Smith had half-realised over two hundred years earlier. After the ephemeral causeway postholes had served their purpose and had been withdrawn the taller 'A' posts acted as lunar sighting-devices showing the moon's progress across the horizon. When the moon rose between the first, right-hand, and second post it was a quarter of the way between its midpoint and its northern extreme. Between the second and third posts it was a third of the distance. Six posts were needed to complete the journey from midpoint to the most northerly rising but Hawley never excavated the area of the fifth postholes and the sixth would have been destroyed when Stonehenge's earthen ditched-and-banked avenue was laid out. Despite these lacunae the existence of the four 'A' Holes provides strong support for Newham's brilliant deduction.[43]

Prehistoric iconoclasm is not unknown. Centuries later when the first bluestone circles were put up inside the henge the north-eastern entrance was widened by levelling a 7.6m long stretch of the bank east of the causeway and tumbling the turf, soil and chalk back into its section of the ditch, filling it. Two important results followed. With the broadened entrance now 18.3m across the axis of Stonehenge veered almost 4° eastwards from the original 46°33′ to a new 49°54′, an orientation quite close to that of the midsummer sunrise (Fig. 16). It was a modification which deliberately transformed Stonehenge from a lunar to a solar monument. The second outcome was spectacular. It caused the Heel Stone to be virtually on the line of the changed axis.[44]

The argument for a lunar alignment, involving the Heel Stone, in the first phase of Stonehenge is not invalidated by the discovery in 1979 of a wide hollow just to the west of the outlier. A large stone had been withdrawn from it at an unknown date.[45] This stone, now known as Stone 97, may have been put up during the bluestone circles time of Stonehenge when the axis was converted to a solar alignment. The Heel Stone and Stone 97 standing side by side would have formed an astronomical 'window' framing the rising midsummer sun. This explanation, however, would not account for the removal of the stone if this had been effected at some prehistoric date.

The 1979 excavation produced no evidence that the stones had stood together. A second possibility is that the hole was a pit in which the Heel Stone itself had once stood before being manoeuvred into a more satisfactory position.[46]

There is even a third and equally plausible explanation. The azimuth or compass-bearing of Stone 97 from the centre of Stonehenge was 46°, nicely placed on the axis of the first henge and just halfway between the Heel Stone and the most northerly rising of the full moon at midwinter. Such a marker could have acted as a second lunar foresight, supplanting the four timber, perishable posts, A–D that had been arranged to record the moon's movements. The situation of Stone 97 would have warned observers that the major moonrise would occur two years after the moon appeared to its left. There may once have been a third stone actually standing in line with the extreme major moonrise but, if so, its stonehole would have been eradicated when the ditch for the avenue was trenched in Stonehenge's second phase.[47]

With the transformation of the axis from a lunar to a solar alignment the presence of Stone 97 could have been an irrelevance, even a distraction, and uprooting would have left the Heel Stone as a solitary outlier, an approximate foresight to the sunrise with no hint of a former lunar orientation. Any continuing belief today that the stone was originally planned to indicate the summer solstice can be maintained only by a refusal to admit that the present axis of Stonehenge on which the Heel Stone nearly stands is not the original one.[48] Stone 97's rôle is debated in Chapter Nine.

Today the Heel Stone is better understood but in the process it has suffered. Deprived of its popular name, stripped of its solar function, and perhaps not even in its primary position the weathered, leaning pillar has only reluctantly revealed its purpose.

It should not be called the Hele Stone, the Heel Stone or the Friar's Heel. It is wrong to term it the Sun Stone or Pointer or Marker or Index Stone. Petrie's 'Stone 96' is numerically helpful but uncharismatic.

As the outlier is unlikely to be renamed the Merlin-Moon Monolith it should be allowed to return to its former anonymity. And somewhere across the circle the Friar's Heel lies undiscovered.

Fig. 16 The widened north-east entrance of the later Stonehenge.

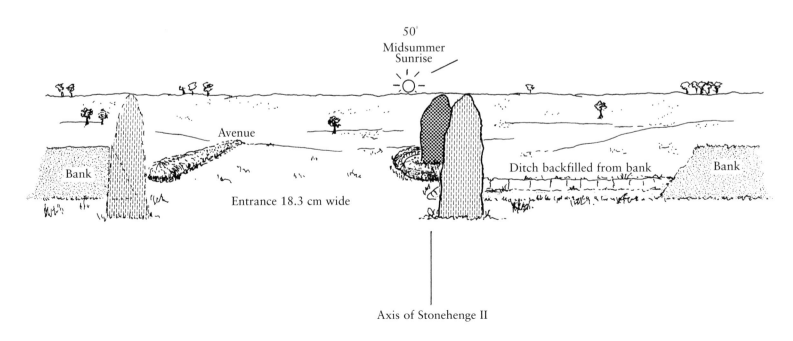

50°
Midsummer
Sunrise

Avenue

Bank

Entrance 18.3 cm wide

Ditch backfilled from bank

Bank

Axis of Stonehenge II

Why, this is very midsummer madness. W. Shakespeare, *Twelfth Night*, III, iv, 62.

It must also be asked, when three good plans of Stonehenge already existed: by Aubrey in 1666; by Stukeley in 1723; and John Wood in 1740, why it was not until 1770 that John Smith observed that the Heel Stone stood in line with the midsummer sunrise.

The sun's regular yearly cycle from midsummer to midwinter and return is such an obvious one and so well-known to prehistoric people that it seems puzzling that perceptive fieldworkers such as John Aubrey and William Stukeley should not have noticed how close the Heel Stone stood to the orientation of the midsummer sunrise. The solution lies partly with the British calendar and partly with mechanical unreliability.

In 1666 John Aubrey made the first good plan of Stonehenge. He noted the presence of the outlier at the north-east and he distinguished between it and the Friar's Heel in the circle itself. Yet he made no reference to the correlation between the outlier and the summer solstice.

Aubrey, of course, knew that Midsummer Day was 24 June, the birthday and Feast Day of St John Baptist. 'It was a Custome for some people that were more curious than ordinary to sitt all night in the Church porch of their Parish on midsomer-eve, that is, St John Baptist's eve; and they should see the apparitions of those that should die in the parish that year come and knock at the dore'.[49]

But in 1666 24 June was not one of the days of the midsummer solstice.

In the seventeenth century Britain was still using the Julian calendar of 46 BC which by miscalculation had been losing a day every 163 years since its inception. In 1582 Roman Catholic countries in Europe corrected this by adopting the new calendar of Pope Gregory but in those vehemently anti-papist days Protestant states ignored the innovation and it was not until 1752 that Britain and her colonies reluctantly accepted the necessity for change. Russia, even more orthodox and isolationist, remained non-Gregorian until 1918. The lonely island of Foula in the Shetlands still does. There, Christmas Day is celebrated on 6 January, twelve days later than the rest of the Christian world.

Because Britain in 1666 was following the Julian calendar, at that time ten days behind the correct date, Aubrey's '24 June' in reality was 14 June. On that day the sun was rising over 4°, nearly 6 m, to the east of the Heel Stone, well away from the solstice. Aubrey, unaware of the discrepancy, inevitably recognised no relationship between the stone, 24 June and the longest day.

This was not the cause of Stukeley's oversight. He had discussed Stonehenge with several astronomers and had a fair understanding of possible alignments there. His 1723 manuscript contains an undated note, 'The Entrance of Stoneh. is 4° from the true N.E point, they set it to the N.E. loc. that is the suns utmost elongation in Somer Solstice'.[50] This is the earliest astronomical reference to Stonehenge and was probably made after Stukeley had discussed some of the problems of Stonehenge with colleagues.

One page 105 of the manuscript, in a different hand, is an interpolated small sheet containing calculations of where the sun would rise 'on the Longest Day' in the latitude of Stonehenge. The note is signed 'Wyng', almost certainly Tycho Wyng (1696–1750), a noted astronomer and the Coroner for Rutland from 1727 to 1742. In his diary Stukeley, who had moved from London to Grantham in 1726 when his fieldworking days were behind him, recorded that he 'had spent many agreeable hours at Stamford and Pickworth with Mr Tycho Wyng and Mr Edward Weaver, the great Lincolnshire astronomer'. Both Wyng and Weaver visited Stukeley in September 1725 when he was living at Stamford.[51]

Stukeley, therefore, was in possession of good solar data and could have been expected to notice how close the Heel Stone stood to the midsummer alignment. He did not, not because of the Julian calendar, but because of his faulty compass. He was well aware that in 1723 the longest day of the year was not 21 June but 11 June, the Feast Day of St Barnabas, ten days before Midsummer Day. His notes made during his survey of the Devil's Arrows in 1725 prove this. 'Boroughbrig fair is now on S. Barnabas, the summer solstice . . . the great panegyre of the Druids, the midsummer meeting . . . the remembrance hereof is transmitted in the present great fair held at Burroughbridge on St Barnabas' day'.[52]

> On St Barnabas
> Put the scythe to the grass,
> Barnaby bright
> The longest day and the shortest night.
>
> J. Vince, *Discovering Saints in Britain*, Princes Risborough, 1979, 32

Stukeley had made a survey of Stonehenge. 'I examined their [the Druids] works for several years together with sufficient accuracy with a theodolite' and he concluded that there had been an error in the layout of the circle.[53]

> The works of *Stonehenge* generally vary to the right hand from cardinal points, and that to the quantity of 6 or 7 degrees. The principal diameter or groundline of *Stonehenge*, leading from the entrance, up to the middle of the temple, to the high altar (from which line the whole work is form'd) varies about that quantity southward of the north-east point.[54]

He believed that those responsible for the plan had blundered by about 7° south of 45°, an azimuth of 52°.

Even before his talks with Wyng and Weaver Stukeley had taken other astronomical advice. 'I remember I open'd this affair, near 20 years ago [*c.* 1720] to Dr *Halley*, who was of the same sentiment'. Edmond Halley, the Astronomer Royal who predicted the re-appearance of the comet subsequently named after him, had compiled charts of magnetic deviation. Stukeley's knowledge of these may explain his own reference to the Druids and their compasses.[55] He suggested that the reason for the irregularity of the bearings at Stonehenge was because 'the Druids us'd a magnetical compass . . . and the needle vary'd so much, from the true meridian line'.[56]

It is known today that the sarsens of Stonehenge were erected in the pre-iron Early Bronze Age and the existence of prehistoric magnetic compasses can be discounted. Instead, the cause of Stukeley's misalignments can be attributed not to the Druids' imperfect instruments but to his own inaccurate theodolite.

> In the manuscript he records 27 bearings in the Stonehenge region, of which 20 can be identified as true bearings from the Ordnance Survey maps. For these his bearings give a mean error of about 1° 30' westwards of the true bearings, but with a standard deviation of about 3° probably because the compass pivot was worn or rusty or both.[57]

This was a misfortune but Stukeley must still be honoured as a pioneer. Before his solstitial conjecture any astronomical comments about stone circles had been based either on the number of stones in a ring, nineteen suggesting the lunar cycle of 18.61 years, 29 or 30 the days in a lunar month or on the shape of a ring, a crescent symbolising the moon, a circle the sun. Even Stukeley himself having visited the great megalithic complex at Stanton Drew in 1723 speculated that two circles there 'consisting of 30 stones, and the other of 12, seem to mean the Solar month and Lunar year'.[58]

The change in his astronomical thinking, for the first time considering the possibility of discovering sightlines at Stonehenge and elsewhere, may have come to him following his conversations with astronomers. But his faulty compass led him to think that the Heel Stone stood off the line of the midsummer sunrise.

Astronomically, he was an innovator, the initiator of proper astronomical studies, simply failing to detect the proximity of the Heel Stone to the summer solstice because of his defective surveying equipment. No one before him had thought of looking for celestial alignments and it was his work that influenced John Wood and John Smith in the following decades.

In 1752, after Wood but before Smith, the calendar was reformed. The change took place on 2 September, the next day becoming 14 September. Confusion was widespread. There were arguments as to when bills became payable, there were tears over uncelebrated birthdays, fears that almost half a month's wages had been forfeited, that everyone had lost a week and a half of their lives. The national cry was, "Give us back our eleven days". But the calendrical change led John Smith to his flicker of fame.

Wood had been wrong about the Heel Stone and the moon because his plan, precise in its relationship of stone to stone, was wrong in alignment by some 10°. Smith was wrong about the Heel Stone because he thought it had been raised as a solar marker. Neither, however, was as wrong as William Shakespeare.

In 1594 or 1595, twelve or thirteen years after the Catholic countries of Europe had corrected their calendars, he wrote the comedy, *A Midsummer Night's Dream*. In it he casually set his Midsummer's Day in the month of May (Act IV, scene I, line 139).

Because of Titania's reference to 'the middle summer's Spring' (Act II, I, 82) it has been suggested that instead of the calendrical midsummer Shakespeare set his lovers' play at Whitsuntide or 15 May because this was the time of weddings and of the lewd May revels that in 1583 were condemned by the puritanical Philip Stubbes:

All the yung men and maides, olde men and wives, run gadding over night to the woods, groves, hils and mountains, where they spend all night in plesant pastimes . . . I have heard it crediblie reported, and that *viva voce*, by men of great gravitie and reputation, that of fourtie, threescore, or a hundred maides goyng to the woodes ouer night, there have scarsely the thirde part of them returned home againe undefiled.[59]

It is poetically appropriate that in a discussion of the Heel Stone and the manner in which it has been misidentified and misinterpreted as a midsummer marker that the *Midsummer Night's Dream* should be radiant not with sunshine but with moonlight. It should have been the Heel Stone rather than Bottom who so desperately called out, 'A calendar, a calendar! Look in the almanac; find out moonshine, find out moonshine' (III, I, 55–7).

Monuments themselves are subject to Forgetfulness, even while they remain . . . they usually stand rather as dead objects of popular wonder, and occasions of Fables, than as certain Records of Antiquity. W. Charleton, *Chorea Gigantum*, 1663, 5.

Plate 43 The prostrate Slaughter Stone with the Heel Stone beyond.

Chapter Nine

The Slaughter Stone

SACRIFICE AND SUNSHINE

In all matters of archaeology it is constantly found that certain questions are better left in abeyance, or bequeathed to a coming generation for solution. The 'Slaughtering Stone' appears to be an admirable example of this class.

F. Stevens, *Stonehenge Today and Yesterday*, 1916, 31.

The coarse pillar of the Heel Stone, numbered Stone 96[1] leans some 77 m from the centre of Stonehenge. About 31 m to its south-west, by the entrance, lies the wrinkled, pock-marked slab of the Slaughter Stone, Stone 95, half-buried alongside the apparent end of the bank. Large and heavy, 6.6 m long, 2.1 m wide, 0.8 m thick, and 28 tons of elephantine sarsen, its position is anomalous, neither in the middle of the causeway, nor at either of its edges. It is not on the Neolithic axis of the monument nor on its Bronze Age realignment. Unfortunately, an optical illusion misled several commentators who did not realise how eccentrically the stone was placed (Fig. 17).

Its very name is pseudo-romantic. Its prostrate condition is confusing. Its location is deceptive. Even the constructional phase to which it belonged is a matter of dispute.

THE NAME

The stone was never regarded as a sacrificial altar until the late eighteenth century. William Camden and Inigo Jones did not give it a name, the latter merely referring to 'the [four] great stones which made the entrances', locating two of them outside the causeway. From his half-forgotten notes Jones made about them thirty-five years after his visit in 1620 the dimensions, 'seven foot broad, three foot thick and twenty foot high' [2.1 × 0.9 × 6.1 m] correspond so closely to those of the Slaughter Stone that it is likely that the architect had measured it. Misgivings have been expressed about his tall portals at the corners of the entrance to the henge. 'There can be little doubt that he had made a mistake'. This may be too harsh a judgement. As well as the internal Slaughter Stone two stones may have survived outside Stonehenge for some decades after Jones's observations.[2] No other stones correspond to Jones's words.

John Aubrey did identify the pillar and the Heel Stone but only as 'the two great stones marked 'a' [the Slaughter Stone, a title not yet given to it], 'w' [the Heel],

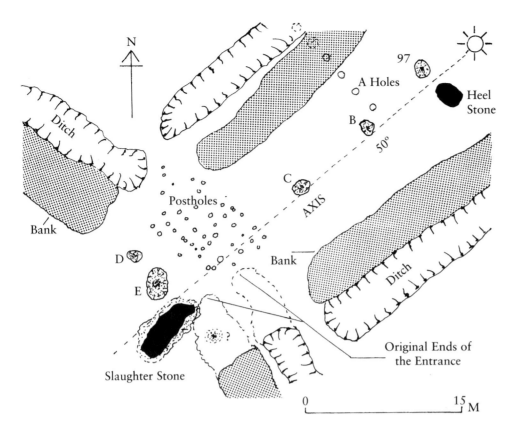

Fig. 17 The Slaughter Stone, Stonehenge and the re-aligned solar axis.

one whereof (sc. 'w') lieth a good way off, north-eastward from the circularish bank'.[3]

Sixty years later the Slaughter Stone was still anonymous. 'One at the entrance', wrote Stukeley, is 'a very large stone, at present flat on the ground', perhaps collapsed because of the digging of treasure-hunters or by the 'unfortunate colony of rabbets lately transplanted thither'. John Wood, prosaically terming it 'Stone G', believed it was intentionally prone, 'laid flat with a Design that it's Surface should be Level with the Surface of the natural Earth' unlike the erect Heel Stone, his Stone R.[4]

Almost a quarter of a century later John Smith contradicted Wood. Plagiarising Stukeley as usual he observed, 'Rabbits burrow under it, which may have caused it to sink under the surface of the earth; this stone formerly stood erect and was square at top'.[5] But it remained nameless.

Towards the end of the eighteenth century, however, the proto-Christian, mild-mannered druids of antiquity favoured by the Age of Reason were ousted by a belief in a more savage past.[6] In a reaction against the sedate neoclassicism of the Augustans the age of romantic credulity preferred fantasies to philosophy, the macabre to meditation and torture to contemplation. In the decades of Lewis's *The Monk* (1796) and Mary Shelley's *Frankenstein* (1818) stone circles became thronged with bloodstained priests engaged in ceremonies of disembowelling and augury.

In his *Spanish Tragedy* of 1588 the Elizabethan playwright Thomas Kyd had written 'Blood is a beggar'. Two centuries later gothick imagination also demanded gore and Stone 95 provided it. In 1776 the author of *A Description of Stonehenge* enthused about 'a large stone lying within the entrance of the area, which in all likelihood served by way of a table, upon which the victims were dissected and prepared'. In

1799 Edward King called Stone 95 'the slaughtering-stone', a slab 'on which the victims were immolated'. There was worse. 'It is not without reason suspected that they proceeded to even more criminal lengths, and finished their horrid sacrifice with a still more horrid banquet'.[7]

> It is the sacrificial altar, fed
> With living men – how deep the groans!
>
> W. Wordsworth. *The Prelude, XIII*, 1805, 331–2

It might be wondered why it was Stone 95 rather than the Altar Stone, Stone 80, at the heart of Stonehenge that was selected as the stone of sacrifice but the Altar Stone was unsuitable. Being a dressed, polished block of pale-green sandstone, long and smooth-sided, it was quite unlike the Slaughter Stone whose rough pits and hollows and crevices offered the impressionable mind gruesomely evocative receptacles for the gushings of blood before eviscerated corpses were borne to the Altar for the final rites.

DID THE STONE EVER STAND?

William Cunnington was convinced that the pillar had fallen or been pushed over. In 1802 he wrote to a colleague, the Rev. James Douglas, Kentish antiquarian and author of *Nenia Britannica* (1796), describing his excavation of the sarsen in May. 'I made the men dig under the prostrate stone so as to examine it thoroughly . . . and can attest the fact that the aforesaid stone was placed in an erect position. That part of the stone which stood in the ground was rough, but those parts which were exposed were stippled like the others'.[8] He estimated that the stone was 6.5 m long and that with a hole over a metre deep it would have stood 5.4 m above ground.

The following year on 12 April 1803 in a letter to his friend, John Britton, he elaborated. 'I will pledge myself to prove that Mr King's "slaughtering stone" stood erect. . . . I dug round it, and also into the excavation where it originally stood when erect . . . By digging I found the excavation in which the end A [the NE base] was placed . . . on the east side you may see similar irregularities as you must have noticed, on the butt ends of the upright stones of the fallen trilithons'. The stone had fallen inwards. The investigation, however, had given no clue as to when or why the stone had been displaced.[9]

Over a hundred years later in 1920 when Hawley re-excavated the stone very little more was learned about its history. All around the sarsen was a trench about a metre wide filled with Cunnington's spoil and rubbish but there was also evidence of even earlier interference. The slab had been toppled into a hastily-dug and inadequate pit so short that it left the ends of the stone propped on the sloping edges. In the unintended cavity beneath it, 25 cm deep, 'we found a bottle of port left under the stone, presumably by him [Cunnington] out of consideration for future excavators. The seal was intact, but the cork had decayed and let out nearly all of the contents', an upset endured by the excavators with unfortified stoicism.[10]

None of this explained why the stone should have been levelled but it is feasible that it had stood inconveniently in the way of carters and waggoners coming to Stonehenge to plunder the smaller stones. This was a practice that may have dated from mediaeval times. Hawley discovered that just to the north-west of the Slaughter Stone the causeway had been churned up to a depth of 20 cm by Tudor and Stuart treasure-seekers, perhaps even Inigo Jones and his companions who dug there in 1620 leaving broken glazed platters and glass bottles behind them.[11]

Years after his investigations Jones himself lamented that the stones were

not only exposed to the fury of all devouring Age, but to the rage of men likewise, [and] have been more subject to ruine. For, being of no extraordinary proportions, they might easily be beaten down, or digged up, and at pleasure, made use of for other occasions. Which, I am the rather enduced to beleeve, because since my first mesuring the work, not one fragment of some then standing, are now to be found.

A decade later, in 1666, John Aubrey on his plan of Stonehenge noted several 'pathes worne by Carts' across the bank and ditch.[12]

The depredations continued well into the eighteenth century and the continued passage of wheeled vehicles laden with stones weighing four tons or more had caused considerable damage as Hawley realised. He had been unable to find the holes in which Jones's four portal stones had stood. Uncharacteristically, he speculated about what had happened.

The soil in the depression at the entrance, already mentioned, would be very soft, especially when water collected in the cavity. Wheels of heavy vehicles would sink into it and become bogged, and possibly the vehicle would be upset. The deep ruts on the north-west of the causeway show that the road was much used and that it was deflected from the soft cavity and even mounted the edge of the rampart to avoid it. To ensure a safe road four fallen stones might have been taken from the monument and placed here to mark the firm ground, but not being placed in holes they gradually disappeared. Aubrey mentions only three, and in Smith's plan, dating about 1770, none is shown; so it may be inferred that all had gone by that time.[13]

The Slaughter Stone may have been thrown over because it was an obstruction, surviving only because of its bulk and weight. A line of drill-holes across one corner shows that an attempt had been made to break it up but by 1750 it was safe. Stone-robbing ceased around the mid-eighteenth century perhaps from a Romantic dread of spectral reprisals. Petrie remarked that although some sarsens and bluestones had fallen or been shifted 'no stones are missing since Wood's plan of 1747'.[14]

Cunnington's and Hawley's excavations by themselves were not enough to demonstrate with certainty that the Slaughter Stone had stood. They were suggestive but not conclusive. Luckily, literature and art combine to prove that Stone 95 had originally been upright.

The written words are unequivocal. The dimensions given by Inigo Jones for the four stones he said stood at the entrance are so similar to those of the Slaughter Stone that it must be probable that he actually saw it standing. If it had been almost buried in the earth he would not have known, without digging, that it was 'three foot thick'. He also wrote that the stones were 'twenty foot high' rather than 'long', an obvious indication that they were standing.

This is confirmed by that fine fieldworker, John Aubrey. His meticulous plan of Stonehenge, drawn in 1666, reveals what harm had been done since 1620 with one of

Jones's four entrance stones missing. In 1663 he had been shocked to realise that diagrams 'donne by memorie only' were unreliable. His subsequent draughts were more trustworthy and it is likely that his plan of Stonehenge was faithful to what actually existed 'as it remains in the present yeare 1666'.[15]

He clearly referred to the Slaughter and Heel Stones as 'the two great stones'. By going on to describe two Station Stones, numbers 91 and 93, as 'but about six foot high' the implication must be that his 'great one, fig. 6', the Slaughter Stone, was even taller and, therefore, erect.[16]

If there were no more than Jones's and Aubrey's records the matter might still be considered not entirely resolved. Recently the two men have been condemned as 'proto-archaeologues' – surely the most preposterous solecism ever inflicted upon archaeology – who 'seem to have drawn Stonehenge restored, or as they imagined it to have looked when originally built'.[17] History is against this.

Some fifty years before Jones, around 1568–9, Joris Hoefnagel, a topographical artist who specialised in perspective drawings of monuments, a rare technique for his time, seems to have visited Stonehenge, perhaps in the company of his friend and Flemish compatriot, Lucas de Heere. Four Elizabethan half-aerial illustrations of Stonehenge from the north-west have survived to commemorate the occasion: not Hoefnagel's which has been lost, but de Heere's, and a derivative watercolour by William Smith as well as an engraving dated 1575 by 'R.F.' and 'an incompetent re-engraving for the 1600 edition of Camden's *Britannia*'.[18] Of these, de Heere's and Smith's show only the sarsen circle but both 'R.F.' and the Camden include extra features. There are obvious absurdities in the Camden: a walled castle in a mountainous background instead of an Iron Age hillfort in the gentle Wiltshire plains, presumably a misunderstanding of the Latin 'castrum'; trilithons linked together like a mediaeval mass gallows; and with stones missing or misplaced. Despite these blunders by an indifferent copyist, the engraving does have merits: it shows Station Stone 93 in the foreground; it shows the bank and ditch, albeit as a wall; and it includes two stones standing just outside the ring at the north-east, 'two stones at the entrance to the Avenue' (Fig. 18). As they are close to the circle and inside the ditch and bank they must be the Slaughter Stone and an adjacent pillar, the now-missing Stone E, rather than the Slaughter Stone and a misplaced sketch of the Heel Stone.[19]

In the 'R.F.' engraving the two sarsens are erect boulders and in Camden, 1610, twenty years before Inigo Jones, they are upstanding pillars. His nephew, John Webb, using Jones's posthumous notes, corroborated this. 'He hath described in his Draught two Stones ... these were the two parallel stones that *stood* [my italics] upon the inside of the Trench, at the Entrance from the North-East'.[20]

The stonehole found by Cunnington, the records of Jones and Aubrey, the drawing by R.F. and the sketch in Camden, all concur that as late as AD 1666 the Slaughter Stone was a high, upright pillar. The opinion that 'this stone had been tipped out of its hole ... a very long time ago, during the first centuries after the construction, perhaps because it interrupted the heel stone view' appears to be both chronologically and archaeologically mistaken.[21]

Facts also militate against the comically coital conjecture that the Slaughter Stone was pushed over during the Bronze Age to allow the midsummer sun to cast a shadow from the phallic Heel Stone to reach the 'unobstructed Goddess [Altar] Stone inside the stone womb' and consummate a sacred marriage.

It is a prostrate consummation devoutly mistaken because of (a) the sketches of R.F., 1575, and Camden, 1610; (b) Jones writing of the 'height' rather than 'length' of the Slaughter Stone, an observation confirmed by Webb and, independently, by John Aubrey; (c) C-14 assays from antlers in the stonehole of Stone E, of 1935 ± 40 bc (OxA-4838) and 2045 ± 60 bc (OxA-4837), *c.* 2550–2450 BC, show that the pillar had been set up rather than toppled in the Bronze Age. It would have blocked the path of the seminal and miscast shadow.[22]

TO WHICH PHASE OF STONEHENGE DID THE SLAUGHTER STONE BELONG?

Until recently it was supposed, without proof, that the stone had been part of the first phase of the monument. The publication of the radio-carbon assays from the hole of Stone E resolved the uncertainty. The Slaughter Stone was a contemporary of the

Fig. 18 Stonehenge from Camden's *Britain*, 1610, showing both the Slaughter Stone (a) and its its now-missing partner, Stone E, (b) standing upright.

sarsen circle. There is architectural confirmation.

Being a sarsen whose sides had been dressed with stone mauls, a fact noted by William Cunnington in 1802, it is probable that it was part of the great lintelled circle project, one of scores of boulders dragged from the Marlborough Downs for the building of the gigantic ring in the Late Neolithic.[23]

Although a few sarsens had been incorporated in earlier phases of the henge they had not been shaped. The Heel Stone of Phase I was untouched. So were the Station Stones, four rugged sandstones at the corners of a large rectangle enclosing the bluestone rings of Phase II. What small patches of tooling they do possess 'could have been done after their original erection; and apart from this tooling they are much more like the Heel Stone, in that they are substantially natural boulders'.[24]

Conversely, in Phase III every one of the circle-stones, their lintels, the five trilithons, the returned bluestones, the Altar Stone were hammered, ground with scraping mauls, polished to a smooth finish, particularly on their inner faces. The Slaughter Stone was similarly treated.

'The part of the stone which had been below ground was rough. The part which had been above ground had evidently been dressed in the same manner as the large stones of the main structure. The marks of "tooling" are however almost worn away on the face now uppermost [originally the outer] which has suffered much from weathering'. With nothing to contradict this correlation and with the C-14 assays the Slaughter Stone may confidently be attributed to Phase III.[25]

A COMPANION TO THE SLAUGHTER STONE

> It is almost certain that the Slaughter Stone is the survivor of a pair of upright pillars which formed a gateway to the monument. R. J. C. Atkinson, 1979, 31.

In two of the late Tudor sketches of Stonehenge a tall, thin pillar is shown standing close to the Slaughter Stone. This was not artistic licence. A stonehole was found there by Hawley in 1920. 'We came upon a very large hole roughly 10 ft. in diameter by $6\frac{1}{2}$ ft. deep' [3 × 2 m] with a large packing-stone in it. It was estimated that its stone had stood about 5.3 m high, similar to the Slaughter Stone.[26]

Since the 1950s when stoneholes were allocated letters to distinguish them from Petrie's numbers for surviving stones the pit has been known as Stonehole E. Logically, the system demanded that the hole found near the Heel Stone in 1979, and predicted by Newall fifty years earlier, should have become Stonehole J in sequence to the holes located by Hawley. Instead, it was numbered 97 to tally with the Heel Stone's 96. British archaeology can never be accused of Teutonic inflexibility.[27]

There has been speculation that both Stonehole E and 97 were pits from which the Slaughter Stone and Heel Stone had been withdrawn to be re-erected in their present positions. It is a hypothesis rendered untenable by the knowledge that Stonehole E was occupied by a separate stone as late as AD 1666.[28]

The amazingly perceptive Stukeley anticipated the results of Hawley's excavation by two hundred years. 'There can be no room to doubt but that there was another fellow to it [the Slaughter Stone] . . . and these two made a grand portal'. He also deduced that they had straddled the axis of Stonehenge 'from the altar down thro' the middle of the Avenue', an insight confirmed by modern excavations and surveys 'that the

Slaughter Stone and stone-hole E lie symmetrically on either side of the [second] axis of Stonehenge'.[29]

A small cavity just west of Stonehole E, Stonehole D, was discovered in 1922. Hawley thought it possible that a stone had stood to the south-east of the Slaughter Stone, creating a line of three across the entrance. A suggestion that Stone D had been aligned on the major northern moonrise was in error 'by more than 2°'.[30]

On the reasonable assumption that there had been a pair of high adjacent stones inside the entrance, Stone 96 and E, separated by about 2.6 m, the gap between them would have been of the same width as that of the Heel Stone pair which also stood athwart the axis. This surely was deliberate. But the certainty brings with it further uncertainties. With an entrance widened from 10.7 m to 18.3 m it is puzzling that the pillars should be so close together. Even more bewildering when one considers the admirable balance and architectural harmony contained everywhere else at Stonehenge the Slaughter Stone was set up less than 5 m from the end of the bank to its south-east whereas its partner was more than 7 m from the bank to its north-west. Such spatial imbalance need not have been carelessness.[31]

PURPOSE

A solar alignment may be the solution. For years it has been a canon of popular astronomical – and archaeological – belief that the Heel Stone was positioned to be in line with the midsummer sunrise. It was not. Despite the persistence of wishful thinking this has been known since 1901 when Lockyer pointed out that the 'Friar's Heel' was not on the axis of Stonehenge so that 'the Sun must have completely risen before it was vertically over the summit of the stone'.[32]

Famous photographs such as that by Gerster for the front cover of the 1979 edition of Atkinson's *Stonehenge* showing the sun above the top of the Heel Stone are deceptive. As Chippindale has pointed out they are adjustments. Reality can be disappointing. For an observer at the middle of Stonehenge the sun at its first glimmer on the skyline would appear to the left of the Heel Stone and would have to be fully risen before it reached the sarsen. Any ray or shadow cast then would pass to the left of the circle centre and the expectant Altar Stone. If the outlier had any astronomical function it was lunar, not solar.[33]

Around 3200 BC the ditch and internal bank of a simple henge were constructed on Salisbury Plain. There was an entrance at the south and a wider causeway, 10.7 m across, at the north-east. The axis of the henge through the midpoint of this entrance had a bearing of 46°33'. The Heel Stone did not stand on this axis but was erected in line with the right-hand, south-east, side of the entrance.

At Stonehenge's latitude of 51°10'42" the midsummer sun would have appeared above the low horizon at 49°54'. This was well to the north of the Heel Stone at 51°18', an 'error' of over a degree if the stone had been a solar foresight. Instead, the pillar stood midway between the minor and major risings of the moon as it moved back and forth over the 18.61 years of the lunar cycle.

Centuries later with the emergence of what appears to be a solar cult there was change. People deliberately widened the entrance south-eastwards by throwing 7.6 m of the bank back into the ditch. With a refashioned causeway 18.3 m wide the axis of Stonehenge was transformed, veering from 46°33' to 49°54', an alignment presumably wanted by the workers because it was the orientation of midsummer sunrise. The change also caused the Heel Stone to stand quite close to the new axis.[34] This creation of a broader entrance is revealed most clearly by the six lines of postholes that had filled the space between the terminals of the Neolithic henge. The south-eastern edge of their grid stops about 8 m short of the remodelled ditch and bank to its east.

In 1979 the discovery of Stonehole 97 at 48°21' alongside the Heel Stone created astronomical excitement. It was conjectured that the pair of megaliths had been designed as a solar 'gunsight' some 2.4 m wide to frame the midsummer sunrise. 'The midsummer sun would then rise on an alignment, accidentally or deliberately contrived between the two stones', always assuming that the pair actually stood together, something that the excavation was unable to determine.[35]

If they were contemporaries then, more remarkably still, the sun would have shone between them and then between the Slaughter Stone and its partner, then between stones 1 and 30 of the sarsen circle and 31 and 49 of the inner bluestone ring, pouring down a thin tunnel of stone like the passage of a chambered tomb up to the Altar Stone at the heart of Stonehenge. Astronomically this did happen. If it was designed to do so it is a revelation of considerable astronomical sophistication. But as Stonehenge itself is a model of considerable architectural sophistication the intentional planning of such a solar mechanism would not have been beyond the abilities, or interests, of the builders. To the prehistoric mind the megalithic channel may even have been envisaged as a method that would guide the sun's light into the core of the circle.

If, on the other hand, the link between the sun and the stones was fortuitous it is difficult to explain the position of the Slaughter Stone. At present, lying where it does against the 'bank', it seems to be a fallen portal stone but this is the optical illusion mentioned earlier. It was never close to the genuine end of the entrance. After Hawley finished excavating the infilled ditch he did not replace the rubble but left it inside the henge piled up like a bank that extended to the Slaughter Stone. Possibly he wanted to reproduce the original appearance of the entrance. But visitors to the ring should visualise Stone 95 as it once was, standing free of the upcast and asymmetrically situated as an entrance stone.

There is documentary proof of this. In 1810, long before Hawley and when the widened entrance remained intact, a plan was made of Stonehenge 'by the assistance of an able surveyor' and with 'a strict attention to accuracy'. The draught, one of many excellent maps and plans by Philip Crocker, a former Ordnance surveyor, for Sir Richard Colt Hoare (Fig. 19) shows the 18 m broad space between the banks with the Slaughter Stone lying at least 5 m clear of the south-eastern terminal, well away from where any portal would have stood.[36]

The stone does not seem to fulfil any other function. Rising high and wide it would have blocked any shadow from the Heel Stone entering the circle. William Cunnington III, grandson of the stone's excavator, perceived this. 'If this stone stood erect, it must have entirely concealed the "gnomon" [the Heel Stone] from persons standing in front of the "altar". It would have been impossible to see the sun rise over the gnomon'. Others agreed. 'Had the "slaughtering stone" ever stood erect, it would . . . have been impossible for a person standing on the "altar stone" to have seen the sun rise over the "gnomon"'.[37]

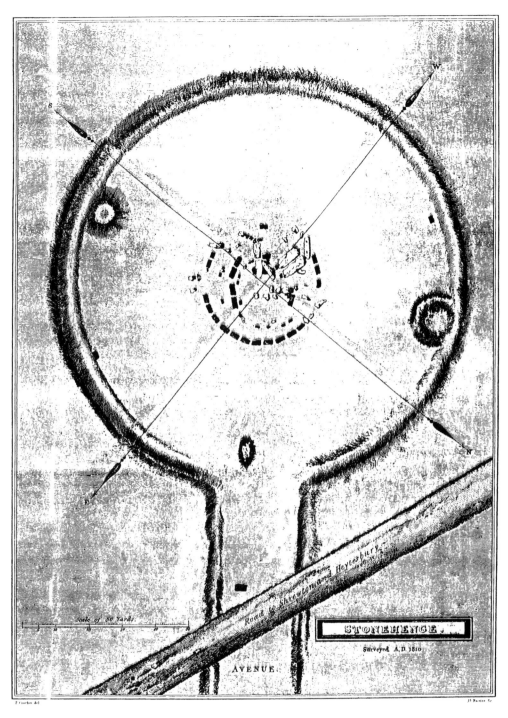

Fig. 19 Philip Crocker's plan of Stonehenge, 1810, showing the Slaughter Stone lying centrally to the widened entrance.

Considered solely as portals the Slaughter Stone and Stone E are not convincing. Standing off-centre on the causeway and less than 3 m apart they would have been strangely cramped as an imposing entrance for processions approaching Stonehenge along the avenue. If, however, they were put up to be in line with the Heel Stone and Stone 97 the thin rectangle of the four stones would have formed a long, narrow passage along the axis down which the rising sun would have shone. If that was the builders' intention then there is a logic to the locations of Stone 95 and the Slaughter Stone as components of a nicely-designed astronomical 'corridor'.

Archaeo-astronomy is a controversial discipline. In spite of the well-known solar 'window-boxes' in Newgrange and Maes Howe there is not one accredited high-precision alignment in the prehistory of western Europe. There are crude orientations on the sun or moon in groups of chambered tombs. There are slightly more refined bearings in stone rows of the Early and Middle Bronze Age. The accumulated data from such rows by Ann Lynch and Clive Ruggles in south-west Ireland and by Ruggles in western Scotland are strongly in favour of approximate solar and lunar sightlines accurate to within half a degree or so, the majority laid out between 1600 and 1200 BC.[38] As the Slaughter Stone belonged to the remodelling of Stonehenge in the Late Neolithic its more precise 'solar rectangle' would precede the rows.

A megalithic and mathematical grace-note can be added. In 1923, digging in the avenue, Hawley came upon two more holes for stones, B and C, in a line between E and the pit of Stone 97. Both stones are missing although C, the southernmost, may have been shown on John Aubrey's plan of 1666.[39]

The distances between the centres of the ragged holes, although impossible to pinpoint with exactness, are intriguing. From C to B is about 8.4 m, B to 97, 8.2 m. The 16.5 m separating E from C is twice the length of the spaces between the others suggesting there may once have been an intervening stone whose hole in the disturbed area of the six lines of postholes, might easily have been overlooked.

One might imagine a row of five standing stones from E to 97 in a line 33.1 m long. This is almost exactly 40 of Alexander Thom's Megalithic Yards of 0.829 m,[40] a length of 33.16 m, with the stones spaced 10 M.Y. apart. If the gap between them was 2.5 m this would be 3 M.Y. Laterally, the stonehole centres of the Slaughter Stone and E are about 4.1 m apart or 5 M.Y. The apparent counting bases of 3 and 5 in these measurements accord well with the thirty stones of the sarsen circle and the five trilithons inside the ring. As the writer remains a resolute disbeliever in any national unit of measurement in prehistoric Britain these observations are offered in a commendable spirit of academic impartiality.

There is physical evidence for the megalithic rectangle but no irrefutable proof that it was astronomically designed. However interesting it is the argument cannot be elevated to the status of a testable hypothesis. But if we cannot certainly link the Slaughter Stone with the sun we can at least cleanse it of its blood.

The orientation of ancient monuments is not popular with some archaeologists, but, if it be a fact that two stones or one stone and a space between two other adjoining stones are in line with a certain sunrise or sunset, the student may justifiably consider theories based on such facts. R. S. Newall. *Stonehenge, Wilts.*, 1955, 14.

Plate 44 The little-known southern entrance with Stonehenge in the background.

Chapter Ten

The Sarsen Horseshoe

A RIDER

The trilithons are not on a circle and the scheme of their placing is obscure.
F. S. Petrie, *Stonehenge. Plans, Descriptions and Theories*, 1880, 6.

A 'STONE CIRCLE' OF OAK POSTS

Stonehenge, this most famous of all British stone circles, is a contradiction. It is a paradox of construction and nationality. It is not a stone circle. It is not British.

Its thick sarsen pillars are tall and statuesque but they were not pounded into shape by masons accustomed to working in hard stone but by carpenters whose natural material was malleable wood. There is also an architectural enigma. Not one of the hundreds of true stone circles in Britain and Ireland had lintels on top of its standing stones. Stonehenge did. Everything was unorthodox.

Not a single 'classical' stone circle had been fashioned by woodworking techniques. Stonehenge was uniquely different. All thirty-five of its lintels on the thirty circle-stones and the five trilithons were held securely by a projecting knob or tenon on the upright onto which the hollowed pit or mortice in the lintel plugged. Such mortice-and-tenon jointing was carpentry. There was a refinement. To ensure complete stability the top of each pillar had chamfered edges like a shallow box or tray within which the bottom of the lintel rested snugly.

In the circle where lintel lay against lintel they were held in place by the tongue-and-groove method, the V-shaped projection at the end of one lintel jutting neatly into the V-shaped cavity at the end of its partner. It was prehistoric engineering of very high quality but it was the handiwork of craftsmen on Salisbury Plain where there was an abundance of trees and an absence of stone. Their expertise was in the building of strong and stable structures of timber and that is what the sarsen Stonehenge was, a wooden circle converted into an astonishment of stone.

This was the first inconsistency. The second is the alien style. The design of Stonehenge was not traditional in Britain. It did have counterparts in Brittany. Nor were the carvings on the sarsens indigenous. In Bronze Age Britain Stonehenge was as out-of-place as a Babylonian ziggurat would have been in Mycenaean Greece.

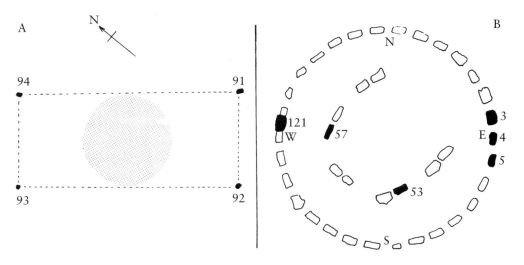

Fig. 20 Architectural features at Stonehenge. A. The rectangle of the Four Stations around the sarsen ring; B. the sarsen horseshoe of trilithons inside the circle. Decorated stones are shown in black.

THE FOREIGN ARCHITECTURE

The constructional elements of Stonehenge's sarsen phase are a perplexing amalgam of a circle, a rectangle, a horseshoe setting and a 'central' stone. Of the three shapes only the first is widespread in Britain. The others are uncommon, almost non-existent, yet there has been virtually no debate about the reasons for the oblong of the Four Stations around the circle and the horseshoe of five trilithons inside the ring (Fig. 20). Nor have the cultural affinities of the Altar Stone been considered.

Not one of the accepted authorities on Stonehenge has attempted to explain why the sarsen circle contains the U-shaped arrangement of trilithons. John Aubrey wondered if the builders had intended there to be not five but seven to form a heptagon related 'to the seaven Planets and seaven daies of the Weeke? I cannot determine, I only suggest'. Stukeley, who innovated the term *trilithon*, 'three stones', thought that the north-east mouth of the horseshoe was left open to be the entrance to the sacred cell. Neither John Wood who only noted the graded heights of the trilithons; nor John Smith, 'originally an Ellipsis, or oval'; Hoare, 'a large oval'; Stone, 'somewhat in horseshoe style'; Cunnington, 'in the form of a horseshoe'; nor Atkinson, 'set in a horseshoe' offered reasons for the unusual design. The detailed *Stonehenge in its Landscape*, 'form a horseshoe', added nothing. In the recent *Stonehenge. Mysteries of the Stones and Landscape* 'At the centre of the monument stands the horseshoe of trilithons' seemed quite adequate.[1]

Stone did stress the enigma but only as a negative. 'In Britain Stonehenge is unique. We have no earlier structure in the same style from which its evolution may be traced, and the design has never been repeated . . . It has no ancestors and no descendants'. He was mistaken. Barclay remarked that the trilithons themselves were unknown elsewhere in Britain but 'examples are to be met with abroad'. So are megalithic horseshoes, rectangles and free-standing, internal pillars.[2]

There are hundreds of stone circles in Britain and Ireland but horseshoes are rare. They are plentiful in Brittany. A possible irony is that, unwittingly, John Aubrey may have recorded the remains of one, customarily thought to be the scanty remains of a northern stone circle, inside Avebury. A resistivity survey appears to confirm a U-shape as against a circular setting there. Other than that uncertain site three internal

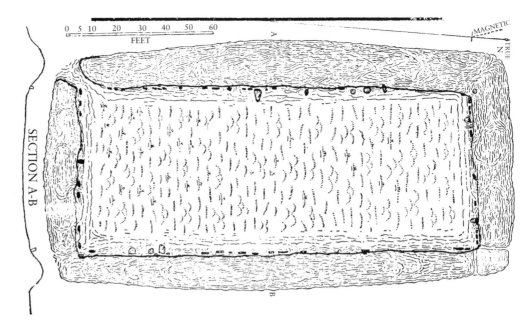

Fig. 21 The rectangle of King Arthur's Hall, Bodmin Moor, Cornwall.

horseshoes of timber are recorded in Britain and Ireland: inside the Arminghall henge, Norfolk, in the ring of posts at Lugg in County Dublin, and in the Machrie Moor I stone circle, on the island of Arran. The hypothetical horseshoe inside the stone circle of Ballynoe, County Down, can be omitted as it is no more than the disrupted kerbstones of two contiguous circular cairns.

In the north of Scotland there is an earthen example at Cowiemuir, Moray, and there are, or were, megalithic sites at Haerstanes, also in Moray, and at Achavanich and Broubster in Caithness, maybe also at Latheronwheel in the same county. On Bodmin Moor in Cornwall there is an immense D-shaped horseshoe on East Moor. Tellingly, this unexpected setting is less than six miles east of King Arthur's Hall, a megalithic rectangle (Fig. 21). The proximity of two such un-British shapes with only 160 miles of English Channel between them and Brittany hints that both may have been the ritual centres of strangers from overseas.[3]

Fig. 22 The rectangle of Lanvéoc, Finistère, north-west Brittany.

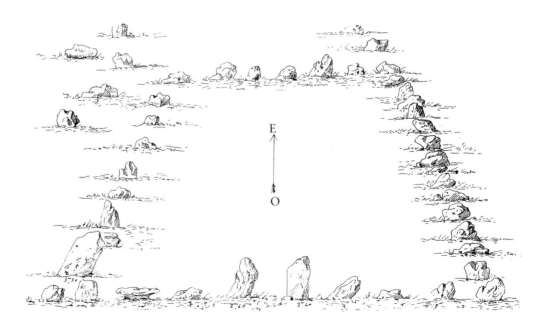

A

Fig. 23 Maps showing the distribution of rectangles and horseshoes in Britain, Ireland and Brittany (see Gazetteer, p. 168).

Rectangles: 1. King Arthur's Hall, Cornwall; 2. Stonehenge, Wiltshire (Station Stones); 3. Landaoudec, Finistère; 4.Lanvéoc, Finistère; 5. Parc-ar-Varret, Finistère; 6. Phare du Créach, Ushant; 7. Ty ar-c'Huré, Crozon, Finistère; 8. Cordon des Druides, Ille-et-Vilaine; 9. Crucuno, Morbihan; 10. Er-Lannic North, Gulf of Morbihan; 11. Jardin aux Moines, Brocéliande Forest, Morbihan; 12. Le Narbon, Morbihan.

Horseshoes: 13. Arminghall, Norfolk; 14. Avebury North, Wiltshire; 15. East Moor, Cornwall; 16. Stonehenge, Wiltshire (Trilithons); 17. Achavanich, Caithness; 18. Broubster, Caithness; 19. Cowiemuir, Moray; 20. Croft Moraig, Perthshire; 21. Haerstanes, Moray; 22. Latheronwheel, Caithness; 23. Machrie Moor I, Arran; 24. Lugg, Co. Dublin; 25. Château-Bû, Ille-et-Vilaine; 26. Pédernec, Côtes-du-Nord; 27. Tossen-Keler, Côtes-du-Nord; 28. Lagatjar, Finistère; 29. Landaoudec, Finistère; 30. Pen-ar-Land, Ushant; 31. Ty-ar c'Huré, Finistère; 32. Le Tribunal, St Just, Ille-et-Vilaine; 33. Champ de la Croix, Crucuny, Morbihan; 34. Er-Lannic South, Gulf of Morbihan; 35. Grand Rohu, Arzon, Morbihan; 36. Graniol, Penhap, Morbihan; 37. Kerbourgnec, St Pierre-Quiberon, Morbihan; 38. Kergonan, Ile-aux-Moines, Morbihan; 39. Kerlescan North, Morbihan; 40. Kerlescan South, Morbihan; 41. Kermario East, Morbihan; 42. Kerzerho, Morbihan; 43. Sainte-Barbe, Morbihan.

Rectangles are even scarcer than horseshoes in these islands. Except for the almost disregarded King Arthur's Hall only the Four Stations at Stonehenge can be quoted as an incontrovertible example although the dozens of minilithic squares and oblongs on Exmoor might be included. Given their nearness to Dartmoor they are more convincingly interpreted as abbreviated forms of double row. So is the now-wrecked east–west oblong of Mattocks Down amongst them, 44.8 × 20 m, of which only one great stone survives. Its partner and the twenty-three lower uprights of the northern side have all gone. It was a typical 'high-and-low' double row.[4]

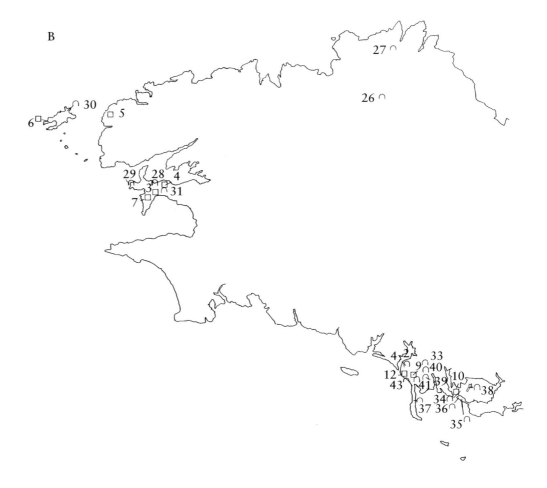

Although remote from its colleagues it shared with them an alignment to cardinal points, there east–west. It is a feature true not only at King Arthur's Hall, but also in Brittany at Parc-ar-Varret, Finistère, both north–south, Lanvéoc, Finistère (Fig. 22), and Crucuno, Morbihan, each oriented east–west. Whether the geometrical triangles, squares and parallelograms on Exmoor owe anything to these angular Breton fashions is a matter for further research.[5]

Definitely excluded as rectangles are the 'Scottish' Four-Poster stone circles whose four stones are seldom at the corners of an oblong but invariably stand on the circumference of a circle proving that this was how the ring was laid out. An arc of a circle can always be drawn through three points with the rare exception of those in a straight line. It is often impossible through four.

Twelve horseshoes, some questionable, and two certain rectangles for the 121,400 square miles of Great Britain and Ireland but more than thirteen hundred stone circles demonstrate how atypical the plan of the later Stonehenge was if created by natives. On the other hand, there are some twenty-nine U-shaped settings and rectangles in Brittany, a département of 10,500 square miles, less than a twelfth the size of the British Isles (Fig. 23). They are associated with Late Neolithic and Early Bronze Age rows of standing stones and ovate megalithic rings known as cromlechs. In the density to the square mile of rectangles and horseshoes in the British Isles and Brittany a ratio of 24:1 greatly favours the last and makes it very probable that the design of the later Stonehenge in at least five of its aspects was influenced by Breton styles: (a) by the geometry and (b) by the astronomy of the rectangle; (c) by the shape of the monumental horseshoe; and (d) by the art; and finally, (e) by the inclusion of an off-centre 'anthropomorphic' pillar for which there are counterparts in north-western Brittany but very few in Britain.

WESSEX AND BRITTANY

Despite the idiosyncracy of its architecture Stonehenge today is considered a British construction. It was not always so. Geoffrey of Monmouth believed that Merlin had carried the stones from Ireland. Inigo Jones thought it Roman. Walter Charleton, Danish. Influenced by the carving of a dagger he noticed in July 1953, Richard Atkinson argued for a Mycenaean designer, later speculating on the likelihood of an architect from Mycenae working 'at the behest of a barbarian British king'. Stuart Piggott was in agreement. Looking to the Aegean for the dagger's likely origins 'its nearest parallels would be in the Mycenaean world of the sixteenth or fifteenth century BC . . . Such a connexion would be by no means improbable in the framework of the prehistory of the period'. Referring to the royal tombs of the Wessex culture he continued that in them 'we find evidence of far-flung commercial contacts stretching to Bohemia, Ireland and the Mycenaean world itself'.[6]

With Ivimy's eccentric exception claiming that the circle was the handiwork of Egyptian astronomer-priests wanting a pollution-free observatory Stonehenge has been accepted as British ever since.[7] The sarsen ring was the visionary handiwork of mighty and wealthy chieftains of the Wessex Early Bronze Age, contemporaries of equally prestigious princely warriors in Brittany.

For years it has been accepted that there were intimate cultural contacts between Wessex and Brittany in the third and second millennia BC. There are lavish graves in the cemeteries of round barrows near Stonehenge and their contents of weapons and opulent personal ornaments are very like those of their Breton contemporaries. Even the handled pot from Winterbourne Stoke 5 bell barrow has its Breton equivalents. The barrow only a mile and a quarter WSW of Stonehenge was excavated by Sir Richard Colt Hoare and his companion, William Cunnington, in July 1809. The mound covered a pit over 4m deep at the bottom of which a funerary garland of twigs rested on an elm tree-trunk coffin by whose skeleton lay a rivetted dagger and gold-pinned wooden sheath, with a second dagger by the man's thigh. The smooth red, four- or five-handled vessel by the skull was unusual and Hoare was aware of its foreign nature. 'This sepulchral urn is different both in shape and colour to any we have ever found in the British sepulchres. It resembles in tint the fine red Samian pottery . . . The rich contents of this tumulus has induced us to crown it with royal honours, and to give it the title of KING BARROW'.[8] There were others.

Wilsford 5, the famous Bush Barrow, half a mile SSW of Stonehenge, was dug into on 11 July 1808. William Cunnington failed to find anything but the following September he came upon the remains of a heavily-built man whose possessions of daggers, flat axe, gold plaques, and dentated bone mounts could all be equated with finds from the dagger graves of the Armorican period in Brittany. Although recent analysis of the daggers has shown this to be an over-simplification the discovery at Winterbourne Stoke 'of another four-handled vessel of Breton type . . . in southern England confirms the cross-channel influence of the Breton workshops'.[9]

In Brittany the Bush Barrow dentated bone mount was reproduced but in gold. The sceptre inside the Kerlagat dolmen at Carnac 'connait encore au Wessex dans le tumulus de Bush Barrow'. Amber pendants have been discovered at Saint-Fiacre, Melrand,

Pleumeur-Gautier, Côtes-du-Nord, and there were others at Kernonen en Plouvorn, Finistère. At Kerguérvarec, Plouyé there was a jet pendant within a circle of lovely honey-coloured barbed-and-tanged flint arrowheads.[10]

Many of the British articles of gold were so similar that Taylor envisaged a single Breton goldsmith working in southern Britain, and suggested that the golden objects might all be contemporary within forty to fifty years. In lovely condition, showing no wear, they were presumably made for and buried with the dead. Burgess also recognised that the pins and daggers were 'so similar as to indicate that they were supplied by the same workshops, probably in Brittany to judge from the number of finds'.[11]

Near Bush Barrow the bowl barrow of Wilsford 7 was a treasure-house. With the skeleton was a grape cup, shale beads, one gold-covered, a shale double-axe pendant, a shield-shaped amber pendant, its convex side grooved. A smaller companion was plain. There were two amber pendants with V-perforations, a spherical cover of sheet gold in two halves, and a pair of perforated fossil encrinites. There was also a more mundane tripartite collared urn.[12]

The adjacent bell barrow of Wilsford 8 was equally rich. Against the burnt human bones on the floor was a small cup with latticed sides, 'An enthusiastic antiquary who was present at the opening of this barrow, fancied that he could trace in this cup a design taken from the outward circle of STONEHENGE'.[13] Amongst the treasure was an amber halberd-pendant bound with four strips of sheet gold and a copper or bronze blade, a gold-covered shale button, a circular bone pendant, one side with sheet gold incised with squares, four pestle-shaped and a bottle-shaped amber pendant, its companion now lost. There were also two circular gold-bound amber discs with V-perforations, three flat amber pendants, a gold-covered bronze pendant in the form of a miniature ingot torc with a V-perforation at its thickest point. Hoare marvelled. 'No barrow that we have yet opened has ever produced such a variety of singular and elegant articles'.[14]

Such largesse of an élite society has its closest counterparts in the rich articles buried with the dead in the large Armorican warrior graves near the north coast of Finistère. Their metal objects of rivetted daggers, flat axes, gold plaques and amber pendants, dentated shaft mountings, handled pots, barbed-and-tanged flint arrowheads are repeated in Wessex. So are the Breton megalithic horseshoes and carvings of axes, daggers and anthropomorphs. At the beginning of the Early Bronze Age 'southern Britain and Brittany presented a single cultural province'.[15]

Divided into two phases[16] the first period of this Armorican barrow culture, c. 1850–1650 bc, c. 2300–2000 BC, was characterised by large tumuli covering inhumations with funerary goods that included four- and six-rivetted daggers whose pommels were profusely decorated with minute gold pins like that in Bush Barrow. Often with them were luxurious articles of gold, amber and jet. 'This . . . suggests that the people buried in Wessex barrows were interacting in their lives with the Breton area at a very early time'.[17] Before then, the beautiful hornblendic gneiss macehead found with a child's cremation at Stonehenge may have come from Brittany. Even earlier French influences have been claimed for the styles of the Early Neolithic Cotswold-Severn chambered tombs, some as close to Salisbury Plain as the group around Avebury.[18]

A plaque akin to those at Bush Barrow is the mistitled 'box' of gold foil in the tumulus of La Motta, Lannion, a mound less than 200 miles from Stonehenge with only 160 miles of the easily-crossed English Channel between them. Even from Carnac the journey would have been no more than 250 miles by land and sea if crossing the

Plate 45 The macehead, probably from Brittany, discovered at Stonehenge.

wilderness of the central Argoat. Four hundred summer sea-miles along the south coast, sailing northwards past the Crozon peninsula, across the Channel and thirty miles up the Christchurch Avon would have been a more comfortable voyage.

The problem with this comfortable model of the Wessex chieftains such as the man from Bush Barrow supervising the construction of the sarsen Stonehenge is that it is wrong. The chronology is now known to be centuries from the truth. At one time with the Armorican dagger graves beginning around 1850 bc, *c.* 2300 BC, and the Wessex rich graves around 1750 bc, *c.* 2150 BC, and with confirming assays from Stonehenge III of 1620 ± 110 bc (I-2384) and 1720 ± 150 bc (BM-46), *c.* 2350–1850 BC, everything fitted together neatly. No longer.

The 'date' of 1620 ± 110 bc (I-2384) obtained from an antler in an unfinished R Hole has been rejected on the grounds of humic acid contamination.[19] The other date of 1720 bc is now only one of a group of much earlier determinations from Stonehenge: 2073 ± 21 bc (UB-3821) from the hole of Stone 1 at the north-east of the ring; and from the horseshoe of trilithons: Stone 53 or 54, 2035 ± 45 bc (OxA-4840); Stone 56, 1720 ± 150 bc (BM-46); Stone 57, 1910 ± 40 bc (OxA-4839); and from Stonehole E alongside the fallen Slaughter Stone 1935 ± 40 bc (OxA-4838) and 2045 ± 60 bc (OxA-4837) (*ibid.*, 524). These newly-acquired assays indicate that Phase 3 of Stonehenge began in the calibrated chronological bracket of 2850–2480 BC centuries before the inception of the Wessex Culture whose rich leaders used but did not build Stonehenge. They inherited the monument from ancestors who many generations before had been in close contact with Brittany.

The heavy ring of sarsens can now be seen standing at a time when megalithic tombs were still being constructed both in Britain and Brittany, angled passage-tombs or *allées-coudées* like Goërem, Gâvres, in use between 2150 ± 140 bc (Gif-768) and 1910 ± 200 bc (Gif-329), *c.* 2950–2100 BC, with anthropomorphic carvings, one a simple rectangle in its passage; or the *allée-couverte* of Crech-Quillé, 1790 ± 200 bc (Gsy-3400), *c.* 2600–1950 BC, with its high-relief 'figure with breasts and a necklace' at the end of its short passage.[20] The popular British origin would not account for the 'foreign' rectangle of the Four Stations, nor the gigantic megalithic horseshoe inside Stonehenge. Nor would it account for the Breton carvings of axes, a dagger and anthropomorphs, or the free-standing Altar Stone. Stonehenge has more in common with the cromlechs of Brittany than with the stone circles of Britain and Ireland.

Breton analogues for Stonehenge's oblong and horseshoe are more clearcut for the latter because the rectangle's known equivalents are nearly all too badly damaged for their exact shapes, dimensions and angles to be reconstructed. Nevertheless, no corresponding blend of geometry and astronomy in a megalithic oblong is known in Britain and Ireland whereas these components are certainly to be found in Brittany.

THE FOUR STATIONS AND THE BRETON CONNECTION

Four sarsen pillars once stood at the corners of a long SE–NW oblong inside the earthen bank of the early Stonehenge. Clockwise from the south-east they were numbered by Petrie 91–94. Stone 91 has fallen, 92 has gone but its hole was located by Hawley in 1921. 93 is a stump. The hole of the missing Stone 94 was found by Richard Atkinson and Alexander Thom in April 1978. Following its discovery it was possible to cite the exact dimensions and angles of the rectangle, always with the proviso that the stones themselves might have been moved in antiquity.[21]

The prehistoric rectangle is near to perfection and had been laid out with great care. Its sides measure 34.2 m from Stone 91 to 92, 79.9 m from 92 to 93, 32.7 m from 93 to 94, and 80.3 m from 94 to 91. The corners are close to right-angles, respectively 89°.42, 89°.55, 91°.03 and 90°.02, forming a regular parallelogram whose long sides lay SE–NW, approximately 140°–320°, the short sides correspondingly aligned SW–NE, 230°–50°.[22]

'Aligned' is intentionally chosen. In 1846 the short SW–NE sides were recognised to point to the midsummer sunrise. In that year the Rev. Edward Duke who introduced the term 'Stations' claimed that stones 91 and 94 had acted as gnomons like the pins of sun-dials. 'The astronomer', wrote Duke, 'taking his station [at Stone 92] . . . at the summer solstice, and turning to the north-east, would see that majestic luminary in all his splendour mounting in the horizon, and making his first appearance over the gnomon' [Stone 91].[23]

Over a century later in 1961 Hawkins, using the impressive novelty of a computer, demonstrated that the long SE–NW sides of the rectangle were virtually in line with the most northerly setting of the moon. Neither his lunar nor Duke's solar orientations were accurate to more than about half a degree, many minutes of arc from astronomical precision but good enough for observers uninterested in celestial minutiae. Coarser sightlines to the same heavenly targets already existed in monuments as diverse as chambered tombs, stone circles and rows of standing stones. To find them established at Stonehenge will surprise no unbiased student.[24]

Until the twentieth century it was never asked why the builders had chosen to set out a rectangle rather than an easier square but in 1906 Lockyer offered an explanation. From the middle of the sarsen circle where the diagonals of the rectangle intersected a line 'over the N.W. stone [Stone 93, not 94 at the NNW] would mark the sunset place in the first week in May'.[25] He was correct.

The SE–NW diagonal from Stone 91 to Stone 93 has a bearing of 297° ± 30′ towards the May Day or Beltane sunset, the very limited declinations of the 'window' from +16°.65 to +17°.2 neatly straddling the 16°.72 declination of the May Day sunset. Thatcher, agreeing with Thom's calendrical analysis of stone circles and rows, stated that 'many of the megalithic alignments in Brittany and in Great Britain point to the sunrise and sunset at those four dates' of early February, The 'Celtic' festival of Imbolc; early May or Beltane; August or Lughnasa; and the beginning of November, Samain.[26]

Coincidence is unlikely. The probability of the May Day line being fortuitous is no more than one chance in ninety. Logic insists that the Four Stations belonged to a phase before the sarsen circle whose thick and tall slabs would have blocked the diagonal sightline.[27] The erection of the circle implies a rejection of the Beltane alignment and it may have been at that time that the rectangle was despoiled, Stone 91 toppled, Stone 93 truncated and Stones 92 and 94 removed.

What has to be emphasised is that there is no comparable monument in Britain or Ireland in which rectangle, diagonal and multiple sightlines combine but there is a strong correlation with the lateral and diagonal alignments in the Crucuno quadrilateral, 33.1 × 24.8 m, 6½ km west of Carnac in Brittany. There the long sides lie neatly east–west towards the equinoctial sunsets and the NE-SW diagonal, 41.6 m long, is in line with the midwinter sunset. In essence its use of a diagonal is a replica of that at Stonehenge. Another rectangle may have existed at Le Narbon just 3¼ km to the

Plate 46 One of the many horseshoes in Brittany, its low stones stand in front of a 'Scottish' Four-Poster at Château-Bû, Saint-Just in Brittany.

WNW. Only five menhirs and tumbled stones survive,[28] typical of wreckage in megalithic Brittany.

There are, or were, other well laid-out rectangles in Brittany such as that at Lanvéoc on the Crozon peninsula in Finistère which also was arranged east–west. Regrettably, in a stony land of impoverished peasants many megalithic sites, although mentioned by antiquarians, have been uprooted and destroyed. Without details of their geometry and astronomy they cannot be used to consolidate the argument for the Four Stations being a structure of Breton inspiration. Fortunately, there are sufficient surviving horseshoes, known as *fer-aux-chevaux*, for their relationship to the U-shaped setting inside Stonehenge to be revealed.

MEGALITHIC HORSESHOES

Inside the sarsen circle of Stonehenge are two horseshoe settings, a lesser one of nineteen bluestones inside a lofty U-shaped enclosure of trilithons, Stones 51 to 60. The horseshoe consists of five lintelled pairs of tall, closely-set pillars, the narrow gap between each trilithon like a strangulated archway. The horseshoe, set NE to SW from open mouth to apex, is 14 m wide and 13.1 m deep. It is graded in height, the terminal pairs 51–2, 59–60, standing 6.1 m high, the central pairs 53–4 and 57–8 opposite, 6.5 m tall but dwarfed by the Great Trilithon 55–6, at the head of the horseshoe, once towering 7.3 m above ground before Stone 55 fell in pre-Roman times bringing its lintel down and flattening the upright Altar Stone at the heart of the ring.

There are carvings of recognisable objects on four circle-stones and two trilithons. This combination of an unusual layout, grading of heights and realistic art has no equivalent anywhere in Britain or Ireland but does exist in Brittany.

Horseshoe arrangements of standing stones are hardly known in Britain, the fragmented possible setting inside Avebury being later interpreted by Stukeley as the remains of a concentric circle. Elsewhere in Britain other U-shapes are rare and remote from Stonehenge. The four or five in northern Scotland are 500 weary land-miles from Salisbury Plain.[29] Critically, with the one exception of Croft Moraig in central

Scotland, the distribution of horseshoes outside Wiltshire is significantly coastal whether in Norfolk, eastern Ireland, on the island of Arran or in northern Scotland. Maritime influence from Brittany is likely.

At least nineteen *fer-aux-chevaux* are known in that region of France, the farthest from Stonehenge the dilapidated Kergonan on the Ile-aux-Moines off the south coast and even that distant site is only 250 sea- and land-miles south of Wiltshire. The nearest is Tossen-Keler at Tréguier on the north coast ninety miles closer. It is not only their shape they share with Stonehenge but grading, an astronomical axis, often towards a cardinal point or to a solar alignment, and representational art.

It has never been asked why such unusual shapes were chosen but it is arguable that they were economically truncated versions of the great megalithic ellipses and egg-shaped rings around Carnac. There, cromlechs like Ménec West contained solar alignments defined by a long or short axis.[30] By 'cutting' such oval enclosures in half a horseshoe would be formed with an open mouth from the marked centre of which an observer would look towards a foresight at the apex of the site. This was emphasised by the simple device of erecting the tallest stones there. An identical principle was used at Stonehenge.

It has already been noted how rare rectangles and horseshoes were in prehistoric Britain and Ireland. In Brittany they jostle. The blend of oblong and *fer-à-cheval* is epitomised at Kerlescan 3 km east of Ménec. Its horseshoe has a convex western but straight eastern side as though its builders were undecided as to whether they were putting up a *fer-à-cheval* or an open-mouthed rectangle.[31]

Twelve kilometres to the ESE on a former hillock in the Gulf of Morbihan a similar conjunction created the oddly-shaped cromlech of Er-Lannic North which, despite its curved south-western arc, appears to have been based on a rectangle.[32] Very relevant to this discussion of such un-British megaliths a gigantic horseshoe stood immediately to its south. Although popular in Brittany it may be that the two shapes never became widespread in Britain and Ireland because of the presence in those islands of so many stone circles.

Like Stonehenge the Breton horseshoes were assembly-places at times of festival. The huge Ménec cromlech at Carnac and the nearby cromlechs of the vanished Kermario and the spectacular Kerlescan, all three vast enclosures but hardly 3 km apart, were still used for seasonal gatherings in the last century, the winter solstice celebrated at Kerlescan, the vernal and autumnal equinoxes at Kermario, and midsummer's day at Ménec. At Stonehenge the trilithons were aligned towards the midwinter sunset.[33]

The megalithic horseshoe is supreme amongst the ruck of stones around it. Standing inside its overbearing archways one is hardly aware of the surrounding circle and, emphasising its pre-eminence and importance, it was almost certainly erected before the ring. Because of the great size of its ten uprights it would have been difficult to construct once the enclosing circle was in place.[34]

There is a caveat. The outer ring is an exact circle, a perfection difficult to achieve if the trilithons were already standing obstructively. It is feasible that the holes for the stones of the ring were dug out first with wide gaps left at Stone 11 at the precise south and, significantly at Stone 21 at the precise west where the hole is slightly out of true and with a discordant ramp which sloped upwards from inside the circle. That stone could not have been hauled upright once trilithon 57–8 was in position.

The immense pillar 56 of that trilithon may have been erected from the west. An excavation in 1956 found a long ramp running directly to Stone 56 whose base was 2.4 m deep in the ground. The pillar was possibly set up either sideways or turned when erect, perhaps to avoid existing stones of the ring. It is noticeable that every one of the circle-ramps slope in from outside except Stone 21 which slopes down from the centre of the ring.[35] Whatever the truth of the sequence of construction it is likely that for a time the great horseshoe stood alone on Salisbury Plain, solitary, awesome and alien.

It was the dominant feature of Stonehenge, the centrepiece of a ring of stones that were lintelled in imitation of the ring-beamed framework of a timber building.[36] Presumably for architectural consistency native woodworkers added unnecessary lintels to the horseshoe, forcing the uprights to be placed in closely-set pairs. Despite this, the monstrous setting remained singular and foreign.

It has to be asked why such an unexpected shape was chosen. The bizarre design had no precedent in Britain and it altered what had been traditional at Stonehenge. The orientation of the axis was changed from the long-established north-east to the novel south-west in an arrangement unlike anything else in Wessex but one which was to be the major feature of the monument. Outlandish and astonishing the horseshoe is most persuasively explained as an innovation from overseas.

The rectangle of the Four Stations has parallels with oblongs in Brittany. The U-shaped arrangement of the trilithons matches the *fer-aux-chevaux* there. The carvings at Stonehenge are unequivocal evidence of a Breton origin.

THE MEGALITHIC ART

Carvings on stone circles in Britain are northern and abstract. Except for Stonehenge no ring south of the Lake District is decorated. Art in megalithic circles is to be found mainly in Scotland where untranslatable cupmarks and cup-and-ring marks were ground out on stones standing in positions associated with the moon or sun. Such non-representational motifs are quite dissimilar from those at Stonehenge which are analogous to the formalised symbols of weaponry in Brittany.[37]

At Stonehenge there were carvings only on stones at the cardinal points of east, south and west. Near the east of the circle Stone 3 has motifs of three axes and a lattice pattern on its outer face. The meshed design is similar to the interlocking squares or 'figurines' inside the eastern passage-tomb of Mané Kerioned at Carnac. Exact east was emphasised by the cluster of axes on Stone 4. Atkinson accepted 'about a dozen' of the claimed twenty-six. The adjacent Stone 5 has one axe. The so-called 'knife-dagger' and 'torso' on Stones 23 and 29 may be no more than the result of differential weathering of the sarsens. 'In the opinion of some archaeologists both marks are of doubtful human origin'.[38]

At the south of the trilithon horseshoe the innermost side of Stone 53 bears the image of the famous dagger and fourteen or more axes. Opposite it, at the west and also facing inwards, Stone 57 carries a heavily-worn quadrilateral like 'an old-fashioned tea-cosy', first recognised by Newall in 1953 and likened by Atkinson to the rectangular anthropomorphs of Brittany, 'a cult figure, possibly a mother-goddess'. 'Its appearance at Stonehenge provides one more link between Wessex and the Breton peninsula'. There seems to be a smaller replica below it. A very weathered third

Plate 47 The rectangle on Stone 57. The 'Charlie Chaplin' axe can be seen just above it.

rectangle was recognised in 1958 on the underside of the fallen Stone 120, the lintel of Stones 19–20 directly behind trilithon 57–8.[39]

The rectangle on Stone 57 seems to have a small loop like an inverted U on its upper edge and this has been compared with cognate 'heads' on many Breton carvings. Careful inspection, however, suggests that the 'carving' may be a natural fissure that the mason integrated with his own carving. The loop is not as neatly-shaped and defined as the rectangle, it is not symmetrically placed at the centre of the top line as all Breton examples are, it is not continuous, and its right-hand end stops short of the figurine whereas the left side passes through the rectangle's rim and runs deeply down to a large solution hole in the left-hand corner of the carving. There is an identical, and natural, 'loop' inside the rectangle's top righthand corner. Prudence demands that only the rectangle should be accepted as man-made.

Such 'rectangles', once termed *boucliers* (shields) or *marmites* (cooking-pots), are now accepted as anthropomorphic symbols carved on stelae in early Breton passage-tombs such as Barnenez, Ile Guennoc, Ty-ar-Boudiquet at Brennilis, and Kercado. They occur on a score of slabs inside chambered tombs and on five menhirs (Fig. 24). The images were not restricted to the earliest Neolithic passage-tombs, *dolmens à couloir*, but were still being produced up to the inception of the Bronze Age. 'There is undeniable evidence of some sort of cult of a figure in the late neolithic of western Europe, and that figure is usually female. There is no doubt that interest in this figure is evidenced on the walls of megalithic tombs in northern France'.[40]

The shape is believed to be the formalised body of a female guardian of the dead, a weapon-bearing protectress often juxtaposed against an axe of stone or metal or a bronze dagger. The figure is sometimes a simple square or a square with a rounded top portraying a head like the rectangle on Stone 25 of the magnificently ornamented passage-tomb of Gavr'inis which is so clear that it has been termed 'la déesse en écusson'.[41] Alternatively, a square might have a central indentation in imitation of the necklaces carved below pairs of rounded breasts in high-relief in *allées-couvertes*

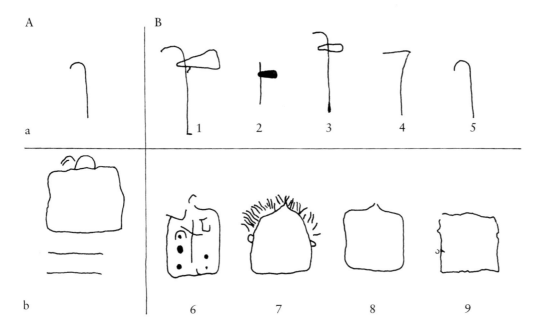

Fig. 24 Some carvings of axes and anthropomorphs on Breton megaliths. A.a. the Stonehenge carving of a shafted axe; A.b. the anthropomorphic rectangle (from Castleden, 1993). B. some Breton carvings: 1–5, axes: 1. Mané Kerioned East; 2. Barnenez; 3. Mougau-Bihan; 4. Mané Kerioned East; 5. Mané Lud. 6–9, anthropomorphs: 6. Les Pierres-Plates; 7. Ile Longue; 8. Ile Longue; 9. Mané Bras.

like Prajou-Menhir and Kerguntüil. Some have 'handles' halfway down their sides, presumably arms, and inside many of the outlines, as at Les Pierres-Plates, are incised circles representing breasts.

They exist on menhirs like St Samson-sur-Rance, in the tombs of megalithic passage-tombs and *allées-couvertes*, and, significantly, on cromlechs and horseshoes such as Er-Lannic and Tossen-Keler. Axe-carvings exist at Tossen-Keler, Kergonan and Er-Lannic. No daggers are known on the horseshoes in Brittany but they do occur in conjunction with anthropomorphs or with 'breasts' in *allées-couvertes* on the north coast such as Mougau-Bihan and Kerguntüil, tombs whose floruit of 3100 to 2100 BC overlapped the sarsen phase of Stonehenge, *c.* 2850–2480 BC. There are also simple rectangles without loops at the passage-tombs of Mané Bras and Penhap, and at the *allée-coudées* of Goërem, Gâvres and Les Pierres-Plates. There are whole series of conjoined, plain squares at Kercado and Mané Kerioned.

Perhaps the closest example in time, space and associations to the art at Stonehenge occurs in the Early Bronze Age *allée-couverte* of Prajou-Menhir near Lannion, Côtes-du-Nord, in whose vicinity so much Armorican gold and weaponry have been found. There, in a cramped terminal cell, were carvings of paired rectangles surmounted by handled daggers and a possible axe. Confirming the female symbolism of these motifs pairs of embossed breasts were contained in adjacent cartouches. The simple rectangles, the axe, the daggers duplicate the art at Stonehenge with only the English Channel and a few land-miles between them.[42]

Doubts have been expressed about the interpretation of the rectangle on Stone 57 suggesting that the carving may have been 'executed by a late visitor, perhaps even after the collapse of the stone in 1797, who wished to leave a commemorative inscription in a prepared panel'.[43]

There is no inscription and practical considerations argue against the idea of a recent date. Sarsen is intractable. To grind out a panel 114 cm square and at least 1 cm deep was an exercise in tedium. Atkinson calculated that it would have taken a man a fortnight. E. H. Stone reckoned that a worker could remove 74 cm^3 in an hour. Even labouring non-stop ten hours a day a man would have taken almost three weeks to scrape, pound and polish the minimum of 13,000 cm³ of the rectangle. It is unlikely that the 'graffitist', even if exhausted, would then have failed to add his name.[44]

There have been other criticisms of the interpretation of the rectangle as an anthropomorph. While admitting that 'there are no similar British examples' an ingenious alternative proposed that the carving with its attached loop might portray a Stonehenge sarsen, maybe even trilithon 57 itself, 'and the rounded projection in the middle of the upper side a representation of the tenon'.[45] It is plausible and possible especially as the inward-sloping 'shoulders' of the rectangle do have a similarity to the entasis-like inverted triangles between the tops of the trilithon archways.[46]

Feasible though it is supporters of this explanation must satisfy substantial objections. It has already been noted that the 'loop' is probably a natural fissure in the stone. Secondly, whether the carving is an anthropomorph or a silhouetted sarsen it is still a form of representational art inimical to British abstract styles. It was also pecked and ground out on a pillar that was set at the cardinal point of west. Presumably the situation was deliberately chosen, intended to create a balanced symmetry with the dagger and axes on the trilithon at the south, and the axes at the east. Finally, there is at least one other 'anthropomorph at Stonehenge, exposed on the fallen lintel 120. Its gentle loop does echo the 'heads' of Breton figurines but is the feeblest depiction of a Stonehenge tenon.[47]

The authenticity of the 'rectangle' as an anthropomorph is confirmed conclusively not only by its close likeness to those known in prehistoric contexts in Brittany but also by the proximity of the 'crook' just above it. In Brittany some handled stone axes known as *houlettes*, 'shepherds' crooks', were economically carved as a simple shaft with a curved head but no axe-blade, in outline resembling Charlie Chaplin's walking stick. One was carved on Stone 57. Stylised axes and 'goddesses' were frequently set together, protectress and weapon, in tombs such as Mané Lud, Table des Marchands, Petit Mont, Grah Niaul and Pierres-Plates and their conjunction at Stonehenge is another reflection of that monument's Breton origins.[48]

The trilithon carvings at Stonehenge were planned as a composition. For a devotee inside the horseshoe, facing the south-west, the weapons of a dagger and axes on Stone 53 were to his left. To the right were the anthropomorphs and it is not sacrilegious to regard them in the same way as the crucifix is visualised by Christians today, as personified symbols of holiness. Enhancing this impression of sacred space, redolent of life, death, fertility and sunset, the skeuomorph of a chalk axe was recovered from the ramp of Stone 56 alongside the rectangle and a chalk phallus was found close to Stone 57 itself.[49]

With carvings of weapons and figurines on either side of him a suppliant would have faced what today is an almost unremarked, unconsidered Breton connection at Stonehenge, the Altar Stone. This 5 m long sandstone pillar now lies half-buried beneath the bulk of the fallen Trilithon 55 but originally it stood erect near the centre of the circle. In 1802 Cunnington may have found its stonehole.[50] The pillar has been regarded as the embodiment of the guardian of the dead.

There are, or were, other 'central' stones in Wiltshire: the destroyed 'Obelisk' inside Avebury's southern circle; perhaps one also at Winterbourne Bassett; another at Tisbury. In Britain the major concentration of such pillars is southern and, almost predictably, close to the sea, some in Cornwall, a dozen in the Irish south-western counties of Cork and Kerry. Such internal stones are rare elsewhere in these islands[51] but are well-known in the north and west of Brittany where they stand inside the

Plate 48 A carving of a dagger with an axe to its right below graffiti on Stone 53.

Plate 49 The anthropomorphic carving of breasts and a necklace inside the *allée-couverte* of Crech-Quillé, Brittany.

chambers of passage-tombs such as Ile Guennoc, Barnenez and Ty-ar-Boudiquet. These free-standing pillars are considered to be megalithic versions of the female guardian of the dead, an interpretation entirely explicit at the slab with carved breasts and necklace standing at the junction of passage and burial-chamber in the *allée-couverte* of Crech-Quillé near the north coast of the Côtes-du-Nord.

In Britain 'protectresses' also occur, memorably in yet another maritime context, on the island of Anglesey where the chamber of the Bryn Celli Ddu passage-tomb contains an isolated pillar described as 'unique in the British Isles. It might perhaps be compared to some of the decorated menhirs in Brittany'.[52] At a nearby passage-tomb, Barclodiad y Gawres, 'the apronful of the goddess', Stone 22 at the juncture of passage and chamber 'is a tall stone with the entire front surface decorated with a well-organised design which could be interpreted anthropologically'. The carving is so striking that it has been termed a representation 'of the Mother Goddess herself watching over the dead'.[53] Such examples create a persuasive Breton origin and sepulchral function for the Altar Stone at Stonehenge, an awesome personification of the power of death, the centrepiece of a sacred horseshoe of colossal sarsens upon whose sides images of the protectress of the dead merged with the setting of the midwinter sun behind the Altar Stone at the darkening death of the year.

CONCLUSIONS

The architectural and artistic evidence strongly supports the belief that the sarsen phase of Stonehenge was designed in a Breton style, possibly by Bretons themselves. The geometry and astronomy of the Four Stations has many parallels in Brittany but few in Britain. The trilithon horseshoe is even more compelling proof because British counterparts are hundreds of miles from Stonehenge whereas such settings are more numerous and much nearer in Brittany. The grading of the horseshoe towards an astronomical event, the midwinter sunset, is analogous to the aligned and graded *fer-aux-chevaux* of Tossen-Keler, Kergonan and others. The repertoire of representational art: anthropomorphs, axes, dagger and 'crook' has its only source in Brittany. The Altar Stone appears more Breton than British.

The entire design of the final Stonehenge was foreign, revolutionary, and inimical to indigenous styles. It may well have been the handiwork of intrusive and powerful leaders from Brittany. When Cato Worsfold wrote *The French Stonehenge* in 1898 his title may have been more appropriate than he realised.

Stuart Piggott's prophetic words so many years ago are remarkable.

We have indeed no option but to regard the Wessex Culture as the result of an invasion from Brittany. By invasion we do not visualise bloody battles in which Breton warriors with grooved daggers ended the lives of archaeologically decadent but stubbornly British beaker-folk . . . Nevertheless it was more than the entry of a boatload of traders. If not a military conquest, it was at least an annexation . . . a dominant and intrusive aristocracy who for some centuries at least lorded it over the native element.[54]

And built Stonehenge?

GAZETTEER TO CHAPTER TEN

*Indicates an uncertain site

RECTANGLES

England

1 King Arthur's Hall, Cornwall; (3) SX 130 776. Johnson and Rose, plan, 28, 29.

2 Stonehenge. Station Stones, Wiltshire; (3); SU 122 422. Petrie, 1880, plan, 37.

Brittany

3 Landaoudec, Finistère; (4); 2 km N of Crozon. Pontois, 115–16, sketchplan, 116.

4 Lanvéoc, Finistère; (4); 5 km NNE of Crozon. Giot 1960, 120.

5 *Parc-ar-Varret, Finistère; (3); 1 km NNW of Porspoder. Gilbert 1962, 224, no. 15.

6 Phare du Créach, Ushant; (4); 2$^{1}/_{2}$ km W of Lampaul. Giot *et al.*, 1979, 410.

7 Ty-ar-c'Huré, Crozon, Finistère; (4); 1 km SE of Morgat. Pontois 1929, 98, 115, 117.

8 *Cordon des Druides, Ille-et-Vilaine; (5); 5 km NNE of Fougères. Gilbert 1962, 220–1, no. 6.

9 Crucuno, Morbihan; (2); 3 km NNW of Plouharnel. Thom *et al.*, 1973, 450–4, plan, 451.

10 Er-Lannic North, Gulf of Morbihan; (3); 2 km S of Larmor-Baden. Le Rouzic, 1930, plan, 4.

11 *Jardin aux Moines, Brocéliande Forest, Morbihan; (2, 5); 2$^{1}/_{2}$ km ENE of Néant-sur-Yvel. Briard 1989, 41–56, plan, 43.

12 *Narbon, Le, Morbihan (4) 1$^{1}/_{2}$ km SSW of Erdeven. Sherratt, 1998, 132.

HORSESHOES

England

13 Arminghall, Norfolk; (4) TG 240 060. *PPS 2*, 1936, 1–51, plan, 6.

14 *Avebury North, Wiltshire; (5) SU 103 699. Ucko *et al.*, 224–7, plan, 225.

15 *East Moor, Cornwall; (5); SX 222 778. Johnson and Rose, 29.

16 Stonehenge, Wiltshire; (2); SU 122 422. Petrie 1880, plan, 37.

Scotland

17 Achavanich, Caithness; (1); ND 188 417. *RCAHM-Caithness*, 1911, no. 293, plan.

18 Broubster, Caithness; (3); ND 048 608. *RCAHM-Caithness*, 1911, no. 163, plan.

19 Cowiemuir, Moray; (4); NJ 371 631. *PSAS 40*, 1905–6, 192–4, plan, 192.

20 Croft Moraig, Perthshire; (2); NN 797 472. *PPS 37*, 1971, 1–15, plan, 14.

21 Haerstanes, Moray; (4); *c.* NJ 27. 60. *PSAS 40*, 1905–6, 204.

22 *Latheronwheel, Caithness; (4); *c.* ND 179 342. *Trans Inverness Sci Soc 7*, 1915, 343.

23 Machrie Moor I, Arran (4); NS 912 324. *PSAS 121*, 1991, 61, plan.

Ireland

24 Lugg, County Dublin; (4); O 032 246; *PRIA 53C*, 1950, 311–32, plan, Plate XXXIII.

Brittany

25 Château-Bû, Ille-et-Vilaine (3); 15 km NE of Redon. Burl, 1995, 252, no. 354.

26 *Pédernec, Côtes-du-Nord; (4); 12 km WSW of Guingamp. Gilbert 1962, 201–3.

27 Tossen-Keler, Côtes-du-Nord; (2); originally just W of the Château d'Eau, 13 km NE of Lannion. Now at Tréguier, 18 km ENE of Lannion. *L'Anthropologie 72*, 1968, 5–40, plan, 12–13.

28 Lagatjar, Finistère; (2); 9 km WNW of Crozon. Pontois, 110, plan.

29 Landaoudec, Finistère; (4); 2 km N of Crozon. Pontois, 115–16, plan, 116.

30 Pen-ar-Land, Isle of Ushant, Finistère; (2); 3 km ENE of Lampaul. Briard 1990, 50–1, plan.

31 Ty-ar c'Huré, Finistère (4); 3 km SSW of Crozon. Pontois, 1929, 115.

32 Tribunal, Le, St Just, Ille-et-Vilaine; (1); Briard, 1990, 57.

33 Champ de la Croix, Crucuny, Morbihan; (2); 4 km N of Carnac-Ville. Thom and Thom 1978, 119–20, plan.

34 Er-Lannic South, Gulf of Morbihan; (4); contiguous with Er-Lannic N (no. 10). Le Rouzic 1930, planche 1.

35 Grand Rohu, Arzon, Morbihan; (4); 6 km W of Sarzeau. Merlet 1974, 26–9, 31, plan, 29.

36 *Graniol, Pen Hap, Morbihan; (4); $9^1/_2$ km WNW of Sarzeau. Merlet 1974, 19–20, plan.

37 *Kerbourgnec, St Pierre-Quiberon, Morbihan; (3); 4 km N of Quiberon. Thom and Thom 1977, 7, 22; 1978, 20–1, plan.

38 Kergonan, Ile-aux-Moines, Morbihan; (1); $1^1/_4$ km S of landing-stage. Merlet 1974, 7–19, 34, plan, 9.

39 Kerlescan North, Morbihan; (4); $3^1/_4$ km NE of Carnac-Ville. Thom and Thom 1978, 92–6, plan, 96.

40 Kerlescan South, Morbihan; (1); 100 m S of Kerlescan North. Thom and Thom 1978, 92–7, plans 93, 94.

41 Kermario East, Morbihan; (4); $2^1/_2$ km NE of Carnac-Ville. Giot 1960, 123.

42 Kerzerho, Morbihan; (4); 1 km SE of Erdeven. Gilbert, 1962, 229.

43 Ste. Barbe, Morbihan; (4); 1.7 km WNW of Plouharnel. Lukis 1875, 26.

PART THREE

The Making of a Stone Circle

Plate 50 *(previous pages)* A view from Scafell towards the lowlands.

Plate 51 *(above)* Swinside from the west.

Chapter Eleven

Swinside, Cumbria

STONE CIRCLE, STONE AXE AND SUNRISE

In the neighbourhood of Millum, at a place called Swinside, in the estate of William Lewthwaite, Esq, of Whitehaven, is a small but beautiful druidical monument; it is circular, about twenty yards in diameter; the stones of which it is composed are from six to eight feet high, all standing and complete. A little to the south, is another of larger dimensions, but not in so perfect a state: the neighbouring people call those places by the emphatical names of Sunken Kirks.

William Hutchinson, *A History of Cumberland*, 1794, 529.

THE FACTS

Swinside is one of the finest of all stone circles. It stands in fortunate, almost unmolested loneliness at the south-west corner of the Lake District five miles north of Millom and twenty-three miles ssw of the famous stone circle of Castlerigg at Keswick, separated from it by the Langdale mountains (Fig. 25). Being so out of the way neither Aubrey nor Stukeley knew of it. It was first mentioned by Hutchinson in 1794 and did not appear in Camden's *Britannia* until 1806. 'Being in a remote and unfrequented corner of the district, these remains have received little attention'.[1]

South-west Cumbria is a low-lying tract of limestones, good for farming but cut off from the major region of the Lake District by the Scafell range and by the long mountain of Black Combe three miles to the south-west of Swinside 'and the sense of cultural isolation of the region from the north is embodied in the old Furness saying, "Nowt good ever came round Black Combe"'.[2] Yet it had charms.

It is said that the crest of the mountain offered more expansive views than any other upland in England. Wordsworth, nudging the banal, marvelled at the prospect.

> This Height a ministering angel might select,
> For from the summit of BLACK COMB (dread name
> Derived from clouds and storms!) the amplest range
> Of unobstructed prospect may be seen
> That British ground commands . . .
>
> *View from the Top of Black Comb*, 1813

There has been better poetry and the mountain deserved better.

Superstition had it that Black Combe was a magical place. Bees hibernating in its heathered slopes were said to awaken and hum melodiously on Christmas Eve. More menacingly, Black Combe was the habitation of a heathen spirit, Hob Thross, 'rough body', who demanded thickly buttered porridge in return for undertaking menial tasks

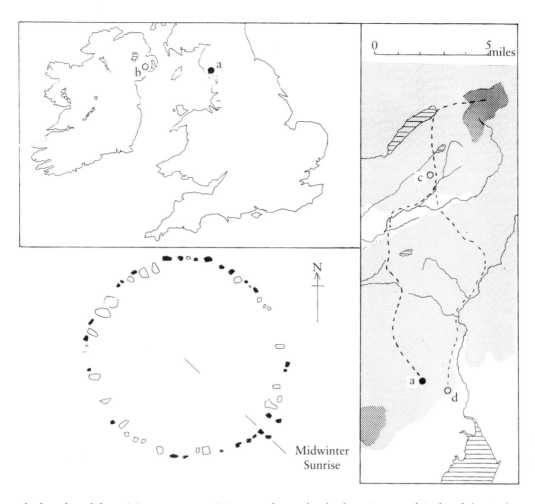

N

Midwinter
Sunrise

Fig. 25 Map and plan of Swinside stone circle, Cumbria. a. Swinside; b. Ballynoe; c. Brats Hill; d. Ash House Wood; e. Scafell; f. Wastwater; g. Black Combe; h. Duddon Sands.

before breakfast. More potent spirits may have dwelt there in people's fearful minds when Swinside was being erected.

The circle stands in a swampy meadow at a height of 204 m 'surrounded by mountains of a dreary aspect'. Raven Crag is just to the west. To the north-east are the craggy peaks of Dunnerdale Fells. Sombre heights hiding Wrayslack, 'the secluded valley', rise to the east where, between the ring and its encircling uplands, the Black Beck flows smoothly southwards before twisting and turning abruptly east to the waters of the Duddon Sands three miles south of Swinside.

The name derives unromantically from *Swinesat* and *Swynesheud*, the summer pasture for pigs. Less prosaic is the legend that the stones cannot be counted although this belief in universal innumeracy dates only from the present century. A much older story explained that the alternative name for the circle, Sunken Kirk, was a venerable memory of the time when a Christian church was being erected only for the Devil to drag the stones down into the earth every night until, in despair, the builders abandoned the project leaving only the tops of the columns jutting from the ground.

Wordsworth, minimally more poetical than at Black Combe, saw the result.

> That mystic Round of Druid frame
> Tardily sinking by its proper weight
> Deep into patient Earth, from whose smooth breast it came!
> *The River Duddon, Sonnet XVII, Return*, 1820

There were other submerged churches in Britain. There is Chapel o'Sink in Aberdeenshire and, supposedly, there was a second ring nearby at Tofthills 'where not a stone remains and the absence is accounted for by the story that the spirits have caused the circle to sink underground'. There was a natural rock between Sancliff and Coningsby in Lincolnshire reputed to be the site of an engulfed church. Twenty-five miles to the south there was another lost temple near Ickleton, Cambridgeshire.[3]

Unlike these mythical disappearances Swinside has not vanished and Dymond made a good survey of the site in April 1872, undertaking an equally meticulous plan of Stanton Drew 200 miles to the south in the same Spring. In 1877, he returned to Swinside to add useful details of the heights and breadths of the stones. The ring is a true circle about 28.6 m in diameter. Of a possible original 64 stones some 54 remain, 28 still standing, quite closely set about 1.5 m apart. The tallest, a tapering pillar 2.3 m high stands close to true North. Opposite it is a broad slab, 1.8 m in height, that was split by a rowan tree years ago. The tree has withered into death leaving the stone with a deep vertical crack as witness to its Pyrrhic victory. At the south-east of the ring is an entrance composed of two circle-stones and a pair of outlying portals.[4]

The circle was surrounded by a buttress or rude pavement of smaller stones, raised about half a yard from the surface of the earth and providing support for the shallow-set stones.[5] Sheep sheltering by them from the weather created hollows that caused several stones to collapse and the fact that they have all toppled inwards implies that they originally stood at the inner edge of the bank which eighteenth- and nineteenth-century ploughing reduced to today's inconspicuous state. There are wide gaps at the ENE and WSW suggesting that stones had been removed from the circle to allow access with a plough or a mowing-machine. In his excavation Dymond noticed that the sub-soil was very irregular, perhaps a second indication that the interior had been disturbed by agricultural activity.[6]

The ring was partly-excavated by Dymond, Collingwood and three men from mid-day Tuesday, 26 March 1901 until the close of the following evening. They dug two long, intersecting 46 cm-wide trenches, NW–SE, NE–SW, across the ring with a curious zig-zagging pattern of others between south-east and south-west, an investigation of some 51 m² of the central area. Within the circle the trenches represented less than a thirteenth of the 642 m² of the interior.

Below the grass and turf was a thin layer of soil under which yellowish marl or 'pin-nel' varied from 15 cm to 75 cm in depth, being deepest at the entrance which had been dug into earlier around 1850. Wherever it was uncovered the gravelly marl was wavily uneven, presumably the result of ploughing. The bases of the circle-stones rested on the pinnel, held firmly in their holes by small cobbles with others heavily packed around the sides. The only finds were a nut-sized lump of charcoal just north-east of the centre with others near the entrance, a minute splinter of decayed bone near the first bit of charcoal and two pieces of red stone. There were also some contemporary glazed sherds and a Lancaster halfpenny dated between 1789 and 1794 lying in the uppermost turf layer.[7]

Unrecorded by Dymond there are possible outlying features at Swinside. About a quarter of a mile from the south-east of the ring is a prostrate slab 1.5 m long with an apparently shaped base. What look like packing stones lie around it. As there are similar stones in its vicinity they may be the fallen relics of a series of trackway markers leading to the Duddon Sands.

Near Swinside were other stone circles. 'Many Druidical circles exist in this district', wrote Hutchinson but they have been destroyed and they were coastal, standing on the far side of the fells from Swinside. At Annaside a little to the south-east of Gutterby and some six miles south-west of Swinside beyond Black Combe there had been a ring of twelve stones in a circle about 12 m across. All that remains is one huge but badly battered boulder 1.37 m high and 3 m wide, too big to break and cart away. Less than a mile to the south-east and five miles south-west of Swinside was the now-destroyed Kirkstones whose thirty stones once formed two concentric circles. A mile to the north-east at Hall Foss, just north of *Stangrah* or Grey Stones Farm, 'are the remains of a druidical monument, called the *Standing Stones*, forming a circle of 25 yards [23 m] diameter, consisting of eight massy rude columns; some have lately been broken, and taken away'.[8] Not one remains. The three rings stood at the corners of an almost perfect isosceles triangle three-quarters of a mile wide and a mile long. Little survives. Only one circle, at Ash House Wood, was close to Swinside, a mile to its south-east.

Dymond puzzled over Swinside. 'Whatever may have been the purpose for which some other structures of this class were set up, 'Sunken Kirk' must have been destined to be a *locus consecratus*, not necessarily connected with sepulture, but devoted to certain ceremonial observances'.[9] Restrained speculation over the known facts about the ring and its environment can introduce some humanity.

A RECONSTRUCTION

Five thousand or more years ago, two hundred brief generations, a party of men, stocky, strong-muscled from living in the strenuous fells, left the settlement of huts and cattle stockades that huddled together in the shelter of the hillsides. It was early autumn. Already the crooked, bulky oaks were losing their leaves, those of alders were darkening and on the evergreen junipers purple-black berries were ripening.

The men looked to the sky for signs. People's existence was shaped by the inhuman and wanton forces there that sent storms or quiet rain, gales or still days, snow or warm sunlight. From a stone circle, open to the sky, men could manipulate those forces through rituals that brought peace and averted misfortune.

Above the trees and bushes, above the crowding hills, dark-brown buzzards circled for hours, flying low above the moors. Eagles soared lazily. Coal-black ravens, omens of disaster, tipped their wide wings, turned sideways, rolled over, croaked and rattled in melodramatic acrobatics to attract their mates. Had one landed in front of the men the party would have turned back.

Over their heads the clouds were thickening as autumnal rains warned of the coming winter. Cool winds bent the grasses as the party went to the hillsides to choose stones for their intended circle. Physical and psychological demands decided the place for it. It should be near the settlement but hidden from it, often on previously cultivated ground that had proved to be fertile. It had to be close to suitable stones, situated not far from water, a river, stream or spring, standing amongst a fastidiously selected skyline of hills. There were three to the north at NNE, north-east and ENE. Black Combe was due south-west.[10]

While some men went on the short walk to the stone-littered slopes of Raven Crags others began hacking into the slight slope with wooden levers, antler picks and cattle shoulder-blades as scrapers, fashioning a level platform, cutting into the higher soil at the west, heaping up cobbles at the lower east. The shelf-like arenas of other great circles were as carefully prepared. Some, like Ash House Wood, were within walking distance of Swinside. Others were far away. Ballynoe was on the other side of the Irish Sea. But there was a cultural blueprint to these rings, circular, spacious, many-stoned, flat, with distinctive entrances. These were the long-established fashions of their region.

There were times when nothing could be done, when the skies were bloated with surly clouds whose days of rain left cattle standing hoof-deep in mud. But at last the area was cleared of littered stones. The turf was stripped. From a central point a circle was scratched and gouged out in the bared earth using a local unit of measurement, a 'Cumbrian Yard' of about 0.794 m, perhaps based on the stride of some long-dead ancestor. For any distance longer than 5 m it is arguable that the Yard was multiplied by three to make a more practical 'Rod' of 2.38 m.

There are inbuilt problems in modern attempts to determine such lengths, not the least being the inability of today's surveyors to be sure that their calculated diameter of a ring is the one intended by the builders as they laid a succession of rods over lumpish soil to a neat point that became the 'centre' of a roughly-dug stonehole. And there were prehistoric errors. Imprecise reproduction after reproduction of the original yardstick led to trivial variations in the measure for other groups but Swinside's, like the others, was one unique to the Lake District, not a crude approximation of an unrelated 'foreign' unit of measurement.

Paradoxically, it is the recognition of different, strictly parochial measurements elsewhere, a Perth Yard of 0.96 m in central Scotland, a Beaker Yard of 0.73 m at Woodhenge and Stonehenge, a Cork Yard of 0.95 m in south-west Ireland, that gives unconscious support to the belief that societies in Late Neolithic and Early Bronze Age Britain and Ireland used such variable local measuring-lengths for their structures.[11]

The people could count. In the Lake District they computed in fours, the number of Rods in the stone circles demonstrating this, being laid out in multiples and halves of that number: 40 for the long diameter of Brats Hill whose yardstick of 0.8 m was only 6 mm longer than Swinside's; 42 for Castlerigg with an error of −1 mm; 42 for Elva Plain, a +4 mm discrepancy; 136 for the immensity of Long Meg and Her Daughters, unsurprisingly erring by +2.16 cm; 42 for Studfold, −1.3 cm; and 36 for Swinside, the last being an exact multiple of 0.794 m. Given the uncertainties implicit in these dimensions it is remarkable how minimal the divergences were. Which of the rings was planned with the original yardstick will probably never be known.

Hole after deepish hole was dug, the perfect circle divided into equal quadrants by four markers at the north, east, south and west. It was symbolism. There was no Pole Star to guide those planning the ring. Nor did they have any interest in establishing exact cardinal points as the imprecision of their 'north' shows, being 3° to 4° away from the meridional north-south line.[12]

The sun was the cause. From compulsions beyond our understanding, being incapable of entering their animistic image of the world in which every natural thing, rock, tree, river, rainbow, had life, the builders of Swinside integrated the design of their circle with the direction halfway between the midsummer sunrise at the north-east and the midsummer sunset at the north-west. They erected the tallest stone there.

Had the northern skyline been flat the position would have been at the True North. It was not. Nature seldom provides level horizons on dry land and it did not at Swinside. There the immediate north-eastern hills are much higher than the distant slopes of Corney Fell to the north-west, delaying the emergence of the midsummer sunrise, and this uneven topography caused the observed 'midpoint' to be shifted to the east of True North. It was certainly to the north that the observers looked rather than to the south and the midwinter sunrise and sunset. The looming height of Black Combe at the south-west dominated the horizon, pushing the 'south' well to the east whereas the southernmost block was positioned a little to the west.

Stone after stone was brought to the circle, a mixture of glaciated granites and many local porphyritic slates or 'grey cobbles'. Averaging 2 m in length and about 5 tons in weight they were roped on to sturdily-built sledges and dragged along a portable 'railway' of long timbers, pairs of bark-stripped tree-trunks being lifted after the load had passed and carried forward to extend the moveable track closer and closer to the site. Stoutly meshed cables of leather with a breaking strain of a third of a ton were hauled by teams of workers. A score of men could pull the lashed stone with others attending to the rails.

As the stones reached the prepared, firmly-trampled platform workers were ready to erect them. With the heaviest slab no more than about six tons in weight it demanded the organisation of skilled teams but not gangs in their hundreds. At its most critical angle, almost but not quite upright, the pillar had a dead weight of some 2700 lb. For a short while a well-built man could exercise a pull of 100 lb. With two dozen or so labourers on the ropes and a few others propping heavy wedges behind to prevent the block falling backwards a gang of thirty could accomplish the task.

There were many stones in the ring, closely-grouped, almost shoulder to shoulder in crude imitation of the unbroken banks of henges in eastern England. The existence and appearance of those earthen enclosures were known to the occupants of Swinside because the strangers who raised those earthworks came year by year to the Lake District to obtain precious axes shaped from the tough, almost unbreakable stone of the mountains.

Calculations indicate that there may have been as many as sixty-four stones at Swinside, sixteen in each quadrant. Although there are gaps today there is still a good run of stones between north-west and north-east where, with the inclusion of a missing stone whose hole has been detected, sixteen would have stood. There is a similar persuasive arc between east and south. With the postulated counting-system of 4 used by the designers of Swinside four sets of sixteen, ($[4 + 4 + 4 + 4] \times 4$), would be plausible.

Most of the stones are flat-topped, varying unsystematically in height, but five are sharply peaked, one at the north and, perhaps significantly, four near the collateral points of north-east, south-east, south-west and north-west where the tiniest, a neat triangle, is no more than 3 m high. The tallest is the peaked pillar at the north. Despite its height it is elegantly slender. It tapers. Facing it at the south, is the broad block, heavy, thick, flat-topped.

Completing this finely-arranged, lovely stone circle a well-defined entrance was constructed at the south-east where adjacent circle-stones 2.1 m apart had two portal-stones set up a metre outside them forming an impressive, rectangular portico through which celebrants would pass to enter the circle for their seasonal rituals.

The people who planned the circle had not been limited by space when deciding on the size of the ring and they designed an enclosure of 640 m² that was spacious enough but not over-large for its participants. Setting aside the northern half of the ring for those performing the rituals, and allowing a comfortable 2.6 m² of outstretched arms for each of the onlookers Swinside could have accommodated a congregation of well over a hundred. This is far more than the number of workers needed to build the ring and implies that women as well as men, possibly even strangers, took part in the ceremonies. The new circle was an unroofed enclosure, open to the sky, the means of communication with the forces of nature whose caprices could endanger life. The air, not the earth, was their home and it was to the sky that the people appealed.

Like the crucifix, the chalice and the pyx, sacramental articles of the Christian church, the stone axe, symbol of life and death, was central to the activities. Its manufacture on the mountain of Scafell Pike twelve miles to the north was one of the reasons for building Swinside. Swinside stood at the south-western end of one of two mountainous routes from Scafell Pike at the heart of the Langdales and one of its functions was to be an entrepôt and staging-post for the distribution of stone axes to the Furness peninsula some miles to the south and, more adventurously, to north-eastern Ireland.[13] Close to the ring but lying on a different route from the mountains, was the supposedly contemporary and architecturally similar stone circle of Ash House Wood overlooking the waters of the Duddon Sands. From that bay a tortuous channel flowed into the Irish Sea.

Furness with its fells, fertile soils and patchwork of farmsteads was an important centre for Swinside. A high proportion of roughout axes have been found there, a much greater concentration than elsewhere in Cumbria. Three or four have been recorded in the vicinity of Shap and the Stainmore Gap that provided a route to eastern England. Ten came from the settlement of Ehenside Tarn on the west coast near Egremont.[14] But many more lay five miles south-west of Swinside in the neighbourhood of Kirksanton with its standing stones, burial chamber and the Bronze Age stone circles of Lacra on Great Knott. Over thirty, both roughouts and well-finished polished axes, were discovered further south on the Furness peninsula with its tarns, becks and rich earths that attracted Neolithic settlers as the 'Yorkshire' chambered tomb of Skelmore Heads near Ulverston and the stone circle of the Druid's Temple on Birkrigg Common show.[15]

Southern Furness with its scatter of axes is a devious fifteen miles from Swinside but only six south-west of the Druid's Temple and 'the circles and the axes thus hang together and seem to demand explanation as the relics of a single people'. There are no stone circles on the peninsula south of the Druid's Temple and Collingwood wondered whether there had not been rings of timber there. 'Its heavier soil and scantier stone would make this not unlikely'.[16] It was feasible. Less than twenty-five miles to the south-east in an equally stoneless countryside there was an indisputable prehistoric ring of birch poles and oak posts at Bleasdale near Garstang in Lancashire. It is sadly neglected.

The Furness region was the last stage of a series of portages on foot and by water from Scafell Pike to the shelter of the lower Hollow Stones, on to the stone circle of Brats Hill on Burn Moor, further miles to Swinside, perhaps then on to the Druid's

Plate 52 Scree slopes on Scafell, the source of the axes.

Temple, ending on the south-west coast of Furness at the ten-mile-long beaches of Walney Island, 'the haunt of dolphins', raucous with the screeches of thousands of large and brutally murderous black-backed gulls gliding smoothly from their nests of matted seaweed and grass in a perpetual search for fish, frogs, carrion.

Late Neolithic pottery, including a grooved ware sherd, have been recovered on the island at temporary settlements such as North End and Hillock Whinns with its many scores of flint tools. Cow Leys Scar at the south had both flint and stone axes. It could well have been at such places with their abundance of abrasive sand and water that the roughout axes were given their final treatment, gracefully shaped and polished before some of them were loaded into boats to send them to Ireland.[17]

It was only twenty-five direct miles from Scafell Pike to south Furness. In reality, traversing scree-slopes, clambering fell-sides, following the easiest contours, using rivers that curled around impeding hills, crossing moors, passing the half-buried bones of animals killed by wolves, sheltering wearily, resting at each stone circle, the journey was twice that distance and probably four times that number of days.

For centuries men had been exploiting the good stone in the mountains of the Lake District for their heavy, thin-butted axes, first simply picking out shattered pieces from the scree-slopes, later digging out shallow pits, loosening the rocks with fire. There were two major sources, Great Langdale and Scafell. In the Langdales there were 'factories' at the Pike of Stickle, at Harrison's Pike, and others such as the northernmost, Thunacar Knott, which lay at the beginning of a vertiginous descent by High Raise, Greenup Gill and Stonethwaite Beck to Borrowdale, Derwent Water, present-day Keswick and the Castlerigg stone circle from which central staging-post the axes could be carried to the north-west and to the east. Scafell Pike, four miles to the west of the Langdales was better placed for the passes that led to the west coast and the south.

It is not known how the miners regarded the mountains, whether as mundane quarries or as deistic bodies making gifts of stone to the mortals that came to them. There are hints. Even where there were safe seams to be worked other dangerous overhangs and gullies were exploited. 'The mechanical properties of the rock were little different

Plate 53 A view of the mountains from the lowlands.

from those in other parts of the complex, yet it seems that those making the axes sought out especially inaccessible locations'.[18] Extracted from those situations with their spectacular views such difficult, almost unobtainable material may have been peculiarly special, embodying the power of the mountain in its uniqueness. An axe made from it may never have been used as a tool.

The land was friendless, implacable. Men had died there. Except for the moans of wind against the rocks and boulders it was a silent world. And almost empty. Until the late autumn and the trills of returning snow buntings there was only the noiseless flight of a lonely ring ouzel to break the blandness of the sky. But sometimes behind the bird came a powerful peregrine falcon, speckled like chain-mail, hurtling towards its victim, stopping, dropping like a deadly stone, down and under the soft underbelly, talons tearing. The strength and speed of the bird, its ruthlessness, made its slate-grey feathers prized. Any miner having them was envied as he scrambled amongst the litter of stone.

It was summertime work to be ended before the autumn rains. Men had to stay on the high peaks, breaking, flaking, rough-shaping, sleeping in the brilliance of starlit nights under lean-to shelters. Parties brought the workers food, took away axes. Cattle that had been herded on to the hillsides for summer grazing became pack-animals when the season ended.[19] Then the men could leave.

Neither north nor south offered an easy way out of the mountains. In either direction the higher slopes were desperately steep and made worse by the slithers of scree underfoot. There were sheer falls of rock but the track, if it deserved the quality of such a name, to the south was perhaps the more dangerous.

The difficulty was not only the terrain. There were axes to be carried. Even when almost four-fifths of the fine-grained tuff had been flaked on site to reduce the tool to a near-finished state it still weighed about a pound and a half.[20] Bulgingly uncomfortable on a man's back a pack of them affected balance, making walking an exercise in caution. Not unexpectedly, travel by water was preferred but first the mountains had to be descended.

In that world every place had a personality and a name. Scafell Pike, 'the hill with summer pasture', the highest mountain of the entire range, rose in a savage and immense landscape in which men were midgets. There was a horrid, sometimes beautiful terror in the pinnacles of naked rock, the unprotected drops, waterfalls, the dizzying heights below which great tarns seemed no bigger than a raindrop in a dried leaf. The peaks were awesome and they were threatening for laden men.

From Scafell Pike, at 978 m the highest mountain in England, to the safety of the lake of Wastwater, 'the valley with water', was no more than two miles but the journey was long in time and edged with danger. The Pike and its sister mountain, Scafell, were only three-quarters of a mile apart but they were separated by the Mickledore chasm, 'the great passage', a short but very narrow ridge between deep precipices. After a sharp and treacherous descent the group veered north-westwards down another steep scree-slope for a grim scramble of half a mile to the natural amphitheatre of Hollow Stones, a patchwork of grass and monstrous boulders below Scafell Crag. After a rest the way became easier for the porters as they trudged along the grasses of Brown Tongue under the dark cliffs of Lingmell, 'the hill of heather', and finally to a gentle descent to the welcome view of Wastwater.

This route from Scafell Pike had to be taken whether the axes were being carried to the stone circle of Ash House Wood or to Swinside. From Wastwater both companies had to cross Burn Moor, later to be known as 'the moor with burial-places', with an unavoidably steep climb of a mile before levelling out onto the plateau of the moor, skirting Burn Moor Tarn and Boat How – where in centuries to come there was to be a Bronze Age settlement – before coming to the great stone circle of Brats Hill, the first of the depôts on the journey from the mountains.

Sometimes there were equinoctial storms with curtains of dark clouds, thunder, lightning that blasted trees, burnt dwellings, lit the countryside in sharp flashes of overexposed light. And there were days that drifted as natives and visitors relaxed, axes transferred to new teams of bearers for the next stage of the trek southwards along the abrupt downhill tramp to where modern Boot lies. Here the trails divided. For Ash House Wood Penny Hill to the east had to be reached, then on past the pyramid of Harter Fell to Grassguards, High Tongue and down to the River Duddon, 'the valley of gloom', its waters rushing from Wallowbarrow Gorge ravine, swirling and flooding between the alders and willows along its rocky sides. To Ash House Wood was a further fifteen miles.

This now-destroyed stone circle was not far south-east of Swinside. Eighteenth-century reports state that the ring was rather larger than its near-neighbour 'but not in so perfect a state' and of smaller stones. It stood on a high, fairly even terrace with a steep slope to its south. The ground appeared to have been levelled. Of the twenty-two stones seen by Hutchinson only two survive, set in a layer of smaller stones, their centres about 31 m apart, perhaps an intended forty Cumbrian Yards. The taller is 1.2 m high, its partner 1 m. Other large boulders lie at the bottom of a gill to the north, evidence of nineteenth-century destruction. There was an entrance at the south-east through which the Duddon Sands were visible.[21]

To reach Swinside from Boot was less demanding than the way to Ash House Wood, a simple journey of twenty miles, two or three days in good weather. The River Esk, 'the water', could be used for eight winding miles before disembarking, hefting burdens onto shoulders, walking steadily towards the lower slopes of Corney Fell. The ground was uphill but not fierce, just upwards and across Blackbarrow and Kinmont Becks, steeper up to Stoneside Hill and then a final stretch curving around the northern side of Swinside Fell and down to the stone circle.

It is likely that some of the axes brought there may have been intended for Ireland where there is almost a replica of Swinside at Ballynoe near Downpatrick: large, circular, of many stones and with a portalled entrance; the ground had been levelled.

On a fine day, from the summit of Black Combe, 'the dark crested mountain', there was an astonishing panorama of sea, island and of mountains miles away. The builders of Swinside would see the shape of Snaefell on the Isle of Man and, far across the sea, the sharp silhouette of Slieve Donard in the distant Mourne Mountains. Eighty miles of Irish Sea separated the rings of Swinside and Ballynoe but the crossing was made easier by the existence of the Isle of Man halfway between the Duddon Sands and Dundrum Bay a few miles from Ballynoe.

On the Isle of Man the tussocked outline of Snaefell rose as a landmark and in fair weather experienced navigators could have reached it in a long summer's day, one man steering, eight paddling 10 m-long, skin-lined boats capable of five knots hourly. Flexible, lightweight vessels of this kind were adaptable, and superlative to handle in difficult waters.[22]

There was a long established tradition of crossing from the British mainland to Ireland. There were 'Scottish' Neolithic tombs on the Isle of Man itself, Castell-yn-Ard, The Kew, Ballafayle, King Orry's Grave, and there was a late and aberrant stone circle at Meayll Hill in the south-west corner of the island. Tides, currents, safe coves for landing all were well known by the centuries of the Late Neolithic.[23]

From the Isle of Man the angular peak of Slieve Donard guided the seafarers westwards towards Dundrum and the secure harbour of its Inner Bay. Returning, they steered towards the equally dominant outline of Scafell.[24]

Following the arrival of the first, pioneering parties there was an innovation. By agreement with suspicious natives propitiated by gifts and promises of safety, a great stone circle had been built, an imitation of Swinside. The site was cautiously selected. It was at the remote centre of a ring of few chambered tombs: Audleystown, Slidderyford, Ballyalton and others, none closer than five miles and the novelty of a foreign stone circle may have caused curiosity rather than antagonism.

The enterprise may have hoped to establish a Cumbrian beach-head from which Irish inhabitants might be persuaded that the axes of volcanic tuff from Scafell were stronger and more desirable than the sharper but more brittle porcellanite from Tievebulliagh mountain fifty miles to the north. If so, it failed. Few Cumbrian axes have been identified in Ireland, their acceptance obstructed by conservatism.[25]

Ballynoe was no more successful. Not long after its construction it was abandoned. Natives came to the foreign ring, desecrated it by raising two round kerbed burial-cairns inside it. Years later the cairns themselves were vandalised in the Bronze Age. The mounds were flattened. Their kerbs were interrupted to make room for a long, untidily rectangular cairn with a triple cist at its western end and probably another at the east. Burnt bones of young adults were left in them. Even they were disturbed. In historic times the capstones were dragged away for buildings, the cists were exposed

and the site was left in shabby decay, overgrown, only its ring of tall stones
remaining as witnesses of an ancient ambition.

Swinside was luckier. Isolation saved it. Until recent centuries there was no
interference. Perhaps Nature protected it. The circle had always been more than a
temporary halt like a Wells Fargo post, always had more importance to its makers
than just a warehouse from which axes could be stored and bartered at propitious
times of the year. Spirits of intercession guarded it. Arcane codes were built into it.

The tallest stone is the tapering, peaked pillar at the north. Despite its height it is
gracefully lean. Facing it at the south, is a thick, almost square flat-topped stone.
Neither had been shaped but they had been chosen for their contrasting appearance.
They created a combination of a high, thin, pointed pillar and squatter, broad block,
a juxtaposition of opposites known in many other megalithic rings and rows in
Britain, Ireland and Brittany. The opposition of a lithe pillar facing a lower, wider slab
has been interpreted as the combination of 'male' and 'female' principles which, at
Swinside, also emphasised the cardinal points, the corners of the sun's world. Similar
male and female stones also alternate in the two circle-stones and the pair of portals
outside them in a rotation of tall-pointed, low-flat, tall-pointed, low-flat, a statement
of spirituality for anyone entering the ring. It was fertility symbolism safeguarding the
fecundity of the land, the strength of cattle, the survival of children.[26]

Plate 55 The south-east portalled entrance.

There was also an astronomical alignment. From the centre of Swinside the line of the southern circle-stone and outlying portal has an azimuth of 134°.5 towards the heights of Kirkby Moor six miles away, the direction of the midwinter sunrise.[27] In the thin light of that dawn axes may have been brandished in supplication, arms raised to the sun, dances, celebratory rites enacted in recognition that the new year was beginning, men and women combining in acts of sympathetic magic to ensure that life, light and warmth would return.

Such a complexity of elementary numeracy, measuring-rods, opposed male and female stones at cardinal points, regard for hills, and subtle calendrical alignments, innocence, sensitivity and the awareness of a living world reveal something of the intricacies of mind and beliefs that controlled the lives of the people of Swinside.

So far from being 'rude stone monuments', unplanned and casually thrown up; so far from being celestial observatories for astronomer-priests; these were centres of magical protection. Swinside was a perfection of the encircling landscape built in stone, a unity of the physical and the imagination, a symbol of the determination of man to survive against the threatening spirits that loomed everywhere, invisible, high, inhabiting and affecting the precarious and dangerous world of the sky.

Overhead, seen by all the people watching it for omens, dark against a fading moon, an owl circled, noiseless, searching, swooping upon its kill, contentedly returning to its nest as bright sunlight lit the stones and made shadows of the men and women moving inside the circle.

At Swineshead, a very high hill . . . is a druidical temple, which the country folk call 'Sunken Kirk', i.e. a church sunk into the earth. It is nearly a circle of very large stones, pretty entire. No situation could be more agreeable to the Druids than this; mountains almost encircle it, not a tree is to be seen in the neighbourhood . . . This monument of antiquity, when viewed within the circle, strikes you with astonishment, how the massy stones could be placed in such regular order either by human strength or mechanical power. R. Gough, Camden's *Britannia, III*, 1806, 432.

ABBREVIATIONS

Ant	*Antiquity*
Arch	*Archaeologia*
Arch J	*Archaeological Journal*
CA	*Cornish Archaeology*
CAS	Cornwall Archaeological Society
CBA	Council for British Archaeology
Curr Arch	*Current Archaeology*
GM	*Gentleman's Magazine. Archaeology*
JBAA	*Journal of the British Archaeological Association*
JIA	*Journal of Irish Archaeology*
JRAI	*Journal of the Royal Anthropological Association*
PPS	*Proceedings of the Prehistoric Society*
PSAL	*Proceedings of the Society of Archaeologists of London*
PSANHS	*Proceedings of the Somerset Archaeological and Natural History Society*
PSAS	*Proceedings of the Society of Antiquaries of Scotland*
PUBSS	*Proceedings of the Bristol University Spelaeological Society*
RCAHM	Royal Commission for Ancient and Historical Monuments
TCWAAS	*Transactions of the Cumberland & Westmorland Antiquarian and Archaeological Society*
UJA	*Ulster Journal of Archaeology*
WAM	*Wiltshire Archaeological Magazine*
YAJ	*Yorkshire Archaeological Journal*

NOTES

INTRODUCTION

1 Rogers, P. (ed.) *Johnson and Boswell in Scotland. A Journey to the Hebrides*, New Haven and London, 1993, 72. For doubts about the antiquity of folk-tales, see Harte, J., 'Folk Memory', *3rd Stone 31*, 1998, 5–9.
2 'Traces of our remote ancestors' *GM, I*, 1886, 210–11. [from, *GM 1*, 1861, 498–507].
3 Walker, J. K., *GM, II*, 1886, 25–6 [from, *GM, II*, 1843, 361–5].
4 Linton, W., *Colossal Vestiges of the Older Nations*, London, 1862, 22.

CHAPTER ONE

1 *Ant 41*, 1967, 174.
2 Grinsell, 1976, 29; *Folklore 43*, 1932, 362–75.
3 Lambrick, G., *The Rollright Stones*, Oxford, 1983, 46–7.
4 *Arch J 49*, 1892, 154; see also Hutton, R., *The Pagan Religions of the Ancient British Isles*, London, 1991, 247–83.
5 Evans, A. J., 'The Rollright Stones and their Folklore', *Folk-Lore 6*, 1895, 6–50, 34–47. Hook Norton, AD 916: Swanton, M. (ed.) *Anglo-Saxon Chronicle (A)*, London, 1996, 98.
6 Corpus Christi College, Cambridge, MS 313, Pt. II, f. 66v; Ravenhill, T. R., *The Rollright Stones and the Men who Erected Them*, Birmingham, 1932, frontispiece, 2–3. The extract is misquoted in Thomas Hearne's *Remarks and Collections, VIII, 1722–5*, Oxford Historical Society, 1907, 113. *In Oxenefordensi pago sunt magni lapides, hominum manu sub quadam quasi connexitate disposti. Set a quo tempore, set a qua gente, set ad quid memorandum vel significandum fuerit factum hoc, nescitur. Ab incolis autem vocatur locus ille Rolendrith.*
7 Leland, J. *c.* 1535–43, *The Itinerary*, ed. Smith, L. T., Carbondale, 1964, vol. 6, fol. 20; Crawford, O. G. S., *Long Barrows of the Cotswolds*, 1925, 212–13.
8 Camden, 1610, 374–5. For the evolution of historical thinking, see Kendrick, T. D., *British Antiquity*, 1950; Piggott, S., *Ancient Britons and the Antiquarian Imagination*, 1989.
9 Drayton; Selden; see: Ravenhill, *The Rollright Stones*, 55.
10 Holmes, R., *Witchcraft in British History*, 1976, 71. James VI and I: Briggs, R., *Witches & Neighbours. The Social and Cultural Context of European Witchcraft*, 1996, 29, 191; For Calvin, see Trevor-Roper, H. R., *The European Witch-Craze in the 16th and 17th Centuries*, 1969, 64.
11 Witches at the Rollright Stones: Turner, M., *Folklore & Mysteries of the Cotswolds*, 1993, 101. Prosecutions: Briggs, K. M., *The Folklore of the Cotswolds*, 1974, 130.
12 The Long Compton 'witch': Turner, *Folklore & Mysteries*, 110.
13 Bottesford: Dare, M. P., *The Church of St Mary the Virgin, Bottesford, Leics, and Its Monuments*, 1947, 40, 45–6; Brand, J., *Observations on Popular Antiquities, III*, 1870, 82.
14 The Camden Wonder: Clark, Sir G., *The Camden Wonder*, 1959; Williamson, H. R., *Historical Whodunits*, 1955, 164–80; Brooks, J. A., *Ghosts and Witches of the Cotswolds*, 1981, 67–78.
15 Rollo and the battle of Hook Norton: Swanton, M. (ed.) *Anglo-Saxon Chronicle*, London, 1996, 98. Rollo, AD 876: 'F' chronicle, 74; Hook Norton, 'A', 98. Chronicle 'D', 99, has AD 914.
16 Lambrick, G., *The Rollright Stones. Megaliths, Monuments, and Settlement in the Prehistoric Landscape*, London, 1988, 41.
17 Ralph Sheldon: Plot, R. *The Natural Historie of Oxfordshire*, 1677, 336; Aubrey, 1665, 72. Dr Toope: *ibid.*, 112.
18 St Patrick: *ibid.* 123. Druids: *ibid.*, 24. For biographies of John Aubrey as a scholar and antiquarian, see: Hunter, M., *John Aubrey and the Realm of Learning*, London, 1975; Powell, A., *John Aubrey and His Friends*, London, 1988. 2nd edn. For a more general account of his life, see: Tylden-Wright, D., *John Aubrey. A Life*, London, 1981.
19 Daniel Defoe, *A Tour Through the Whole Island of Great Britain*, ed. Furbank, P. N. and Owens, W. R., New Haven and London, 1991, 178, 196–7.
20 Roger Gale: Lukis, 1887, 153–5.
21 Stukeley, 1776a, 48.
22 Stukeley, 1740, Preface, vii.
23 Piggott, S., 1985, 105–6.
24 Stukeley, 1743, 10, Tab 6.
25 Druid's Cubit: Stukeley, 1740, 6, 10. Merrymaking: *ibid.*, 1743, 13; *ibid.*, 1776, I, 108.
26 Parry: Lukis, 1887, 158.
27 Chippings: Turner, M., *Folklore & Mysteries*, 100–1; Evans, A. J., 'The Rollright Stones and their Folklore', 23. For the cattle-drovers' routes, see: Godwin, F., and Toulson, S., *The Drovers' Roads of Wales*, 1977, 136–48. It also contains references to the prehistoric standing stones that were used as nineteenth-century landmarks.
28 For folk-stories about the Rollright Stones, see: Evans, A. J., 'The Rollright Stones and their Folklore', also: Grinsell, 1977.
29 Aubrey, 1665, 107.
30 For Nennius, see: *British History and the Welsh Annals*, ed. and tr. Morris, J., 1980, 42, no. 73.
31 King Edgar, Canon 16, see: *Ancient Laws and Institutes of England*, ed. Thorpe, B., 1840, 396. 'Frid-splot': a plot of ground 'encircling some stone, tree or well considered sacred, and therefore offering sanctuary to criminals': Stuart, J., *The Sculptured Stones of Scotland, II*, Edinburgh, 1867, xxxvi.
32 William Parry: Lukis, 1887, 157.
33 Elder tree: *Brewer's Dictionary of Phrase and Fable*, 1978, 410; *Culpeper's Colour Herbal*, 1983, 65–6. Mother Shipton: Windsor, D., *Mother Shipton's Prophecy Book*, 1990, 1–2.
34 The witch and Shipton-under-Wychwood: Costello, D., *Holidays with Hobgoblins*, 1861, 215–22; Ekwall, E., *The Concise Oxford Dictionary of English Place-Names*, Oxford, 419, 540.
35 The King Stone: Taunt, H. W., *The Rollright Stones: the Stonehenge of Oxford*, 1907, 43; Turner, M., *Folklore and Mysteries*, 99. For phallic stones, see: Cutner, H., *A Short History of Sex Worship*, 1940, 171–2.
36 Cotswolds trackway: Beesley, T., *Trans. N. Oxford Arch Soc I*, 1855, 61–73, Grundy, G. B., *Oxfordshire Record Society 15*, 1933, 94–5; Fox, C., *The Personality of Britain*, Cardiff, 1938, 63. Welsh uplands: Taylor, 1979, 164–5. Clun valley: Chitty, L., 'The Clun-Clee ridgeway; A prehistoric trackway across South Shropshire', in Foster, I. LL. and Alcock, L., (eds) 1963, 173.
37 Bonney, T. G., *GM, II*, 1886, 4.
38 Fergusson, 1872, 124–6.
39 Mr Bliss: Ravenhill, *The Rollright Stones*, 14. Replaced stones and sign: Taunt, *The Rollright Stones*, 23.
40 Inner faces: Ravenhill, *The Rollright Stones*, 14. Continuous wall: *ibid.*, 15; Gale, in Lukis, 1887, 153. Cheekbone: Ravenhill, *The Rollright Stones*, 42. Excavation: *Trans Birmingham & Warks Arch Soc 5*, 1927, 305.
41 Astronomy: Taunt, *The Rollright Stones*, 23; Bloom, J. H., *Folk Lore, Old Customs and Superstitions in Shakespeare Lands*, 1930, reprinted 1976, 92; Lockyer, 1909, 36; Ravenhill, *The Rollright Stones*, 38, 40.
42 Ley-lines: Watkins, A., *The Old Straight Track*, 1925, 171–2; Devereux and Thomson, 1979, 103. Dowsing: Graves, T., *Dowsing*, 1976, 169–74; Graves, T., *Needles of Stone*, 1980, 46, 54, 56, 152, 218; Graves, T., *Dowsing and Archaeology*, 1980, 43–4. The Dragon Project: Michell, 1982, 104; Robins, D., *Circles of Silence*, 1985. Witchcraft: Graves, T., *Dowsing and Archaeology*, 1980, 152; Turner, M., *Folklore & Mysteries*, 101–3; Wilcock, J., *A Guide to Occult Britain*, 1976, 148–52.
43 'Gateway': Thom, Thom and Burl, 1980, 136. Stars: Thom, 1967, 65, 100, S6/1. For the changing rising positions of Capella between 2500 and 1000 BC, see: Hawkins, 1966b, 2300–2500 BC, 32°.8; 2000 BC, 32°.2; 1500 BC, 24°.6; 1000 BC, 14°.8.
44 Burl, 1976, 292–7.
45 Flints: *Oxoniensia 28*, 1963, 92. Excavations and fieldwork: Lambrick, *The Rollright Stones*, 48, 70–80.
46 *Ibid.*, 41–8; Burl, 1993, 181 *et al.*
47 Burl, 1988b.
48 Lambrick, *The Rollright Stones*, 121–4.
49 Lynch, F., 'The megalithic tombs of North Wales' in Powell (ed.) *et al.*, 1969, 138–9, 204.
50 Lambrick, *The Rollright Stones*, 85; Clough and Cummins, 1988, 187.
51 Dates for the Devil's Quoits: Barclay, A. *et al.*, *Excavations at the Devil's Quoits, Stanton Harcourt, Oxfordshire, 1972–3 and 1988*, Oxford, 1995, 42, 46, 88.
52 Lambrick, *The Rollright Stones*, 61, 112.
53 *Sunday Telegraph*, 4 June 1991; *Daily Telegraph*, 6 June 1991.

CHAPTER TWO

1 Sizes of great stone circles: Burl, 1976, 366–71; Ménec: Burl, 1985b, 158.
2 Bainbridge: Haverfield, F., 'Cotton Iulius F.VI. Notes on Reginald Bainbrigg of Appleby . . .', *TCWAAS 11*, 1911, 361–2; alternative name for Castlerigg: MacMichael, J. H., 'Castlerigg', *Notes & Queries*, 1904, 396.
3 Denham Tracts: *The Folk-Lore Society 35*, 1895, 244–53.
4 Lady Selby: Bateson, E., *A History of Northumberland, I*, 1893, 161.
5 Thomas Fuller: Westwood, 1992, 381–2.
6 Stone numbers cited by various surveyors: Camden, 1695, 831; Aubrey, 1665, 115; Stukeley, 1776b, 47; Hutchinson, W., *The History and Antiquities of Cumberland I*, Carlisle, 1794, 226; Wordsworth, W., *The Complete Poetical Works of William Wordsworth*, Macmillan, London, 1899, notes, 844 (p. 725); Lukis, W. C., *PSAL 10*, 1883–5, 313; Collingwood, R. G., 1933, 173; Thom, Thom and Burl 1980, 42, L1/7.
7 Witches and Michael Scott: Sullivan, J., *Cumberland & Westmorland. Ancient & Modern*, 1857, 128.
8 Folk-stories: Grinsell, 1976, 164–5. fiennes, *c.* 1712, 171–2; Smith, G. 'Long Meg and Her Daughters', *GM 22*, 1752, 372.
9 Breton art: Burl, 1985b, 36, 71, 94. (see also: Chapter Ten). Megalithic art in Britain: Morris, 1989.
10 Stukeley, 1776b, 47.
11 Druidical folly: Ffynch, M., *Portrait of Penrith and the East Fellside*, 1985, 184. Storm: Sullivan, *Cumberland & Westmorland*, 128. Lacy: Hutchinson, *History and Antiquities of Cumberland*, 225.
12 The two internal cairns: Hodgson, K. S., *TCWAAS 35*, 1935, 79; Bainbridge: Haverfield, 'Cotton Julius', 361; Aubrey, 1665, 116; Stukeley, 1776b, 47; Camden, 1695, 831; Fell, C., 'Summer excursion', *TCWAAS 47*, 1947, 231. Castlerigg: Stukeley, 1776b, 48.
13 Fergusson, J., 1872, 135; Stukeley, 1776b, 47; Hutchinson, *History and Antiquities of Cumberland*, 246.
14 Geology: Woolacott, D., 'Note on the rocks of the stone circles at Keswick and Long Meg, near Penrith', *Proc. Univ. Durham Phil. Soc. 3*, 1909, 12–13.
15 Clare, T., *Archaeological Sites of the Lake District*, Ashbourne, 1981, 9.
16 Watson, G., *The Long Meg Druidical Circle near Penrith, Cumberland. A Suggested Theory of its Geometrical Construction, and Adaptation Sun-Worship*, Penrith, 1900, 1–3.
17 Thom, 1967, 67; Soffe, G. and Clare, T., 'New evidence of ritual monuments at Long Meg and Her Daughters, Cumbria', *Ant 62*, 1988, 552–7.
18 Falling of stones: Clare, 1975, 7.
19 Long Meg's carvings: Simpson, Sir J. Y., 1897, 19–21; Beckensall, 1992, 7–14.
20 Frodsham, P. N. K., *TCWAAS 89*, 1989, 1–19.
21 Bradley, 1993, 65.
22 Watson, G., *The Long Meg Druidical Circle*, 4; Morrow, J., *Proc. Univ. Durham Phil. Soc. 3*, 1909; Thom, 1967, 99; Hawkins, 1966b.
23 'Solar' spiral carvings: Brennan, 1983, 72, 190–5. Castlerigg: Frodsham, P. N. K., *Northern Archaeology 13/14*, 1996, 112, 113.
24 Burl, 1988b, 197.
25 Burl, 1988b, 199–201.
26 Burl, 1976, 69.
27 Crawford, O. G. S., 'Long Meg', *Ant 8*, 1934, 328–9; Topping, P., 'The Penrith henges', *PPS 58*, 1992, 249–64. 263.
28 Broomrigg: Waterhouse, 1985, 107–13.
29 Estimates of size: Burl, 1988b, 188.
30 Collingwood, 1933, 178.
31 Crone, A., 'The Clochmabenstane, Gretna', *TDGNHAS 58*, 1983, 16–20. 18.
32 Bunch and Fell, *PPS 15*, 1949, 1–20. 15.

CHAPTER THREE

1 Multiple rings: Burl, 1976, 117–19; Burl, *3rd Stone 30*, 1998.
2 English Heritage press release, 10 November 1997. There were reports the following day in the *Daily Mail*, the *Daily Telegraph*, the *Guardian*, the *Independent* and the *Times*.
3 Stukeley, 1776b, 173.
4 T. P., 'An account of the remains at Stanton-Drew, in Somersetshire', *GM*, Pt. II, 1785, 761.
5 Avebury found by accident: Aubrey, 1665, 18; Stanton Drew: *ibid.*, 65.
6 Druids and Stanton Drew: *ibid.*, 46, 68.
7 The name of Stanton Drew: Long, W., 'The druidical temple at Stanton Drew, commonly called the Weddings', *Arch J 15*, 1858, 210; Dymond, 1896, 23; Grinsell, *The Folklore of Stanton Drew* 1973, 11; Lohan, K., 'The Hauteville Quoits', *Family Tree Magazine 7 (1)*, 1990, 29.

8 Stanton Drew church: Johnson, W., *Byways in British Archaeology*, 1912, 46–7.
9 Stukeley, 1776b, 169.
10 Aubrey, 1665, 46; Legg, R., *Stanton Drew Great Western Temple*, Wincanton, 1998
11 The hanging tree: Stukeley, 1776a, 149.
12 John Strachey: McGarvie, M., 'John Strachey, FRS and the antiquities of Wessex in 1730', *Trans Anc Mons Soc 27*, 1983, 77–104. 103.
13 Dovecote: Stukeley, 1776b, 171–2.
14 Landscaped stone circles: Stukeley, 1776b, 174–5.
15 Stanton Drew and the five planets: Wood, J., *An Essay Towards a Description of Bath, I*, 1749, 151.
16 Pythagorean system: *ibid.*, 153.
17 Stanton Drew as a university; Wood, J., 1747, 7–9; Wood, J., *An Essay*, 157–8.
18 C. W. Dymond: Grinsell, L. V., *The Megalithic Monuments of Stanton Drew*, Bristol, 1994, 3.
19 Circles, not ellipses: Thom, Thom and Burl, 1980, 116–17.
20 Laying-out of the NE circle: Grinsell, L. V., *Stanton Drew Stone Circles*, London, 1956, 2.
21 Dymond, 1896, 34.
22 Varying estimates of the diameter of the central ring: Stukeley, 1776b, 172; Wilkinson, Sir J. G., 'The rock-basins of Dartmoor . . .' *JBAA 16*, 1860, 114, plate 8; Thom, 1967, 40, S3/1; Wood, J., *An Essay*, 149; Crocker: Hoare, Sir R. C., *The History of Modern Wiltshire, II*, 1826, 52–3; Dymond, 1896, 35.
23 Bosing: Atkinson, R. J. C., *Field Archaeology*, London, 1946, 32; Stukeley, 1776b, 171.
24 Strachey: McGarvie, M., 'John Strachey', 103–4.
25 Parched grass: Morgan, C. L., 'The stones of Stanton Drew; their source and origin', *PSANHS 32 (2)*, 1887, 410.
26 Aubrey, 1665, 67, 69.
27 Short avenues: Burl, 1993, 29–54.
28 Flood plain: Tratman, E. K., 'Investigations at Stanton Drew', *PUBSS 11 (1)*, 1966, 40–2.
29 The church and the Cove: Johnson, Note 8, 46.
30 finds from the Cove: Dymond, 1896, 13.
31 Astronomy of the Cove: Long, W., 'The druidical temple', 202.
32 Hauteville's Quoit: Aubrey, 1665, 68; Wood, J., *An Essay*, 149; Morgan, C. L., 'The stones of Stanton Drew', 43–4; Brentnall, H. C., 'Sarsens', *WAM 51*, 419–39.
33 Long, W., 'The druidical temple', 205.
34 Stukeley, 1776b, 173.
35 Mercer, R., 'Norton Malreward', *Arch Review for 1969, Groups XII, XIII*, 1970, 24; Stukeley, 1776b, 173.
36 *Ibid.*, 170.
37 Morgan and Hauteville's Quoit: Dymond, 1896, 18.
38 Cove conglomerate: Kellaway, 1971, 34.
39 Lot's wife: Aubrey, 1665, 46.
40 The Weddings: Stukeley, 1776b, 174.
41 The old piper: Bord, J. and C., *Atlas of Magical Britain*, 1990, 49–50.
42 Stukeley, 1776b, 174.
43 Wood, J., *An Essay*, 148.
44 Aubrey, 1665, 46.
45 *Ibid.*, 68. For a discussion of the oak effigy, see: Fryer, A. C., *Wooden Monumental Effigies in England and Wales*, London, 1924, 29, 60.
46 Strachey: McGarvie, M., 'John Strachey', 103–4.
47 Nennius, *Historia Brittonum*, *c.* 796, ed. Morris, J., Chichester, 1980, 35; Fergusson, 1872, 152–3.
48 Accidental find at Stanton Drew: Gay, Rev. R. *c.* 1660, *A Fool's Bolt Soon Shot at Stonage*, in: Legg, R. (ed.) *Stonehenge Antiquaries*, Milborne Port, 1986, 7–37. 41.
49 Layer of ironpan: Tratman, E. K., 'Investigations at Stanton Drew', 40–1.
50 Burl, 1988c, 15–16.
51 Pitts, M. and Whittle, A. W. R., 'The development and date of Avebury', *PPS 58*, 1992, 203–12; Burl, 1995, 82.
52 Stukeley, 1776b, 170.
53 Grinsell, L. V., 'Somerset barrows. Part II: North and East', *PSANHS 115*, 1971, 44–137.
54 Avebury replaced by Stonehenge: Burl, 1979a, 240–4.
55 Dimensions of the ditch, see Chapter Three, note 2. Nature of the soil, Morgan, C. L., 'The stones of Stanton Drew', 44.
56 Wood, J., *An Essay*, 150.
57 *Ibid.*, 149.
58 Dowsing: Smith, R. A., 'Archaeological dowsing', 47; Underwood, G.,

'Archaeology and dowsing, II, 67'. Both in Graves, T., (ed.) *Dowsing in Archaeology*, Wellingborough, 1980.

59 Spacing of multiple sites: Thornborough: Clark, G., *PPS 2*, 1936, 1–51; Avebury: Burl, 1979a, 151; Priddy: Tratman, E. K., *PUBSS II (2)*, 1967, 110; Grey Wethers and the Hurlers: Thom, Thom and Burl, 1980, 104, 74; King Arthur's Down and Tregeseal: Barnatt, 1982, 19, 164; Wendron: Lukis, Rev. W. C., *The Prehistoric Stone Monuments of the British Isles. Cornwall*, London, 1885, Plate V; Bathampton: Quinn, P, *3rd Stone 2*, 1997, 11–12.

60 Lockyer, 1909, 166–74.

61 *Ibid.*, 166–77.

62 Watkins, A., 'Portfolio 5. Camps in alignment, II, 2. Figs. 1–3', 1928; Hereford Reference Library; Devereux and Thomson, 1979, 18.

63 Dymond, 1896, 40.

64 Thom, 1967, 100, S3/1.

65 Burl, 1987, 14–16.

CHAPTER FOUR

Neither Boscawen-Un nor the Merry Maidens are recorded in *Antiquity* or *PPS*. The four circles are described in *Cornish Archaeology 19*, 1980, 17–30, and in *Cornish Archaeology 25*, 1986, 69–71.

1 Borlase, W., *Antiquities, Historical and Monumental of the County of Cornwall*, London, 1769, 191.

2 Three, nine and nineteen: Schimmel, A., *The Mystery of Numbers*, Oxford, 1993, 164–79.

3 'Poore throughfare': Leyland, J., *The Itinerary, 1535–1543, I–III*, 1710–12, ed. Smith, L. T., Carbondale, South Illinois, 1964, I, Pt. II, 171, fol. 77. Travellers: Norden, J., *A Topographical and Historical Description of Cornwall*, 1603–7, 22; Carew, R., *The Survey of Cornwall*, 1602, ed. Halliday, F. E., London, 1969, 138.

4 Holed stone: Borlase, W., *Antiquities, Historical and Monumental*, 179. Rosemodress: Weatherhill, C., *Cornish Place Names and Language*, Wilmslow, 1995, 38.

5 Grading of the Merry Maidens: Mercer, R., 'The Neolithic in Cornwall', *CA 25*, 1986, 35–80. 69.

6 Barnatt, 1982, 155.

7 Lewis, A. L., 'Prehistoric remains in Cornwall, II', *JRAI 35*, 1905, 427–34.

8 Lord Falmouth: Lockyer, 1906, 268. Dead horse: Weatherhill, C., and Devereux, P., *Myths and Legends of Cornwall*, Wilmslow, 1994, 140.

9 Athelstan: Hayman, 1997, 12.

10 Mordred: Weatherhill, C., *Cornish Place Names and Language*, 26–43. Sites of the battle of Camlann: Lacy, N. J. (ed.), *The New Arthurian Encyclopaedia*, Chicago and London, 1995, 68–9.

11 Dans Maen: Borlase, W., *Antiquities, Historical and Monumental*, 194. Oldest reference: Grinsell, 1976, 54.

12 The stone dance: Hunt, R., *Popular Romances in the West of England*, London, 1856. Quoted in: Michell, J., *The Old Stones of Land's End*, London, 1974, 61.

13 Holed stone: Borlase, W., *Antiquities, Historical and Monumental*, 179. Lewis, 1905, 429.

14 The Pipers: Hurling: Weatherhill and Devereux, *Myths and Legends of Cornwall*, 141. Excavation: Borlase, W. C., *Naenia Cornubiae*, Truro, 1897, 107. The stones: Barnatt, 1982, 226–9; Straffon, C., 'Where is the third Piper?, *Meyn Mamvro 6*, 1988, 4–6.

15 Goon Rith: Barnatt, 1982, 229; Michell, J., *The Old Stones*, 66.

16 Tregiffian: *CA 7*, 1968, 80; *Arch J 130*, 1973, 259; *Radiocarbon 18*, 1976, 39.

17 Hills at the Merry Maidens: *Meyn Mamvro 12*, 1990, 11; Straffon, C., *Pagan Cornwall. Land of the Goddess*, St Just, 1993, 23.

18 Astronomical alignments: Lockyer, 1909, 269–76.

19 Absence of astronomy: Thom, 1967, 100, S1/14; Barnatt, 1982, 158–9.

20 Ley-lines: Michell, J., *The Old Stones*, 62–3.

21 Lethbridge as a scholar: *Ant 46*, 1972, 5. The pendulum: Lethbridge, T., *The Legend of the Sons of God*, London, 1972, 19–23. An interesting account of Lethbridge's experiments with a pendulum appears in the Foreword by Colin Wilson in, *The Essential T. C. Lethbridge*, eds. Graves, T. and Hoult, J., London, 1980, 12. For his belief that he had discovered a hill-carving of Gogmagog, see: *3rd Stone 27*, 1997, 8–10, 20.

22 Alternative investigations: *Meyn Mamvro 6*, 1988, 7; Straffon, C., *Ancient Sites in West Penwith*, 1992, 5; Hayman, 1997, 220–3, 230.

23 Boleigh stone circle: Lockyer, 1906, 268. Doubts: Barnatt, 1982, 158. Crop-marks: Straffon, C., *Ancient Sites*, 4. There may have been a third circle about 400 yards to the east of the Merry Maidens at Tregurnow,

c. SW437 245: Straffon, C., Letter, *3rd Stone 31*, 1998, 41.

24 Multiple rings: Burl, 1976, 117–19; Burl, *3rd Stone 30*, 1998, 33–7.

25 Astronomical alignments from circle to circle: Thom, 1967, 94, 97–101. Altogether Thom listed sixty associated sites, eight to the moon, ten to stars and thirty-five to the sun.

26 Thornborough: *PPS 2*, 1936, 51. Priddy: Tratman, E. K., 'The Priddy circles, Mendip, Somerset. Henge monuments', *PUBSS 11 (2)*, 1967, 110, Pl. 14.

27 Llandegai: *Ant 41*, 1967, 58–60; *Ant 42*, 1968, 216–21. Dating: *Archaeology in Wales 9*, 1969, 8–9.

28 Name: Weatherhill, C., *Cornish Place Names*, 27; Weatherhill and Devereux, *Myths and Legends of Cornwall*, 141.

29 The overlapping barrow: Barnatt, 1982, 165.

30 Borlase, W. C., *Naenia Cornubiae*, 280–3.

31 Boskednan: Barnatt, 1982, 165–7; 1989, 395–6. Thom, Thom and Burl, 1980, 92–3. Carn Galver: Weatherhill, C. *Cornish Place Names*, 28.

32 Processional way: Barnatt, 1982, 79.

33 Tregeseal entrance tomb: *Arch 49*, 1881, 181–98.

34 *Meyn Mamvro 2*, 1987, 2–6.

35 Kenidjack holed stones: Weatherhill, C., *Belerion. Ancient Sites of Land's End*, Penzance, 1981, 23, no. 26.

36 A mutating 'stone circle': *Meyn Mamvro 2*, 1987, 3.

37 Thom, Thom and Burl, 1980, 99–100.

38 Carn Kenidjack: Weatherhill, C., *Cornish Place Names*, 28.

39 Barnatt, 1982, 162–5.

40 Cupmarked stones at Tregeseal: *Meyn Mamvro 26*, 1995, 3.

41 Tregeseal Central: *Meyn Mamvro 2*, 1987, 2–3.

42 Population: Burl, 1976, 324–5.

43 Peter Pool: *CAS Newsletter 82*, 1996, 1.

44 Tin-mines at Land's End: Norden, J. (1603–7), *A Topographical and Historical Description of Cornwall*, London, 1728, 22.

45 Camden and Boscawen-Un: Camden, 1610, 186, 188.

46 Aubrey, 1665, 70, 104–5; Stukeley, 1740, 54. See also: Piggott, 1985, 100.

47 Athelstan: Todd, M., *The South-West to 1000 AD*, London, 1987, 275. Eamont Bridge: *Anglo-Saxon Chronicle*, tr. Swanton, M. J., London, 1996, 107, Worcester Chronicle D. Triads: Bromwich, R., *Trioedd Ynys Prydein. The Welsh Triads*, Cardiff, 1961. Beiscawen-un: Tregelles, 1906, 381; Borlase, W. C., *Naenia Cornubiae*, 126; Allcroft, 174–5; Michell, J. *The Old Stones*, 17.

48 Iolw Morganw: Michell, J., *A Little History of Astro-Archaeology*, London, 1989, 2nd edn, 36. Modern gorsedd at Boscawen-Un: Miles, D., *The Secrets of the Bards of the Isle of Britain*, Llandybie, 1992. 226–31.

49 Dimensions: Barnatt, 1989, 395. Excavations: Weatherhill, C., *Cornoviae. Ancient Sites of Cornwall and Scilly*, Penzance, 1985, 92; *JBAA 33*, 1877, 198–9.

50 The broken stone: Borlase, W., *Antiquities, Historical and Monumental*, 209, note q.

51 The central pillar: Lukis, W. C., *The Prehistoric Stone Monuments of the British Isles. Cornwall*, London, 1885, 1, Plate II. Cupmarks: *Meyn Mamvro 7*, 1989, 2; *Meyn Mamvro 12*, 1990, 12.

52 Quartz block and astronomy: Lockyer, 1906, 287, 291–2. Candlemass: Barnatt, 1982, 161.

53 Further alignments: Lockyer, 1909, 290; Thom, 1967, 100, S1/a6; Barnatt, 1982, 162.

54 Peters, F., 'The possible use of West Penwith menhirs as boundary markers', *CA 29*, 1990, 33–42.

55 Michell, J., *The Old Stones*, 16, 104–6.

56 Criticism of Michell's selection: Hayman, 1997, 228–9; Williamson, T. and Bellamy, L., *Ley Lines in Question*, Kingswood, 1983, 103.

57 Standing stones: many are listed in volumes of *Meyn Mamvro*, 7, 1988, 11–14; 8, 11–15; 10, 3; 13, 3; 20, 3; 25, 6–7; 29, 3; and 30, 1996, 4.

58 Non-circular rings with 'central' stones: Thom, Thom and Burl, 1980. Black Marsh or the Hoarstones, D2/2, Flattened type A; Boscawen-Un, S1/13, type B; Callanish, H1/1, A; Fernacre, S1/7, D; Glenquickan, G4/12, A; Hurlers Centre, S1/1, Egg II; Kerry Hill, W6/1, complex; Mitchells Fold, D2/1, A.

CHAPTER FIVE

1 Barron, R. S., *The Geology of Wiltshire*, Bradford-on-Avon, 1976.

2 Cunnington, M., *An Introduction to the Archaeology of Wiltshire*, Devizes, 1949, 64.

3 Disc barrow: *ibid.*, 60. Druids barrow: Hoare, 1812, 170.

4 *Ant 1*, 1927, 92–5, 99–100. Cunnington, M. E., *Woodhenge. A Description of the Site as revealed by Excavations carried out there by Mr*

And Mrs B. Cunnington, 1926-7-8, Devizes, 1929.

5 *Ibid.*, 8.

6 *Ibid.*, plates 25–38, pp. 118–45.

7 Grooved ware from Woodhenge: *ibid.*, postholes, B16, C1, 5, 6, 9, 15, 16, F18 [presumably a mistake for F8], 126, 130, 136. For beakers: plates 25, 41, pp. 118–19, 150–1.

8 Turf-lines: *ibid.*, 6.

9 Beakers from Woodhenge: Clarke, 1970, II, 502: 1104F, 1105F, 1106F, 1107F.

10 The ramps of Ring C: Cunnington, M. E., *Woodhenge*, 23.

11 Shapes of the rings: *ibid.*, 15–17; Thom, A., 1961. 'The egg-shaped standing stone rings of Britain', *Archives Internationales d'Histoire des Sciences 14*, 291–302, 294. The accuracy of Cunnington's survey: Cunnington, M. E., *Woodhenge*, 1. See also: Hogg, A. H. A., 1981 'The plan of Woodhenge', *Science and Archaeology 23*, 3–14.

12 Thom's survey: Thom, 1961, 293; Thom, 1967, 73–5, fig. 6.16.

13 Counting base of 4 and the 'Beaker Yard': Burl, 1987, 124.

14 Counting-bases: Burl, A., 'Intimations of numeracy in the Neolithic and Bronze Age societies of the British Isles', *Arch J 133*, 1976, 9–32.

15 Cultoon: MacKie, E. W., *The Megalith Builders*, London, 1977, 104.

16 The Woodhenge sighting-device: Cunnington, M. E., *Woodhenge*, 11, 13, fig 1.

17 Sacrifice: *ibid.*, 9–13; Thom, Thom and Burl, 1980, 130–1.

18 Loss of the Woodhenge and Sanctuary skeletons: Burl, 1979a, 197–8.

19 Thomas, J. *Rethinking the Neolithic*, Cambridge, 1991, 71–2.

20 *Ibid.*, 73. Pollard, J., 'Structured deposition at Woodhenge', *PPS 61*, 1995, 137–56, 152, 149.

21 Human bones at Woodhenge: Cunnington, M. E., *Woodhenge*, 60; Burl, 1987, 101.

22 A roof at Woodhenge: Musson, C. R., 'A study of possible building forms at Durrington Walls, Woodhenge and the Sanctuary', in Wainwright, G. J. with Longworth, I. H., *Durrington Walls: Excavations 1966–1968*, London, 1971, 363–7. See also: Reynolds, P. J., 'Rural life and farming', in Green, M. J. (ed.) *The Celtic World*, London, 1995, 176–209. Piggott, S., 'Timber circles: a re-examination', *Arch J 96*, 1940, 193–222.

23 Burl, 1987, 136.

24 Ritual axes elsewhere than Woodhenge: *PPS 38*, 1962, 231.

25 Neolithic talismen: Thomas, N., 'A Neolithic chalk cup from Wilsford in the Devizes Museum: and notes on others', *WAM 54*, 1952, 452–63.

26 Chalk objects at Windmill Hill: Smith, I. F., *Windmill Hill and Avebury* Oxford, 1965, 130–4. Elsewhere: Burl, 1981, 45.

27 Axe and phallus at Stonehenge: Cleal, in Cleal *et al.*, 1995, 204.

28 Discs: Burl, 1981, 77–8.

29 Fragility of chalk: Cunnington, M. E., *Woodhenge*, 112.

30 West:*ibid.*, 11.

31 'Equinoctial' sunrise: Pearson, M. P., *Bronze Age Britain*, London, 1993, 62.

32 Browne, Sir T., *Hydriotaphia, Urn Burial, or a Discourse on the Sepulchral Urns lately found in Norfolk*, 1658, ed. Herford, C. H., London, 1906.

CHAPTER SIX

1 Gower, J. E. B., Mawer, A. and Stenton, F. M., *The Place-Names of Wiltshire*, Cambridge, 1970, 360; Stukeley, 1740, 8, 47.

2 Roman destruction: Atkinson, 1956, 77; Castleden, 1993, 245–8.

3 Roman material st Stonehenge: Hawley, 1926, 15; Cleal, *et al.*, 1995, 337; Stukeley, 1740, 32.

4 Henry of Huntingdon, *The Chronicle of Henry of Huntingdon*, tr. and ed. Forester, T., 1853. Facsimile reprint, Felinfach, 1991, 7–8. Geoffrey of Monmouth, *The History of the Kings of Britain*, tr. Thorpe, L., London, 1969, 172–4. Robert Wace, *Roman de Brut*, tr. Mason, E., London, 1962, 27–9.

5 Stonehenge bibliography: Harrison, 1901. Welsh bluestones: Harrison, *Geology of Wiltshire*, 1882, 282–91.

6 Works omitted from the bibliography of D. Souden's *Stonehenge. Mysteries of the Stones and Landscape*, 1997, 154–5: Stevens, 1916, 1929; Cunnington, 1935; Newall, 1953; Newham, 1964, Hawkins, 1966a; Crampton, P., *Stonehenge of the Kings*, 1967; Niel, 1975; Stover, L. E. and Kraig, E., *Stonehenge and the Origins of Western Culture*, 1979; Balfour, M., *Stonehenge and its Mysteries* 1979; Fowles, J. and Brukoff, B., *The Enigma of Stonehenge* 1980.

7 Discovery of the avenue and cursus: Stukeley, 1740, 35, 41.

8 Wood, J., 1747, 38; Smith, J., 1771, v, 63–4.

9 Survey: Petrie, 1880, 3. Numbering of the stones: *ibid.*, 9.

10 Excavations at Stonehenge: Hawley, 1921–1928.

11 Bluestones from the Preselis: Thomas, H. H., 1923.

12 The astronomy of Stonehenge: Newham 1964; Newham, 1972.

13 Stonehenge and the dodo: Burl, 1976, 1.

14 The Four Stations rectangle: Thatcher, 1976, 144–6.

15 Standing stones in the avenue: Castleden, 1993, 131–2.

16 Recent radio-carbon dates from Stonehenge: Cleal *et al.*, 1995, 522–6.

CHAPTER SEVEN

1 Colours in prehistoric monuments: Atkinson, Rev. R. J., 1891, *Forty Years in a Moorland Parish*, London 147; Burl, 1981, 152, 165, 167; Lynch, F., 'Colour in prehistoric architecture', in Gibson and Simpson (eds.), 1998, 62–7.

2 Evans, 1966, 136–8.

3 Bartenstein, H. and Fletcher, B. N., 'The stones of Stonehenge – an ancient observation on their geological and archaeological history', *Zeitschrift für Deutsche Geologische Gesellschaft 138*, 1987, 23–32; Thorpe, *et al.*, 123–4; de Luc, J. A., *Geological Travels, III. Travels in England*, London, 1811, 463, 471; Darrah, J., 'The bluestones of Stonehenge', *Curr Arch 134*, 1993, 78.

4 Green, C. P., 'Stonehenge: geology and prehistory', *Proc. Geologists' Assoc 108 (1)*, 1997, 1–10, 2.

5 Cuckoo Stone: Burl, 1987, 44.

6 Stukeley, 1740, 37.

7 Jones, 1655, 34; Aubrey, 1665, 91; Stukeley, 1740, 5.

8 Fiennes, *c.* 1712, 42; Hoare, 1812, 149; Stone, 1924, 143–5. Scarcity of sarsens: Green, C. P., 'Stonehenge', 6.

9 Amesbury 104: Lukis, *WAM 8*, 1864, 155. Pit or grave: *RCAHM-England*, 1979, 1.

10 Arn Hill: Hoare, 1812, 65. Corton: *ibid.*, 102. Boles Barrow: *ibid.*, 87–8; Burl, 1987, 21.

11 Tidcombe barrow: Willis, Mr, 1787 'An essay towards a discovery of the great Ikineld-Street of the Romans', *Arch 8*, 88–99, 1787, 91–2, Note i.

12 Marlborough Down barrows: Barker, C. T, *WAM 79*, 1984, 7–38, 11–17: nos. 3, 4, 5, 7, 8.

13 Timber mortuary houses: Ashbee 1984, 49–51, 126–9.

14 Corton: Hoare, 1812; Boles Barrow: Cunnington, B. H., ' "Blue hard stone, ye same as at Stonehenge", found in Boles [Bowls] Barrow (Heytesbury, I)', *WAM 41*, 1922, 172–4; Hoare, 1812, 87–8.

15 Timber in henges: Richards, J., *Stonehenge*, London, 1991, 88–101.

16 Stonehenge and Brittany: Burl, 1997.

17 Sarsens and bluestones at Stonehenge: Atkinson, 1979, 49–53. The Preselis: Thomas, 1923, 239–60.

18 In favour of glaciation: Judd, 1903; Kellaway, 1971; Thorpe *et al.*, 1991, 121–4; Williams-Thorpe, 1997. Against glaciation: Green, D., 'The Stonehenge bluestones', *Curr Arch 126*, 1991, 251; Selkirk, A., 'Stonehenge bluestones', *Curr Arch 148*, 1996, 143–4; Green, C. P., 'Stonehenge', 7–9; Green, C. and Scourse, J. D., 'The Stonehenge bluestones: discussion', *Proc Brit Acad 92*, 1997, 316–18. (But see Williams-Thorpe, above, 315–16).

19 Bluestones found between Preselis and Stonehenge: Musty, J., 'The blue stones of Stonehenge', *Curr Arch 124*, 1991, 184; Lamb, K., 'The Stonehenge "bluestones" ', *Curr Arch 127*, 1991, 318.

20 Movement of heavy stones: Recumbent stones of circles: Burl, 1970, 68–9. La Hougue Bie: Patton, M. A., 'Megalithic transport and territorial markers: evidence from the Channel Isles', *Ant 66*, 392–5. The Grand Menhir Brisé: Hornsey, R., 'The Grand Menhir Brisé: megalithic success or failure?', *Oxford Journal of Archaeology 6 (2)*, 1987, 185–217; Hadingham, E., *Circles and Standing Stones*, London, 1974, 164.

21 Story of odd coins: Wood, J., 1747, 73–5; Stone, 1924, 140; Grinsell, 1975, 14–15. By 1700 Irish currency was in such a chaotic state that even foreign money was being used. The Treasury acted and 'by a proclamation of 1718 no gold or silver coin was to be paid unless it was weighed'. The Irish 6d had $1^1/_2$d deducted and was devalued to $4^1/_2$d. The source of the story and its approximate date can be suggested. It was not mentioned by Stukeley despite his references to Geoffrey of Monmouth, 48–9. 'How absurd the monkish reports are'. Less than twenty years later in 1740 John Wood was planning Stonehenge and probably heard the tale from Gaffer Hunt of Amesbury who was acting as unofficial guide and supplier of liquor to visitors. His use of 'backside' for 'backyard' was a provincial term, common in Hampshire and probably in Wiltshire. Beakers and stone circles: Burl, 1976, 98–9.

22 A stone circle near the Preselis: Stone, 1924, 65.

23 Preseli lintelled circle: Richards, J. *Stonehenge*, 54–7.

24 Preseli battle-axes: Atkinson, 1979, 176.

25 Medicinal powers: Geoffrey of Monmouth, *c.* 1138, 173; Brome, Rev. J., *Travels Over England*, London, 1701, 44–6.

26 Waterborne experiment: Atkinson, 1979, 113.
27 The journey from the Preselis: *ibid.*, 106–10.
28 Triumphal procession: Crampton, P., *Stonehenge of the Kings*, London, 1967, 7. 'Some form of craft': Balfour, M., *Stonehenge and its Mysteries*, London, 1979, 88.
29 Hawkins, 1966a, 73, 64.
30 Atkinson, 1979, 111–12.
31 Tizard, Capt. T. H., *The Tides and Tidal Streams of the British Islands, the North Sea, and the North Coast of France*, London, 1909, 177, 179, 186–7.
32 Number of stones: Walker and Gardiner, in Cleal *et al.*, 1995, 29.
33 Altar Stone: Ivimy, J., *The Sphinx and the Megaliths*, London, 1974, 81.
34 Dolerites: Thorpe *et al.*, 1991, 122.
35 Spotted dolerite: *ibid.*, 115.
36 Geoffrey of Monmouth and the bluestones: Burl, 1985a, 180; 1987, 132.
37 Gerald of Wales, *c.* 1222, 84.
38 *Ibid.*, 69.
39 Standing stones near Kildare: Evans, 1966, 63, 136–8.
40 Geoffrey of Monmouth, *c.* 1138, 175.
41 Coope, G. R., 'The influence of geology on the manufacture of Neolithic and Bronze Age stone implements in the British Isles', in Clough and Cummins, 1979, 98–101.
42 Battle-axes: Stone J. F. S. and Wallis, F. S., *PPS 17*, 1951, 99–158.
43 Newall: Thorpe, *et al.*, 1991, 108, quoting from an unpublished letter from G. A. Kellaway.
44 fifield Bavant: Stone, J. F. S., *Ant J 30*, 1950, 145–50. Beakers: Clarke, 1970, II, 504.
45 Thorpe *et al.*, 1991, 106.
46 Friable stones: Walker and Gardiner, in Cleal *et al.*, 1995, 29. Cunnington: Judd, 1903, 47–64; Cunnington, W., 'Stonehenge notes. The fragments', *WAM 21*, 1884, 140–2; Burl, 1987, 135. Buried stumps: Cleal, in Cleal *et al.*, 1995, 239.
47 Judd, 1903, 59–60.
48 Dressing of stones on site: Green, C. P., 'Stonehenge: geology and prehistory', 1997, 5.
49 Edington: Jackson, Canon J. E., 'Edingdon monastery', *WAM 20*, 1882, 241–306.
50 Section through Boles Barrow: Cunnington MSS, III, 1801–1809. 'Mr Cunnington's M.S.S. Ancient Wilts, volumes I–XIII', Devizes Museum, 29.
51 Bluestone block: Cunnington, B. H., 'Blue hard stone, ye same as at Stonehenge', found in Boles [Bowles] Barrow (Heytesbury 1), *WAM 41*, 1920, 172–4.
52 Letter to Wyndham: Cunnington, B. H., 'The "Blue Stone" from Boles Barrow', 173.
53 Weight of the bluestone block: P. Saunders, Salisbury Museum, personal communication, 25 March 1997.
54 William Cunnington as a geologist: Cunnington, R. H., *From Antiquary to Archaeologist. A Biography of William Cunnington, 1754–1810*, ed., Dyer, J., Princes Risborough 1975, 109, 154.
55 William Smith: Cunnington MS IV, 53–5.
56 Evelyn: Dobson, A., (ed.), *The Diary of John Evelyn*, II, London, 1906, 83.
57 Chippindale, 1994, 73, fig. 47, *ibid.*, 98.
58 Removal of stones from Boles Barrow: Cunnington MSS, 31; Cunnington, B. H., 'The "Blue Stone" from Boles Barrow', *WAM 42*, 1924, 432.
59 Letter to Britton: *ibid.*, 433.
60 No stones were missing: Petrie, 1880, 5, 16.
61 Wood, J., 1747, 53; plans, 34, 46.
62 Stone 32 and the plans of 1740 and 1877: *ibid.*, 34; Petrie, 1880, Plate 1, 1.
63 The 'dressed' bluestone: Cunnington, B. H., 'The "Blue Stone" from Boles Barrow', 434; Green, 1997, 267; Atkinson, 1979, 50–1.
64 The Museum bluestone from Boles Barrow: Cunnington, B. H., 'The "Blue Stone" from Boles Barrow', 435.
65 Atkinson, 1979, 58–61. Uncertain chronology: Cleal in Cleal, *et al.*, 1995, 169–88.
66 *Ibid.*, 188.
67 Radiocarbon assays: Allen and Bayliss, in *ibid.*, 522–5. From a different source: *Archaeometry 38*, 1996, 391–415.
68 Uncertain date of the arrival of the bluestones: Cleal, in Cleal *et al.*, 1995, 206–7, 230, 212.
69 Green and Scourse, 'The Stonehenge bluestones', 318.
70 The 'missing' bluestones: Niel, 1975, 136.
71 Q and R Holes: Atkinson, 1979, 58–61; sarsen circle: *ibid.*, 49–56.

CHAPTER EIGHT

1 Leaning of the Heel Stone: Hoyle, 1977, 23.
2 Petrie and Hawkins, 1989, 53.
3 Atkinson, 1979, 29.
4 Burl, 1987, 75.
5 Phase of the Heel Stone: Atkinson, 1979, 70.
6 Cleal, in Cleal *et al.*, 1995, 274.
7 Timber structure inside Stonehenge: Atkinson, 1979, 170–1; Burl, 1987, 51–6.
8 The 'Sunstone': Newall, 1953, 4.
9 Cunnington, R. H., 1935, 22.
10 'Hele' Stone: Stevens, F., 1916, 5; Gowland, W., *WAM 33*, 1903, 1–62; Antrobus, Lady F. C. M. *A Sentimental & Practical Guide to Amesbury and Stonehenge*, Salisbury, 1901, 24.
11 Atkinson, R. J. C., 'Stonehenge', *Encyclopaedia Britannica*, London, 1955.
12 Harrison, 1901; Fidler, T. C. 'The astronomical theories as to Stonehenge', *JBAA 37*, 1881, 167–8.
13 Systems of stone-numbering: Petrie, 1880, 9; Wood, J., 1747, 54; Smith, J., 1771, Plate II; Hoare, 1812, 145.
14 Alternatives to the Friar's Heel: Stukeley, 1740, 33; 'the *Crwm Leche* or bowing stone', Anon., *A Description of Stonehenge, Abiry etc*, Salisbury, 1776, 7; Hoare, 1812, 143; Wansey, H., 'Stonehenge', 1796 in Easton, J. (ed.) *Conjectures on that Mysterious Monument of Ancient Art, Stonehenge, on Salisbury Plain*, Salisbury, 1815, 107–11, Smith, J., 1771, 51.
15 Smith, J., 1771, 64, 37.
16 Grand festival: Stukeley, 1723, 112.
17 Stukeley and the midsummer sunrise: 1740, 35, 56.
18 Friar's Heel and the Heel Stone: Smith, J., 1771, 13, 51.
19 Geoffrey of Monmouth, *c.* 1139, 196–8; Wood, J., 1747, 75.
20 Wood, J., 1747. References to his Stone R: pp. 33, 44, 48, 52, 58, 81–2; 'Heil': 17–18.
21 *Crwm leche*: Stukeley, 1740, 33.
22 The outlying Heel Stone: Aubrey, 1665, 76. The Slaughter Stone: *ibid.*, 97.
23 Cropped plan: Aubrey, 1665, 80. Complete plan: Long, 1876, 32. For the interest of readers wishing to examine Aubrey's plan of Stonehenge it must be pointed out that in the Dorset Publishing House edition of 1980, page 80, the edges of the plan have been cropped and some stones are missing.
24 The Friar's Heel: Aubrey, 1665, 95.
25 Long, 1876, 32–40.
26 Stevens, E. T. 1882, 88.
27 Long, 1876, 7–31. 'R. F.': Bakker, J. A., 'Lucas de Heere's Stonehenge', *Ant 53*, 1979, 107–11; Camden, 1610, 251–4; Jones, 1655, 55, 57.
28 Size of footprint: Atkinson, 1979, 204.
29 Wood, J., 1747, 13, 55.
30 Smith, J., 1771, 53; Petrie, 1880, 10, note.
31 Stone 14: Stukeley, 1740, 24, Tab. XIII; Aubrey, 1665, 80.
32 Devil's Arrows: Burl, 'The Devil's Arrows, Boroughbridge, North Yorkshire', *YAJ 63*, 1991, 1–24.
33 Stukeley, 1740, 35; Lockyer, 1909, 62–8.
34 'Or nearly': Stukeley, 1740, 56.
35 Stonehenge and the moon: Wood, J., 1747, 80–1, 95.
36 Smith, 1771, v; Hawkins, 1966a, vii.
37 Midsummer sunrise: Wansey, H., 'Stonehenge', 1796, 61; Duke, Rev. E., 1846, 133; Herbert, A. *Cyclops Christianus*, London, 1849, 98; Stevens, E. T., 1882, 26; Ashbee, P. *The Ancient British*, Norwich, 1978, 152.
38 Confusion: Souden, D., *Stonehenge. Mysteries of the Stones and Landscape*, London, 1997, 124.
39 The Heel Stone as an inexact solar marker: Lockyer, 1909, 68; Stone, 1924, 130; Niel, 1975, 6; Atkinson, 1979, 30.
40 Deceptive photography: Chippindale, 1994, 137.
41 46° 33': Burl, 1987, 77. Long Meg: Burl, 1995, 47. Swinside, *ibid.*, 49; Druids' Circle: *ibid.*, 177. Rollright Stones: *ibid.*, 73.
42 Causeway postholes: Hawley, W. 1924, 30–9; Hawley, W., 1925, 21–50; Newham, 1972, 15–17. Criticisms: Heggie, D. C., *Megalithic Science*, 202, 1981; Cleal, in Cleal *et al.*, 1995, 145.
43 The 'A' Holes: Wood, J. E., 1978, 163; Burl, 1987, 68–70; Petrie and Hawkins, 1989, 53.
44 The changed axis: Burl, 1987, 140.
45 1979 excavation: Pitts, M. W., 'On the road to Stonehenge . . .', *PPS 48*, 1982, 75–132.
46 Astronomical 'window': Castleden, 1987, 102, 129. A pit for the Heel Stone: Burl, 1987, 78.
47 A second lunar foresight. Four posts: Atkinson, 1979; Wood, J. E., 1978, 161- 2. Third stone: Burl, 1987, 40.

48 The present axis of Stonehenge: Atkinson, 1979, 69, 73.
49 Feast of St John Baptist: Aubrey, 'The Remaines of Gentilisme and Judaisme', 1688, in: *Three Prose Works. John Aubrey*, ed. Buchanan-Brown, J., Fontwell, 1972, 207.
50 Summer solstice: Stukeley, 1723, 112.
51 Edward Weaver: *Compact Edition of the Dictionary of National Biography, II*, Oxford, 1975, 2300. Visits to Stukeley: Lukis, 1883, 88.
52 Feast of St Barnabas: Lukis, 1887, 308–9, 376.
53 Stukeley, 1740, 64.
54 *Ibid.*, 56.
55 Stukeley and astronomers: *ibid.*, 57.
56 The druids' compass: *ibid.*, 57.
57 Stukeley's compass: Atkinson, R. J. C., 'William Stukeley and the Stonehenge sunrise', *Archaeoastronomy 8*, 1985, S61-S62.
58 Lunar cycle and month: Toland, 1726, 122; Wood, J., 1747, 80. Shapes of rings, crescent moon, circle the sun: Toland, 1726, 124. Stukeley at Stanton Drew: Stukeley, 1776b, 174.
59 Titania and midsummer: Brooks, H. F. (ed.), *A Midsummer Night's Dream*, London, 1979, lxx. May revels: Stubbes, P., *The Anatomie of Abuses*, London, 1583: Long, G., *The Folklore Calendar*, 1996, 67–8.

CHAPTER NINE

1 Numbering of the Heel Stone: Petrie 1880, 12.
2 The name: Camden, 1610, 252 (1637 edn); Jones, 1655, 57. Jones's mistake: Cunnington, 1935, 24. Burl, 1994, 85–7.
3 Aubrey, 1665, 76.
4 Anonymous stone: Stukeley, 1723, 55; Stukeley, 1740, 33. 'Rabbets': Stukeley, 12. Wood, J., 1747, 53.
5 Smith's plagiarism of Stukeley: Burl 1991, 2. Rabbits: Smith, J., 1771, 51.
6 Owen, A. L., *The Famous Druids. A Survey of Three Centuries of English Literature on the Druids*, Oxford, 1962, 118.
7 Sacrifices: Anon., *A Description of Stonehenge, Abiry &c. in Wiltshire*, Salisbury, 1776, 7. King, E., *Munimenta Antiqua I*, London, 1799, 1549–1209. Immolation: Brown, W., *The Illustrated Guide to Old Sarum and Stonehenge*, Salisbury, 1898, 27. 'Horrid banquet': Maurice, T., *Indian Antiquities VI*, London, 1796, 128.
8 Cunnington, R. H., *From Antiquary to Archaeologist. A Biography of William Cunnington, 1754–1810*, Princes Risborough 1975, 151.
9 Cunnington's letter: Long 1876, 56–7, sketch, 93.
10 Bottle of port: Hawley, W., 'Stonehenge: interim report on the exploration', *Ant J 1*, 1921, 34.
11 Broken bottles: Webb, J., *A Vindication of Stone-Heng Restored . . .*, 2nd edn, London, 1725, 11.
12 Standing Slaughter Stone: Jones 1655, 57; Jones, 1725, 39; Aubrey, 1665, 76.
13 Hawley 1924, 36–7; Cleal, in Cleal *et al.*, 287.
14 Petrie 1880, 16.
15 Aubrey's unreliable memory: Burl, 'Two Early Plans of Avebury', *WAM 85*, 1992, 163–72. His plan: Aubrey, 1665, 80.
16 Aubrey, 1665, 97.
17 'Proto-archaeologues': Hawkins 1966a, 54–5.
18 Drawings of Stonehenge: Chippindale, 1994, 34–5, 37.
19 Bakker, J. A., 'Lucas de Heere's Stonehenge', *Ant 53*, 1979, 107–11.
20 Webb, J., *A Vindication of Stone-Heng*, 16.
21 Interruption of the 'heel stone view': Hawkins 1966a, 55.
22 'Sacred Marriage': Meaden, T., *The Stonehenge Solution*, London, 1992, 165; *ibid.*, *Stonehenge. The Secret of the Solstice*, London, 1997, 127. The Slaughter Stone a standing pillar: sketches, 'R. F.', 1575; Camden, 1610, 252. Written records: Jones, 1655, 63; Webb, 1725, 16; Aubrey, 1665, 97. C-14 assays, Cleal *et al.*, 524.
23 Cunnington in 1802: Cunnington R. H., *From Antiquary to Archaeologist*, 151. Dating of Stone E: Cleal, in Cleal *et al.*, 1995, 204–5, 524.
24 The Station Stones: Burl, 1987, 142–7; Atkinson, 1979, 78.
25 Tooling of the Slaughter Stone: Stone 1924, 119.
26 Hawley, W., 'Stonehenge', 1921, 17–41;
27 Stone numbering: Petrie, 1880, 9. Stone J predicted: Newall, R. S., 'Stonehenge', *Ant 3*, 1929, 75–88. Numbered 97: Pitts 1982, 78.
28 Stoneholes E and 97: Burl, 1987, 77. Stonehole E separate: Hawley, W., 1924, 36; Pitts, 1982, 82.
29 Partner to the Slaughter Stone: Stukeley, 1723, 57. Excavations: Atkinson, 1979, 31.
30 Stonehole D: Hawley, 1924, 46; Cleal, in Cleal *et al.*, 1995, 285. Northern moonrise: Hawkins, 1966a, 139. Lunar mistake: Atkinson, R. J. C., 'Moonshine on Stonehenge', *Ant 50*, 1966, 212–16, 215.
31 Pair of adjacent stones: Stone, 1924, 121. Heel Stone pair: Pitts, 1982, 79,

32. Widened entrance: Burl, 1987, 140.
32 Heel Stone and midsummer sunrise: Lockyer, *Proc Roy Soc 69*, 1901, 143.
33 Chippindale, 1994, 137. A lunar alignment: Wood, J. E., 1978, 163.
34 New axis: Burl, 1987, 140.
35 Sunrise between the two stones: Pitts, M. W., 'The Discovery of a New Stone at Stonehenge', *Archaeoastronomy. Bulletin IV (2)*, 1981, 16–21. Pair standing together: Pitts, 1982, 82.
36 Plan of Stonehenge: Hoare, 1812, 143. Crocker as a surveyor: Marsden, B. M., *The Early Barrow Diggers*, Princes Risborough 1974, 17–18.
37 William Cunnington III: Long 1876, 57. A second opinion: Stevens, E. T., 1882, 87.
38 Evidence of crude alignments in chambered tombs: Burl, 1983, 21–9. In stone rows: Burl, 1993. Irish rows, Lynch, A., 'Astronomy and Stone Alignments in S. W. Ireland', in Heggie, D. C. (ed.), *Archaeoastronomy in the Old World*, Cambridge, 1982, 205–13; Ruggles, C. L. N., 'Stone rows of three or more stones in south-west Ireland', *Archaeoastronomy 21*, 1996, S55–71. In Scotland: Ruggles, *Megalithic Astronomy: a New Archaeological and Statistical Study of 300 Western Scottish Sites*, Oxford, 1984.
39 Holes B and C: Hawley, 1925, 23–4; Atkinson, 1979, 76.
40 Megalithic Yard: Thom 1967, 34–55.

CHAPTER TEN

1 The U-shaped setting: Aubrey, 1665, 82; Stukeley, 1740, 22–5; Wood, J., 1747, 57–80; Smith, J., 1771, 56; Hoare, 1812, 147; Stone, 1924, 1; Cunnington, 1935, 13; Atkinson, 1979, 40; Walker, in Cleal *et al.*, 1995, 29; Souden, D., *Stonehenge. Mysteries of the Stones and Landscape*, London, 1997, 84.
2 Stone, 1924, 33; Barclay, 1895, 127.
3 Rarity of horseshoes: Burl, 1970, 72. Horseshoe at Avebury: Aubrey, 1665, 44–5. Resistivity survey: Ucko *et al.*, 220–7. East Moor: Johnson, N. and Rose, P., *Bodmin Moor. An Archaeological Survey, I*, London, 1994, 28–9.
4 King Arthur's Hall: Lewis, A. L. 'Prehistoric remains in Cornwall', *JRAI 25*, 1896, 2–16; Barnatt, 1982, 196–7. Exmoor: Quinnell, N. V., *Lithic Monuments within the Exmoor National Park: a New Survey for Management Purposes by the Royal Commission on the Historical Monuments in England*, ed. Dunn, C. J., Exeter, 1992. Mattocks Down, a 'high-and-low' double row: Burl, 1993, 89–90, 234.
5 Breton rectangles: Burl, 1993, 89.
6 Stonehenge not British: Geoffrey of Monmouth, *c.* 1139, 196; Jones, 1655; Charleton, 1663; Atkinson, 1956, 84–5; *ibid.*, 1979, 166–7; Piggott, *The Times*, 4 August 1954.
7 Egypt: Ivimy, J., *The Sphinx and the Megaliths*, 1974, 152–9. Stonehenge British: Crampton, P., *Stonehenge of the Kings*, 1967, 59–61; Burl, 1976, 315, and 1987, 150–71; Richards, *Stonehenge*, 1991, 115; Castleden, 1993, 144; Chippindale, 1994, 209; Souden, D., *Stonehenge*, 110–11.
8 Wessex and Brittany: Piggott, S., 'The Early Bronze Age in Wessex', *Proc Prehist Soc 4 (1)*, 1938, 52–106. Handled pot: Grinsell, 1978a, 19. Winterbourne Stoke 5: Hoare, 1812, 122–3; Annable, F. K. and Simpson, D. D. A., *Guide Catalogue of the Neolithic and Bronze Age Collections in Devizes Museum*, Devizes, 1964, 50, nos 263–6.
9 Bronze daggers: *ibid.*, 45–6, nos 168–78; Grinsell, 1978a, 31–5; Taylor, J. J., *Bronze Age Goldwork of the British Isles*, Cambridge, 1980, 87, Wt. 3–6. Recent analysis: J. Briard, in Scarre, C. and Healy, F. (eds), *Trade and Exchange in Prehistoric Europe*, Oxford, 1993, 183–90.
10 Bush Barrow and Wessex: Giot *et al.*, 1979, 41; Taylor, J. J., *Bronze Age Goldwork*, 45.
11 Gold artefacts: *ibid.*, 46, 47; Burgess, 1980, 110, 103.
12 Wilsford 7: Annable and Simpson, *Guide Catalogue*, 44, nos 147–58; Grinsell, 1978a, 35.
13 Wilsford 8: Hoare, 1812, 201.
14 *Ibid.*, 201–2; Annable and Simpson, *Guide Catalogue*, 46, nos 179–92.
15 Single cultural province: Megaw and Simpson, 1979, 223.
16 Two phases: Giot, P.-R., *Brittany*, London, 1960, 128–45; Giot, P.-R., Briard, J. and Pape, L., *Protohistoire de la Bretagne*, Rennes, 1979, 29–107.
17 Rivetted daggers, Giot, 1960, 132–3; Giot *et al.*, *Protohistoire*, 76–7. Handled pots: *ibid.*, 97. Wessex and Brittany, Taylor, J. J., *Bronze Age Goldwork*, 45.
18 Macehead: Castleden, 1993, 282, note 72. Cotswold-Severn tombs and France: Lynch, F., *Megalithic Tombs and Long Barrows in Britain*, Princes Risborough, 1997, 53–4.
19 1620 ± 110 bc: Baylis, Housley and McCormac, in Cleal *et al.*, 518.
20 C-14 assays from Stonehenge: Cleal *et al.*, 204–5. Goërem, Gâvres, Crech-Quillé: Twohig, E. S., *The Megalithic Art of Western Europe*, Oxford, 1981, 179–80, 187. Breton dates: Hibbs, J., 'The Neolithic of

Brittany', in Scarre, C. (ed.) *Ancient France*, Edinburgh, 1983, 323.

21 Four Stations: Atkinson, R. J. C., 'The Stonehenge Stations', *Journal of Hist Astronomy 7*, 1976, 142–4.

22 Dimensions of the rectangle: Atkinson, R. J. C., 1978 'Some new measurements on Stonehenge', *Nature 275*, 50–2.

23 Duke, 1846, 144.

24 Hawkins, 1966a, 110. Coarse sightlines: Burl, 1983.

25 Lockyer, 1906, 93.

26 May Day sunset: Thom, 1967, 110, Epoch 2. Thatcher, 1976, 144–5.

27 May Day diagonal: Burl, 1987, 141–7.

28 Crucuno quadrilateral: Thom, A., Thom, A. S., Merritt, R. L. and Merritt, A. L., 'The astronomical significance of the Crucuno stone rectangle', *Current Anthropology 14 (4)*, 1973, 450–4. Le Narbon: Sherratt, 1998, 132.

29 Horseshoe inside Avebury: Ucko *et al.*, 220–7. Stukeley, 1743, 23. Horseshoes in Scotland: Burl, 1993, 117.

30 Solar alignments in Breton cromlechs: Burl, 1993, 146; *ibid.*, 1995, 260–1.

31 Kerlescan: Burl, 1993, 140–3.

32 Er-Lannic: Burl, 1976, 135–6.

33 Seasonal gatherings at Carnac: Worsfold, T. C., *The French Stonehenge*, London, 1898, 22; Burl, 1993, 144–60.

34 The megalithic horseshoe: Atkinson, 1979, 131; Cleal, in Cleal *et al.*, 205.

35 Ramp for Stone 56: *ibid.*, 207; Castleden, 1993, 161.

36 Timber building: Atkinson, 1979, 170–1; Burl, 1987, 53–5, 172.

37 Cupmarks on recumbent stone circles in Scotland: Ruggles, C. L. N. and Burl, H. A. W., 'A new study of the Aberdeenshire recumbent stone circles, 2: interpretation', *Archaeoastronomy 8*, 1985, S54-S56. Art in Britain: Bradley, 1997, 57.

38 Carvings at Stonehenge: Burl, 1987, 186–7; Bradley, 1997, 137. Lattice: Atkinson, 1979, 209. Mané Kerioned: Burl, 1985b, 152. Stone 5: Lawson and Walker, in Cleal *et al.*, 30–3. Doubtful carvings: Atkinson, 1979, 46.

39 Stone 57: Crawford, O. G. S., 'The symbols carved on Stonehenge', *Ant 28*, 1954, 25–31. 'Mother-goddess': Atkinson, 1979, 45, 179. Third rectangle: Burl, 1987, 210; Castleden, 1993, 209–17.

40 Breton megalithic carvings: Twohig, E. S., *The Megalithic Art of Western Europe*, Oxford, 1981, 60–3, 92.

41 Stone 25, Gavr'inis: Kergal, *L'Allée-Couverte de Gavr'inis. Les Pierres Gravées*, Fontenay-le-Fleury, 1977, 10, 27.

42 Goërem, Gâvres: Twohig, E. S., *Megalithic Art*, figs 84, 123, 134. Kercado: *ibid.*, fig. 93. Simple rectangles, daggers, axe and breasts at Prajou-Menhir: *ibid.*, figs 152, 153. Late date with Bronze Age Seine-Oise-Marne pottery: l'Helgouach, 'Fouilles de l'allée-couverte de Prajou-Menhir en Trébeurden (Côtes-du-Nord)', *Bullétin de la Société Préhistorique Française 63*, 1966 (1967), 311–42.

43 Stone 57's 'eighteenth-century' rectangle: Lawson and Walker, in Cleal *et al.*, 32.

44 Size of the Stonehenge rectangle: Crawford, 'The symbols carved on Stonehenge', 27. Time to carve it: Atkinson, 1979, 127; Stone, 1924, 88.

45 Criticism of the 'anthropomorph: Scarre, C., 'Misleading images: Stonehenge and Brittany', *Ant 71*, 1997, 1016–20. See also: *Archaeology 50 (4)*, 1997.

46 Entasis at Stonehenge: Atkinson, 1956, 23.

47 The carving on lintel 120: Castleden, 1993, 216–17.

48 Juxtaposed axes and 'goddesses': Twohig, E. S., *Megalithic Art*, figs 99, 102, 126, 128, 147, 148.

49 Chalk axe and phallus: Montague, in Cleal *et al.*, 400, 404.

50 Stonehole of the Altar Stone: Hoare, 1812, 150; Burl, 1987, 58.

51 Centre stones in the British Isles: Burl, 1976, 206–7.

52 Bryn Celli Ddu: Lynch, F., *Prehistoric Anglesey*, 2nd edn, 1991, 97.

53 Barclodiad y Gawres: Burl, 1987, 89. Stone 22 regarded as anthropomorphic: Powell, T. G. E. and Piggott, S., *Barclodiad y Gawres*, 1956, 42–52; Lynch, F., 'Barclodiad y Gawres. Comparative notes on the decorated stones', *Arch Camb 116*, 1967, 9; *ibid.*, Note 51, 76; Twohig, *Megalithic Art*, 121.

54 Breton warriors: Piggott, 'The Early Bronze Age in Wessex', 94.

CHAPTER ELEVEN

1 Dymond, C. W., 'A Group of Cumbrian Megaliths', *TCWAAS 5, (O.S.)*, 1881, 39–57.

2 Hutchinson, W., *The History and Antiquities of Cumberland, I*, Carlisle, 1794, 554; Waterhouse, 1985, 43. Black Combe: Hogg, R., 'Factors which have affected the spread of early settlement in the Lake counties', *TCWAAS*

72, 1972, 1–35.

3 Name: Gambles, R., *Lake District Place-Names*, Clapham, 1980, 43. Legends: Grinsell, 1976, 63. Stone circles in Aberdeenshire: Ritchie, J., 'Folklore of the Aberdeenshire stone circles and standing stones', *PSAS 60*, 1926, 304–13; in Lincolnshire: Westwood, 1992, 515; in Cambridgeshire: Johnson, W., *Byways in British Archaeology*, Cambridge, 1912, 30.

4 Dimensions of Swinside: Dymond, C. W., 'A Group of Cumbrian Megaliths', 46, 92 ft [28.0 m]; Thom, 1967, 39, L1/3, 93.7 ft [28.6 m]; Thom, Thom and Burl, 1980, 35, 93 ft [28.4 m]; Waterhouse, 1985, 42, 28.7 m; Barnatt, 1989, II, 353, 29.1 × 27.7 m. Pyrrhic victory: Waterhouse, 1985, 44.

5 'Buttress of rude pavement': Gough, R. trans: Camden's *Britannia, I–IV*, London, 1806, 432.

6 Fallen stones: Barnatt, 1989, II, 353–4; Waterhouse, 1985, 43.

7 The excavation: Dymond, C. W., 'An exploration at the megalithic circle called Sunken Kirk at Swinside in the parish of Millom', *TCWAAS 2*, 1902, 53–63.

8 Destroyed circles: Waterhouse, 1985, 90–3. Annaside: *TCWAAS 1 (O.S)*, 1874, 278; Waterhouse, 1985, 90. Kirkstones: Hutchinson, W., *History and Antiquities of Cumberland*, 554; Waterhouse, 1985, 90. Hall Foss: Hutchinson, W., *History and Antiquities of Cumberland*, 554; Waterhouse, 1985, 90.

9 The purpose of Swinside: Dymond, C. W., 'An Exploration', 60.

10 Hills: Lewis, A. L. 'On three stone circles in Cumberland', *JRAI 15*, 1886, 471–81; Lewis, A. L., 'Stone circles of Britain', *Arch J 49*, 1892, 148. Three hills to the north-east, at 30°, 50°, 64°; no. 81, prominent Black Combe at 320°; entrance and hilltop, 29°. Bewley, R., *Prehistoric Settlements*, London, 1994.

11 Local units of measurement. Beaker Yard, 73 cm: Burl, 1987, 124; Perth Yard, 96 cm: Burl, 1988a, 7–8; Cork Yard, 95 cm: Burl, 1995, 227; Cumbrian Yard, 79.4 cm and Stanton Drew, 92.4 cm: this work. For the problems of recovering prehistoric mensuration, see Heggie, 1981.

12 The 'north' stone at Swinside. Plans by Dymond, C. W., 'A Group of Cumbrian Megaliths', 47.

13 Stone circles as staging-posts: Burl, 1988b, 183–4; Bradley, R. and Edmonds, M., *Interpreting the Axe Trade. Production and Exchange in Neolithic Britain*, Cambridge, 1993, 150–2, 198. Waterhouse, 1985, 4–7.

14 Distribution of Cumbrian roughouts: Collingwood, R. G., 1933, 176; Bradley and Edmonds, *Interpreting the Axe Trade*, 145.

15 Roughouts and polished axes in Furness: *ibid.*, 144, figs 7.4, 7.5. Skelmore Heads: *TCWAAS 63*, 1963, 1–30. Druid's Temple: *ibid.* 12, 1912, 262–74; *ibid.* 22, 1922, 346–52.

16 Timber circles: Collingwood, 1933, 178.

17 Walney Island: Robinson, H., *Walney Island Past and Present*, Abermeurig, n.d.

18 Inaccessible sources: Bradley and Edmonds, *Interpreting the Axe Trade*, 134. For Neolithic technology, see Sahlins, M., *Stone Age Economics*, London, 1974.

19 Cattle and summer grazing: Robinson, H., *Walney Island*, 144.

20 Weight of axes: Bradley and Edmonds, *Interpreting the Axe Trade*, 88, 132, 141.

21 Ash House Wood stone circle: Hutchinson, W., *History and Antiquities of Cumberland*, 529; Waterhouse, 1985, 93; Barnatt, 1989, II, 341.

22 Boats: Bowen, E. G., *Britain and the Western Seaways*, London, 1972, 34–41. For the Ballynoe stone circle: Groenman-van Waateringe, W. and Butler, J. J., 'The Ballynoe stone circle. Excavations by A. E. van Giffen, 1937–8', *Palaeohistoria 18*, 1976, 73–104.

23 Irish Sea crossing: Davies, M., 'Types of megalithic monuments of the Irish Sea and North Channel coastlands', *Ant J 25*, 1945, 125–46.

24 Landmarks: Burl, 1988b, 193–5.

25 Group VI axes in Ireland: Mandal, S. and Cooney, G., 'The Irish stone axe project: a second petrological report', *JIA 7*, 1996, 41–64. Francis, E. L., P. J. and Preston, J., 'The petrological identification of stone implements from Ireland', in Clough and Cummins, 1988, 137–40.

26 Male and female stones: Burl, 1993, 88, 181, 192–3. For ritual in prehistoric Europe, see: Gelling, P. and Davidson, H. E., *The Chariot of the Sun . . .*, London 1969. For social ceremonies in megalith-building people, see: Layard, J., *Stone Men of Malekula*, London, 1942.

27 Astronomy: At Swinside's latitude, 54°.6, an azimuth of 134°.5, and a skyline of 0°.7 corrected for refraction to 0°.26, the declination, −23°.7, is that of the midwinter sunrise. For the calendrically ritual year, see: Hutton, R., *The Stations of the Sun*, Oxford, 1996.

BIBLIOGRAPHY

ALLCROFT, A. H., 1927 *The Circle and the Cross, I*, London.

ASHBEE, P., 1984 *The Earthen Long Barrow in Britain*, 2nd edn, Norwich.

ATKINSON, R. J. C., 1956 *Stonehenge*, London.

——1961 'Neolithic engineering', *Ant 35*, 292–9.

——1979 *Stonehenge*, 2nd edn, Harmondsworth.

AUBREY, J., 1665–93 *Monumenta Britannica, I, II*, ed. J. Fowles, 1980, 1982, Milborne Port.

BARCLAY, E., 1895 *Stonehenge and its Earthworks*, London.

BARNATT, J., 1982 *Prehistoric Cornwall. The Ceremonial Monuments*, Wellingborough.

——1989 *Stone Circles of Britain, I, II*, Oxford.

BECKENSALL, S., 1992 *Cumbrian Prehistoric Rock Art: Symbols, Monuments and Landscape*, Hexham.

BRADLEY, R., 1993 *Altering the Earth*, Edinburgh.

——1997 *Rock Art and the Prehistory of Atlantic Europe. Signing the Land*, London.

BRENNAN, M., 1983 *The Stars and the Stones* London.

BRIARD, J., 1989 *Mégalithes de Haute Bretagne*, Paris.

——1990 *Dolmens et Menhirs*, Rennes.

BURGESS, C., 1980 *The Age of Stonehenge*, London.

BURL, A., 1970 'The recumbent stone circles of north-east Scotland', *PSAS 102*, 56–81.

——1976 *The Stone Circles of the British Isles*, New Haven and London.

——1979a *Prehistoric Avebury*, New Haven and London.

——1979b *Prehistoric Stone Circles*, Princes Risborough.

——1981 *Rites of the Gods*, London.

——1983 *Prehistoric Astronomy and Ritual*, Princes Risborough.

——1985a 'Geoffrey of Monmouth and the Stonehenge bluestones', *WAM 79*, 178–83.

——1985b *Megalithic Brittany: a Guide*, London.

——1987 *The Stonehenge People*, London.

——1988a *Four-Posters. Bronze Age Stone Circles of Western Europe*, Oxford.

——1988b 'Without sharp north . . . Alexander Thom and the great stone circles of Cumbria' in Ruggles, C. L. N. (ed.) *Records in Stone. Papers in Memory of Alexander Thom*, Cambridge, 175–205.

——1988c 'Coves: structural enigmas of the Neolithic', *WAM 82*, 1–18.

——1991 'The Heel Stone, Stonehenge: a study in misfortunes', *WAM 84*, 1–10.

——1993 *From Carnac to Callanish. The Prehistoric Rows and Avenues of Britain, Ireland and Brittany*, New Haven and London.

——1994 'Stonehenge: slaughter, sacrifice and sunshine', *WAM 87*, 85–95

——1995 *A Guide to the Stone Circles of Britain, Ireland and Brittany*, New Haven and London.

——1997 'The sarsen horseshoe inside Stonehenge: a rider', *WAM 90*, 1–12.

CAMDEN, W., 1610 *Britain*, ed. Holland. P., London.

——1695 *Britannia*, ed. Gibson, E., London.

CASTLEDEN, R., 1987 *The Stonehenge People*, London.

——1993 *The Making of Stonehenge*, London.

CHARLETON, W., 1663 *Chorea Gigantum; or the most famous Antiquity of Great-Britain, Vulgarly called Stone-heng*, London.

CHIPPINDALE, C., 1994 *Stonehenge Complete*, 2nd edn, London.

CLARE, T., 1975 'Some Cumbrian stone circles in perspective', *TCWAAS 75*, 1–16.

CLARKE, D. L., 1970 *The Beaker Pottery of Great Britain and Ireland, I, II*, Cambridge.

CLEAL, E. M. J., WALKER, K. E. and MONTAGUE, R., 1995 (eds) *Stonehenge in its Landscape. Twentieth Century Excavations*, London.

CLOUGH, T. H. McK., and CUMMINS, W. A., 1979 (eds) *Stone Axe Studies, Archaeology, Petrology, Experimental and Ethnographic*, CBA Report 23, London.

——1988 (eds) *Stone Axe Studies*, CBA Report 67, London.

COLES, J. M. and SIMPSON, D. D. A., 1979 *Studies in Ancient Europe*, Leicester.

COLLINGWOOD, R. G., 1933 'An introduction to the prehistory of Cumberland, Westmorland and Lancashire north of the Sands', *TCWAAS 33*, 163–200.

CUNLIFFE, B. and RENFREW, C. (eds) 1997 *Science and Stonehenge*, London.

CUNNINGTON, R. H., 1935 *Stonehenge and its Date*, London.

DARVILL, T., 1987 *Prehistoric Britain*, London.

DEVEREUX, P. and THOMSON, I., 1979 *The Ley Hunter's Companion*, London.

DUKE, Rev. E., 1846 *The Druidical Temples of the County of Wilts*, London.

DYMOND, C. W., 1896 *The Ancient Remains at Stanton Drew in the County of Somerset*, Bristol.

EVANS, E. E., 1966 *Prehistoric and Early Christian Ireland. A Guide*, London.

FERGUSSON, J., 1872 *Rude Stone Monuments in All Countries. Their Age and Uses*, London.

FIENNES, C., *c.* 1712 *The Illustrated Journeys of Celia Fiennes. c. 1682–1712*, ed. Morris, C., 1982, London.

FOSTER, I. LL. and ALCOCK, L. (eds) *Culture and Environment. Essays in Honour of Sir Cyril Fox*, London, 1963.

GEOFFREY of MONMOUTH, *c.* 1139 *The History of the Kings of Britain*, tr. Thorpe, L., Harmondsworth, 1980.

GERALD of WALES, *c.* 1222 *The History and Topography of Ireland*, tr. O'Mara, J. J., 1982, Harmondsworth.

GIBSON, A. and SIMPSON, D. D. A. (eds) 1998 *Prehistoric Ritual and Religion. Essays in Honour of Aubrey Burl*, London.

GILBERT, M., 1962 *Pierres Mégalithiques dans le Maine et Cromlechs en France*, Guernsey.

GIOT, P.-R., 1960 *Brittany*, London.

——l'HELGOUAC'H, J. and MONNIER, J.-L., 1979 *Préhistoire de la Bretagne*, Rennes.

GREEN, C. P., 1997 'The provenance of rocks used in the construction of Stonehenge', in Cunliffe, B. and Renfrew, C. (eds), 257–70.

GRINSELL, L. V., 1957 'Archaeological gazetteer', in Pugh, R. B. and Crittall, E. A. (eds) *A History of Wiltshire, I (1)*, 21–279.

——1975 *Legendary History and Folklore of Stonehenge*, St Peter Port.

——1976 *Folklore of Prehistoric Sites in Britain*, Newton Abbot.

——1977 *The Rollright Stones and their Folklore*, St Peter Port.

——1978a *The Stonehenge Barrow Groups*, Salisbury.

——1978b *The Druids and Stonehenge*, St Peter Port.

HARRISON, J., 1901 'A bibliography of the great stone monuments of Wiltshire – Stonehenge and Avebury', *WAM 32*, 1–169.

HAWKINS, G. with WHITE, J. B., 1966a *Stonehenge Decoded*, London.

——1966b *Astro-Archaeology*, Cambridge, Massachusetts.

HAWLEY, W., 1924 'Fourth report on the excavations at Stonehenge', *Ant J 4*, 30–9.

——1925 'Report on the excavations at Stonehenge during the season of 1923', *Ant J 5*, 21–50.

——1926 'Report on the excavations at Stonehenge during the season of 1926', *Ant J 6*, 1–25.

HAYMAN, R., 1997 *Riddles in Stone. Myths, Archaeology and the Ancient Britons*, London.

HERBERT, A., 1849 *Cyclops Christianus*, London.

HEGGIE, D., 1981 *Megalithic Science. Ancient Mathematics and Astronomy in Northwest Europe*, London.

HOARE, Sir R. C., 1812 *The Ancient History of South Wiltshire*, London.

HOYLE, F., 1977 *On Stonehenge*, London.

JOHNSON, N. and ROSE, P., 1994 *Bodmin Moor. An Archaeological Survey, I*, London.

JONES, I., 1655 *The Most Noble Antiquity of Great Britain, Vulgarly Called Stone-Heng*, London.

JUDD, J. W., 1903 'Notes on the nature and origin of the rock-fragments found in the excavations at Stonehenge by Mr Gowland in 1901', *Arch 58*, 1902, 106–18. See also: *WAM 33*, 1903, 47–64.

KELLAWAY, G. A., 1971 'Glaciation and the stones of Stonehenge', *Nature 232*, 30–5.

LEWIS, A. L., 1892 'Stone circles of Britain', *Arch J 49*, 136–54.

——1905 'On the relation of stone circles to outlying stones, or tumuli, or neighbouring hills, with some inferences therefrom', *JRAI 12*, 176–91.

LOCKYER, Sir N., 1906 *Stonehenge and Other British Stone Monuments Astronomically Considered*, London.

——1909 *ibid.*, 2nd edn, London.

LONG, W., 1876 *Stonehenge and its Barrows*, Devizes (see also *WAM 16*, 1876, 1–239).

LUKIS, Rev. W. C., 1875 *Guide to the Chambered Barrows etc of South Brittany*, Ripon.

——1882 *The Family Memoirs of the Rev. William Stukeley . . . I*, Durham.

——1883 *ibid.*, *II*, Durham.

——1887 *ibid.*, *III*, Durham.

MEGAW, V. and SIMPSON, D. D. A., 1979 *Introduction to British Prehistory*, Leicester.

MERLET, R., 1974 *Exposé du Système Solsticial Néolithique reliant entre eux Certains*

Cromlechs et Menhirs dans le Golfe du Morbihan, Rennes.

MICHELL, J., 1982 *Megalithomania*, London.

MORRIS, R. W. B., 1989 'The prehistoric rock art of Britain: a survey of all sites bearing motifs more complex than simple cupmarks', *PPS 55*, 45–88.

NEWALL, R. S., 1953 *Stonehenge, Wiltshire*, London.

NEWHAM, C. A., 1964 *The Enigma of Stonehenge*, Leeds.

——1972 *The Astronomical Significance of Stonehenge*, Shirenewton.

NIEL, F., 1975 *The Mysteries of Stonehenge*, New York.

PETRIE, W. M. F., 1880 *Stonehenge: Plans, Descriptions, and Theories*, London.

PETRIE, W. M. F. and HAWKINS, G. S., 1989 *Stonehenge, Plans, Descriptions and Theories and Stonehenge Astronomy – an Update*, London.

PIGGOTT, S., 1985 *William Stukeley. An Eighteenth Century Antiquary*, 2nd edn, London.

PITTS, M. W., 1982 'On the road to Stonehenge . . .', *PPS 48*, 75–132.

PONTOIS, B. le, 1929 *Le Finistère Préhistorique*, Paris.

POWELL, T. G. E., CORCORAN, J. X .W. P., LYNCH, F. and SCOTT, J. G., 1969 *Megalithic Enquiries in the West of Britain*, Liverpool.

ROUZIC, Z. le, 1930 *Les Cromlechs de Er-Lannic*, Vannes.

RUGGLES, C. L. N., 1988 (ed.) *Records in Stone. Papers in Memory of Alexander Thom* Cambridge.

SHERRATT, A., 1998 'Points of exchange in the Late Neolithic of the Morbihan', in Gibson and Simpson (eds), 119–38.

SIMPSON, Sir J. Y., 1897 *Archaic Sculpturings of Cups, Circles &c . . .* , Edinburgh.

SMITH, J., 1771 *Choir Gaur: the Grand Orrery of the Ancient Druids Commonly Called Stonehenge*, London.

STEVENS, E. T., 1882 *Jottings on Some of the Objects of Interest in the Stonehenge Excursion*, Salisbury.

STEVENS, F., 1916 *Stonehenge Today and Yesterday*, London.

——1929 *Ibid.*, London.

STONE, E. H., 1924 *The Stones of Stonehenge*, London.

STUKELEY, W., 1723 'The history of the temples and religion of the antient Celts', MS. 4.253, Cardiff Public Library.

——1740 *Stonehenge a Temple Restor'd to the British Druids*, London.

——1743 *Abury, a Temple of the British Druids, with some Others Described*, London.

——1776a *Itinerarium Curiosum, I*, London.

——1776b *Itinerarium Curiosum, II*, London.

TAYLOR, C., 1979 *Roads and Tracks of Britain*, London.

THATCHER, A. R., 1976 'The Station Stones at Stonehenge', *Ant 50*, 144–5.

THOM, A., 1967 *Megalithic Sites in Britain*, Oxford.

——and THOM, A. S., 1977 *La Géometrie des Alignments de Carnac*, Rennes.

——1978 *Megalithic Remains in Britain and Brittany*, Oxford.

THOM, A. and THOM, A. S. and BURL, A., 1980 *Megalithic Rings. Plans and Data for 229 Sites*, Oxford.

——1990 *Stone Rows and Standing Stones, I, II*, Oxford.

THOM, A., A. S., MERRITT, R. L. and A. L., 1973 'The astronomical significance of the Crucuno stone rectangle', *Current Anthropology 14 (4)*, 450–4.

THOMAS, H. H., 1923 'The source of the stones of Stonehenge', *Ant J 23*, 239–60.

THORPE, R. S., WILLIAMS-THORPE, O., JENKINS, D. G. and WATSON, J. S., 1991 'The geological sources and transport of the bluestones of Stonehenge, Wilts, UK', *PPS 57 (2)*, 103–57.

TOLAND, J., 1726 *A Critical History of the Celtic Religion and Learning, containing an Account of the Druids*, London, 1814 edn.

TREGELLES, G. F., 1906 'Stone circles', *VCH Cornwall, I*, 379–406.

UCKO, P. J., HUNTER, M., CLARK, A. J. and DAVID, A., 1991 *Avebury Reconsidered. From the 1660s to the 1990s*, London.

WATERHOUSE, J., 1985 *The Stone Circles of Cumbria*, Chichester.

WESTWOOD, J., 1992 *Albion. A Guide to Legendary Britain*, London.

WILLIAMS-THORPE, O., 1997 'Comments following the papers by Drs. Green and Scourse', *Proc Soc. Brit. Acad. 92*, 315–16.

WOOD, J., 1747 *Choire Gaure, Vulgarly called Stonehenge, on Salisbury Plain*, Oxford.

WOOD, J. E., 1978 *Sun, Moon and Standing Stones*, Oxford.

INDEX

Bold indicates a major entry; *italic* indicates an illustration

PHOTOGRAPHIC ACKNOWLEDGEMENTS

Title-page, 30: Cheryl Straffon; 1, 3, 5, 6, 8, 10, 11, 12, 13, 15, 20, 21, 22, 23, 24, 26, 27, 33, 36, 38, 39, 40, 42, 43, 44, 45, 46, 47, 48, 49, 50, 52, 53, 54, 55: Aubrey Burl; 4, 18, 25, 32: Mick Sharp Photography; 7, 9: Richard Wheeler; 14, 16, 17: John Nicoll; 19: West Air Photography; 34: Aerofilms; 35, 51: Homer Sykes/Network; 41: Clive Ruggles